The Informed Republic

The Informed Republic

A Guide To Liberty, Freedom, And Real Self-Government

C.D. Ginsburg

We the People
PUBLISHING

We the People
PUBLISHING

Published by We the People Publishing
www.WethePeoplePublishing.com
Cape Canaveral, Florida

For information about special discounts for bulk purchases or author interviews, appearances, and speaking engagements please contact:

ginsburgradio@gmail.com

First Edition

ISBN Hardcover: 979-8-9893936-0-2
ISBN Softcover: 979-8-9893936-1-9
ISBN Ebook: 979-8-9893936-2-6

Library of Congress: Control Number 2023920402

Editing, book and cover design, produced by Rodney Miles, www.RodneyMiles.com

Cover image: Tanner, Benjamin, Engraver, and John James Barralet. *America guided by wisdom An allegorical representation of the United States depicting their independence and prosperity // Drawn by John J. Barralett ; engraved by B. Tanner*. United States, 1815. [United States: Publisher not identified] Photograph. https://www.loc.gov/item/2010634241/.

"The true principle is ever that of republicanism."

—Thomas Jefferson,
Letter to William Duane August 12th 1810

Dedicated to all those who came before, nearly driven off the cliffs of madness as they tried to save their friends and family with simple truth against trusted lies.

CONTENTS

Preface xv

Introduction 1

Part One: REPUBLICS 7

Republic Defined 8

Republic Evolution in a Nutshell 12

How Republics Fall 14

Liberty 16

Society 19

Community 20

Republic in Retrospect 24

Republic in Form 27

Democracy 31

Citizen 33

Republic from the Perspective of the Free Individual: 35

Part Two: HISTORIES 37

Athens 38

   The Branches 59

     The Ecclesia 59

     The Boule 62

     The Dikasteria 65

   The Thirty Tyrants 73

   The Greatest Macedonian: 78

Sparta 89

    The Political Body 100

    The Classes 103

        Spartiates 103

        Spartan 104

        Perioikoi 104

        Helots 105

    Leagues 109

Unified Greece: Hellenistic period 113

Rome: No More Kings 115

    The Republic 127

The Law: The Twelve Tables Drafting, Development,
and Purpose: 131

    The Laws Of The Twelve Tables: Table I 137

    The Roman Political Branches: 144

        Roman Senate 144

        The Consuls 149

    Polybius on The People: 151

        The People 151

    State Rights 159

    Fall of Rome 160

Part Three: THE AMERICAN REPUBLIC 165

Preamble 166

Altering the Law, A Section Overview 169

The Colonial Republic 182

    Settlers, Migrants, and Inhabitants 182

Goal of the Pioneering Republicans 200

Voting in the Settlements and Beyond 204

Addendum, the Successful Cousin 218

Declarations of Freedom 224

   The Articles 233

   Constituted Treason.. 237

   Constitutional Purpose & Powers 258

The Branches... 266

   Legislature... 266

     House of Representatives.................................... 267

     Senate 267

   Executive 288

   Judiciary.. 291

Bill of Rights.. 296

Presidential Eligibility 310

   The Amendments.. 312

   Amendment I.. 314

   Amendment II... 317

   Amendment III 320

   Amendment IV 321

   Amendment V 322

   Amendment VI.. 323

   Amendment VII... 324

   Amendment VIII 327

   Amendment IX 327

   Amendment X... 328

The Final Outcome.. 332

Standards of Education in Republic 336

   Education.. 336

Conclusion 345
About the Author.. 353
The Declaration of Independence................................. 355
Additional Sources.. 361

PREFACE

THIS WORK IS a general examination of history (not a detailed historical work) to inform the average person (particularly with some existing knowledge) of the actual use and history of *republic*[1] so it might be achieved today in purer form. We do this through:

- historical reviews of happenings and philosophy,
- education in its operation,
- relations to recent (current) events,
- comparisons of its solutions against current systems in use,
- and how a republic is secured.

Truth of republic based on the opinions and historical terminology of modern professionals and experts cannot be found. Therefore, one must examine:

- the stated historical purpose for the community,
- its activity,
- the condition that made one a citizen of republic,
- and what that meant.

---

[1] republic: noun, particularly "A political order in which the supreme power lies in a body of citizens who are entitled to vote for officers and representatives responsible to them," but will be further defined in this book. (From *The American Heritage® Dictionary of the English Language, 5th Edition.*)

There will be focus on the political bodies' so-called governing structures, but this is so we understand more where our bloated and overpowered constructs come from. Most observation of those governing systems will be balanced by relation to how freedom *had* to have restriction in place to reduce a government's capacity of perceived power.

Sources used throughout this work will often be ones accessible and often generally used by the public at large, especially internet sources like Wikipedia. Though many may not find Wikipedia acceptable as a source, the fact remains it and many sources like it are regularly referenced by the populace, making them perfect for examples to share with the reader of the misconstrued public and official narratives. Some sources cited may have changed or are no longer accessible due to the nature of the internet, but diligence will assure that one researching this topic will find many corroborating materials. That said, the corrected perspective this book will present will often come from first person sources and the well-known famous historians of old.

C.D. Ginsburg
Colorado Springs, Colorado
December 2023

INTRODUCTION

IN A MYRIAD of ways, the term *republic* is generally described as:

> "a democratic style system where the leader is elected through popular vote, to an oligarchical form of democracy where the elite rule through representatives in checks and balances."
>
> — Britannica

This is a convoluted definition that constitutes the more modern academic lie of making republics and democracies seem similar while bastardizing republics as tools for the wealthy alone. The term *oligarchic* is often used in relation to a few peoples of wealth and influence. All despite clear evidence to the contrary, such as the U.S. Constitution's operation in which the President is not at all elected by popular vote, but by state-determined selected *electors*, and in which only the representatives are elected by popular vote.

The best simple descriptions of the two concepts (democracy and republic) are as follows:

- **Republic:** An assurance of the native populations' personal freedom and the spirit in which they came together. (This was often done by the use of titled public servants *beneath* the private freemen.)

1

- **Democracy**: The rule by majority opinion in power over the masses for popular preferred classes and their current whim presented as the public will. (This was often done by the use of titled public masters disguised as servants over the privileged civilian. There is no freedom if the majority rules, especially when that majority power is a minority body called "government officials.")

The protection of personal freedom (liberty) of the freeman is the primary real function of a republic.

However, in my opinion a proper definition is:

> **Republic**: A trade protectorate that assures trade with no governing power beyond this duty over its own departments, but for the power to defend liberty at every level. First and foremost, that of the individual doing no harm to others. All domestic security left to the authority of the free armed individual.

This is most notable in the republic of Rome when Brutus was titled the Consul of Rome. Noting the limitation on this public position is imperative in understanding limited governance in liberty-based society. It is often the primary purpose of most republics. Worded another way, the assurance of natural law for the individual to be personally empowered over the collective's governing desires is (should be) paramount in true republics. We don't have much on the other early Consuls of Rome (pointing to the possibility they weren't much in the way of power), and we don't really see the position being akin to a monarchal king, or even akin to a modern president, upon real examination (which we will do a little later in the writing). Consul of Rome was regularly changed every year, though it eventually became a spoils and hereditary seat. The position (consul) was instead more one of a limited power as is defined in Wikipedia's remedial definition of the term:

Ancient writers usually derive the title consul
from the Latin verb consulere, 'to take counsel,'
but this is most likely a later gloss over of the
term, which probably derives—in view of the joint
nature of the office—from con- and sal-, 'get
together' or from con- and sell-/sedl-, 'sit down
together with' or 'next to.'[2]

"Sit down together with" doesn't mean "to follow the lead of" or "lord over." Those literate in liberty understand this is telling us the position only brought the people together in a limited role; one of apparent response or reaction (maybe even for judgment) to disagreement. It is the same thing chiefs and most shamans were limited to doing. We tend to forget in most of these cases the leader didn't get involved in personal or interpersonal matters unless *asked* to arbitrate.

But we have a problem found within the "pros and cons" from the derivation above. *Consul* isn't a Greek term, it is a Latin term based on a Greek concept. *Pro* is Latin meaning "for" or "in favor of" something or somethings being a benefit. *Con* is Latin for "against." Now, how can it mean "together"? A similarity is drawn between it and the Greek prefix *com-*, "altogether," though *consul* takes the Greek meaning over the Roman one for what is most definitely a Roman office. Doesn't matter, because if *sal-* is "sit," *consul* can mean *against agreement*, or to *sit in opposition to*, or to *sit over people having a conflict*. This makes sense when the Consul is one whose advice you seek, and when we realize they are the two commanding generals in war (which is a conflict). Both situations involve a detriment to peace. Thus, *cons*. My assertions here are easily gathered from a simple reading of prefixes and suffixes in a dictionary or on any dictionary website.

This is a foundational behavior for republics being of free individuals who agree to limited leadership in *cases of crisis*, not to enforcement over social behavior or requirement to involve the

---

[2] https://en.wikipedia.org/wiki/Roman_consul#cite_note-PW-2

masses in responses. The term *consul* also encompasses someone who issues advice and has no authority to force compromise and adherence unless he is willing to get his hands personally dirty. The role of a consul is then one of a "public citizen or person."

Brutus' Rome also gives us our first glimpse into the true meaning of the term *republic*. *Res publica* is a Latin phrase meaning "a public matter," as translated by Cicero of Plato's *Politeia* (or *The Republic*)[3]. When one reads *Politeia* they find a discussion between different cultures in Greece debating the meaning of justice and other topics. In that work, we find freemen in a public discussion — a *public matter*. And as you just read, historically the Consul only advised, and in order for a man to be free, his *personal matters* couldn't then be that of the Consul's authority or of the public. Public matters are free-minded discussions (free speech, a pillar of republics and liberty) or events of concern which may need to be addressed by the community. No civil issue presented or remedy prescribed can involve a person who does not want to be involved, and yet if done in everyone's name all *assests* acquired, built, used, and created by the public must be everyone's to use or engage. So, if the community goes to war, you can refuse to go. Yet, if it builds a building, you must be allowed access to it and all publicly funded equipment within, whether you supported the effort or not. For it is *for the public*.

The antiquated view and incorrect statement by Plato that "If you don't focus on politics, politics will focus on you" (paraphrased), is not valid, at least not from the "You need to be engaged in public affairs" mentality of the average politico and one who tows the party line. Republics are by their very nature *optional* and start as opt-out by default. If they didn't, how could you be free? Public matters of concern are things like invasions (thus the limited leadership of Consul), natural disasters, or trade impositions (including things like blockades, banditry, and piracy). A public matter surely isn't morality or behavior, for these are personal, cultural, and religious matters, things which have no place in cooperative public affairs. Such matters

---

[3] *The Republic* (Greek: Πολιτεία, translit. *Politeia*; Latin: *De Republica*) is a Socratic dialogue, authored by Plato around 375 BC, concerning justice, the order and character of the just city-state, and the just man. It is Plato's best-known work, and one of the world's most influential works of philosophy and political theory, both intellectually and historically. — Wikipedia

(personal, cultural, and religious) are often a sub-feature and only apply to those partaking in them, and if deemed "public" would affect those who are not in agreement to a concept or action's stipulations, violate their will, and thus harm the republic.

So, to think the leadership or historical republics were involved in a subservient society, adherent to the will of the majority of "elected representatives," through a presiding "elected" Consul/leader takes false roots in academia from the first moments we have the official activity historically called republic being defined by current standards. We have in truth, an *individual first society*, initially for the founding (ruling) families first and foremost, where the free citizens would meet with a Consul (or chief) who would consult and preside over the meeting on what to do about certain issues, would lead in cases of emergency, and who otherwise had no more political or legal power than anyone else (as we'll see in later chapters).

In time, the natural liberties of every individual are recognized in republic ideology, but the ability for many to separate that fact from a political right assured to natives and not outsiders is what causes the issues we see today. So, how much more is wrong? How much interpretation has ruined the education on the even more recent republic erected by the American Founding Fathers? *There is today an ideological movement which works to intentionally conceal the true history of republic, instead suggesting it was rather the start of the evolution of governmental law and operations, concealing the aspect that government must stay limited in power and scope* — a growth toward collective rule in democracy, a growth they attribute to writings that some say constitute only one percent of all the writings of antiquity.

In truth, government by democracy (majority rule), oligarchy, and monarchy were nothing new to the Founders. What was new, what is supposedly new about America, was the adaptation of the tools of government learned into the individual for their personal empowerment and better management of personal affairs above all other bodies and auxiliaries; not a furthering of external central power's knowledge to better mold the public perception with external leadership or majority social will.

And as stated in the Preface, it will serve us all well to better understand republic as a first safeguard to our liberty.

THE INFORMED REPUBLIC

PART ONE:
REPUBLICS

REPUBLIC DEFINED

IF WE TRULY observe the foundations of republic, it is a maxim-based society where the native individual will is protected from majority rule; while the foreigner, politician, and merchant are highly regulated as to not misuse their limited power/influence to rule the individual through the community facilities and officers (public positions). The law at most levels is self-enforced or at least enforceable at any time by the individual when titled agents are derelict in their duties or not present. Why? Because everyone in the community is usually natural to the community, at least when it is founded. Those who are not natural to the community are generally subject to suspicion and should be, as they are outsiders. That does not mean treated poorly or lesser-than, it means excluded from political actions, observed more closely, and punishable in a different manner than those native to the culture. Outsiders are often and likely vassals or serfs of a foreign power, whereas the republic's people rule the political body or are the sovereign. Republics locked to natural law recognize that so long as the outsider has committed no physical harm or stolen anything and isn't a merchant/official, you can't bind them to your community regulations unless they have officially agreed to follow them. They must willingly submit, and trust in neighbors can take time to establish.

I contend the best republics are always based on *natural law* as their maxim. The dictionary defines *natural law* as:

natural law

NOUN

1. a body of unchanging moral principles regarded as a basis for all human conduct.

2. an observable law relating to natural phenomena.

The second definition is actually the one used by most liberty writers, especially those of the Enlightenment, and it creates the foundation for the true moral principles of human conduct. This is because it includes experience and observation which lead to empiricism. Properly stated, and to the way the Enlightenment that created the New World put it, *natural law* is:

> ... that which is seen to occur in nature as an instinctive reaction to any given situation, and in which it is evident that the individual is always autonomous and must be treated with respect to that autonomy.

Additional definitions to help with understanding this term will be found throughout this work.

Socrates, Plato, and Aristotle emphasized the distinction between "nature" and "law." What civic law commands (laws in public discourse) varies from place to place, but what is "by nature" is the same everywhere. Aristotle is considered by many as the father of "natural law." He states that aside from "particular" (human) laws each people has set up for their community, there is a "common law" or "higher law" that is according to nature. (*Rhetoric* 1373b2–8).

Roman copy of a Greek bronze bust of Aristotle by Lysippos (c. 330 BC)[4]

[4]
https://en.m.wikipedia.org/wiki/File:Aristotle_Altemps_Inv8575.jpg

PART ONE: REPUBLICS

To Aristotle's thoughts *Encyclopedia Britannica* notes:

> There have been several disagreements over the
> meaning of natural law and its relation to positive
> law. Aristotle (384–322 BCE) held that what was
> 'just by nature' was not always the same as what
> was 'just by law,' that there was a natural justice
> valid everywhere with the same force and 'not
> existing by people's thinking this or that . . .'

I find it interesting that the first thing Britannica does is get into the relation of natural law to positive law, which (the latter) includes the protections and permissions granted by a people's government or community, clearly different from what Aristotle is defining. Not surprising, coming from the socialists in England. Even so, Wikipedia manages to get this term right:

> Natural law (Latin: ius naturale, lex naturalis) is a
> philosophy asserting that certain rights are
> inherent by virtue of human nature, endowed by
> nature — traditionally by God or a transcendent
> source — and that these can be understood
> universally through human reason. As
> determined by nature, the law of nature is implied
> to be objective and universal; it exists
> independently of human understanding, and of
> the positive law of a given state, political order,
> legislature or society at large.

The relation of natural law to religious doctrines — which are a tying of the ideal to a specific God and not an anomalous, transcendent source of existence, which includes nature — can be seen as distinct from each other. Often, the term "natural" is wrongfully applied out of the need for a religious text's directives and its specific God to have power over personal behavior through social construct,

11

courts, and governance. As you'll learn in this work, such can only be applied personally, by willful agreement, or with those membered to a religion. It (religious morals) can have no power in the political body involved with multiple beliefs, or with people from outside the "faith" in the republic concept. Thus, the Separation of Church and State practiced by many republics. Remember, the republics of Antiquity were societies of pantheons. Though many would pay alms to a local deity and had civil laws to protect their domestic practices, not everyone had to believe in that deity as great or as their god, nor were such rules necessarily applicable to visitors. This arrangement wasn't always the case, but at what point in time in the community's existence was this respect for other's ideals not happening?

REPUBLIC EVOLUTION IN A NUTSHELL

At its core, *republic* is family-orientated or originated. Example: Imagine your family and several others decide to start a community living near each other. You start in a place where the fathers are head of household, because they do the manual labor or trades, and are the first responders in defending the community. He represents the family in public matters concerning limited issues, because he must confront those issues when there is threat. Trade, infrastructure, bandits, invasions, and so on. However, in all other matters every person (regardless of sex or age) is responsible for their own actions and for making a claim personally and executing actions personally. Damage something and you fix, repair, or reimburse for it. If you murder someone you are either put to death by family of the victim or exiled by the community. These matters are solved in temporary courts called forth by the accuser. That's it. That's the full extent of your law.

The community does not involve itself in personal matters or business agreements. That's wholly up to each individual to deal with, as family, business, and religious matters are personal and no one else's matter unless being used against the community. So, the people may set up rules to assure trade is occurring, and so businesses are not stifled by outside forces. The public involvement in these things comes from the public accusation against a person or body, as well as in a call for arbitration on the issue by a member of the community, not necessarily the titled agents. Both sides' involvement is then at will, though a business or religion has less authority in such matters, as they are a group. Groups can influence and seed power, and thus must not have as much weight before other artificial bodies, such as courts. Power is in public record (public claims) not statutory rules (draconian law).

Through your community's success neighboring traders and merchants begin passing through. Are these people of any of the Foundational Families? No. Should they have a say in domestic policy then? No. Should they be able to speak to any matter that may affect them? Sure, as you cannot truly stop a man from speaking without forcing him quiet. The foreigner may have good insight, but that doesn't mean he should be able to direct how the community deals with those from outside through the domestic auxiliary. The outsiders find lots of opportunity in the community, so they move into the area. They are free to do anything they like except make decisions in public policy, cause war, or aggress on the natives. Why? The families understand through experience and observation that not everyone from outside the community believes what they believe or thinks as they do. In fact, lots of the outsiders seem to think the persons holding titles are superiors to the populace due to skill or a trust. This is odd in your community as you *all* understand you are all of founding blood. If you are all of shared foundational blood of the community how can any of you be above another? Titles are for public service. The moment the foreigners are a threat or behaving in a manner affecting community safety and tranquility you can act with force and without public declaration as these are not equals in the forum (public court of record), though often you will make a public statement. This is the pre-eminent ideal of a republic.

HOW REPUBLICS FALL

- Foreigners begin to arrive more and more.
- They start to treat the locals as tyrants for enforcing their local laws, and for being aggressive with troublesome, uneducated, despotically loyal "migrants."
- They disrespect local customs, and even try to disrupt and end such traditions.
- In time they begin to influence Founding Family members who sympathize with the foreigners or who desire more power among their peers and wealth in their hands. This is the beginning of democracy toward tyranny, despotism, or monarchy.
- They begin to abuse their positions of trust which are not supposed to change or alter the foundations of the community. The cancer is implemented throughout in order to gain further influence with foreigners and their governments. The once-loyal native is more drawn to power.
- They treat their follow native as ignorant and close-minded.
- Eventually, the traitor gives the foreigner power to alter public policy through lesser laws, drawing their claim to power on the common laws once reserved for the few instances relating to harmful damages.
- Built on titled positions once limited to a specific function only, or used for praise not authority, properly educated natives knew the first-time law was altered to benefit a foreign ideal that violated the community's maxims and the originating community was dead if not avenged swiftly through force by the native(s).

This is both the beginning and ending (when not vigilantly upheld) of a republic. As you proceed in reading this work it will be shown that assuring the outsiders a voice to the titled roles can help lessen the jealousy of outsiders. However, if the titled do not obey the limitation of the offices of power, then democracy will still lead to collapse of the often-successful republic. Much of this is the reason for the Enlightenment's relation to basic freedoms of speech, worship of one's preferred religion, civil government separate from religion (separation of church and state), and low-regulated to totally-free trade.

LIBERTY

Statue of Freedom (model, 1854–1857; cast 1860–1862) by Thomas Crawford crowns the United States Capitol dome[5]

---

[5]

https://en.m.wikipedia.org/wiki/Statue_of_Freedom#/media/File%3ASt atue_of_Freedom%2C_Washington%2C_D.C.jpg

In moving forward, the biggest problem in understanding just how free-minded and politically-voluntary a republic is, seems to be in the lack of understanding of liberty as much as how natural law is obfuscated. *Liberty* in the minds of some seems to imply some allowance by society, some permission from the social construct or community. However, this is totally counterintuitive to the foundational writings of America or any republic's foundational history, mostly because of the actual definition itself:

liberty

['lɪbərdē]

NOUN

1. the state of being free within society from oppressive restrictions imposed by authority on one's way of life, behavior, or political views

This is even according to Google's own search engine, mind you.

Merriam-Webster defines liberty as:

1: the quality or state of being free:

    a : the power to do as one pleases

    b : freedom from physical restraint

    c : freedom from arbitrary or despotic control

    d : the positive enjoyment of various social, political, or economic rights and privileges

    e : the power of choice

—https://www.merriam-webster.com/dictionary/liberty

Under every tyranny the later additions to the definition of *liberty* such as, "a right or privilege, especially a statutory one," or basically it being a "permission" takes over as the norm among the populace, generally because it fits the authoritarian's narrative that they permit you because the people permitted them to do so in perpetuity as a willing posterity. It also plays to the serf's terror in what may happen in a truly free society, which in their minds is only ever a nightmare despite the historical proof to the contrary. Yet, if one is allowed or given a "privilege" under statute(s), doesn't this imply they are still restricted, imposed upon, even oppressed by the statute(s)? In what way does this meet the words in the primary definition of "being free from" or "freedom"?

Maybe most get overly focused on the term *society*? This too tends to be used to confuse the natural interaction of republic.

SOCIETY

society[6]

[suh-sahy-i-tee]

noun, plural societies.

1. an organized group of persons associated together for religious, benevolent, cultural, scientific, political, patriotic, or other purposes.

2. a body of individuals living as members of a community; community.

I would love to give you the original definition in so much pertaining to this subject. In some places, I do and will. However, even trying to get the original roots for words like society, which the dictionary breaks down into "soci(us) partner, comrade + -etās, variant of -itās- -ity" are distorted when trying to run a linguistic translation, and we even see here "-etas" isn't clarified, because it implies "action" of the connected term. Research shows it's basically an abstract like "-ness" implying one thing has a related quality to something else, like society meaning "of us." Yet, if you observe such root breakdowns as are shared even in the dictionary forms, we still can see a disconnect from how the words are used. This is important because without adhering to the original root, anarchy to redefine and hide meanings takes control. Then we get corruption and confusion. This must be avoided. In the case of the root to the word "society," we still get the understanding of partners, or in comradery. The primary definition tricks us to think this must be structured in agreement by it being "organized." So, we must look to the second definition shared to get somewhat closer to the historical root, and away from the authoritarian modern term which uses community. So, what is community?

---

[6] http://www.dictionary.com/browse/society

COMMUNITY

community⁷

[kuh-myoo-ni-tee]

noun, plural communities.

1. a social group of any size whose members
reside in a specific locality, share government, and
often have a common cultural and historical
heritage.

Love how they toss government in there? Yet, wait! If we go back
to look at the definition of the word "social" (do this on your own),
we will see a similar definition to society! Mainly implying a
companionship. In short, society already means "close group." So, we
can realize easily that society is a companionship, that is generally
thought to be under some behavioral unwritten agreement.

Yet here we still must deal with two words shared within these
definitions: society, with the definition of community; and
community with the definition of society (or social group). This is
never good linguistics and makes relation of terms suspect. A proper
definition for a real word cannot contain the word itself. As such we
must determine the proper, or original meaning to "community." We
will find this in the link above, a couple of definitions down from the
modern primary definition:

a social, religious, occupational, or other group
sharing common characteristics or interests and
perceived or perceiving itself as distinct in some
respect from the larger society within which it
exists.

---

⁷ http://www.dictionary.com/browse/community

Ah! There's the keyword, "common." There is no need for agreement or structure in society or community. There simply needs to be *commonality*, people doing things similarly. In the case of republics, that commonality is the right to exist, to not be threatened into social compliance, by retaining the inherent freedom to abstain from groupthink/activity and respond to any threat freely, exactly as nature leaves all things to do. In the grander sense, it was taught by the American Founders of the Enlightenment, and the Enlightenment as a whole by minds like Locke, Newton, Voltaire, and Machiavelli that a free people will and must exist *in liberty*. Thus, liberty is the commonality of true republics. A fact you will see later in this work, too.

This means *liberty* must then precede and overrule common statutes (laws), the laws most communities have, as they are not developed until after consensus, or "agreement;" nor are they applicable until there is a structure which binds the statutes. Despite popular opinion society builds structure, structure does not build society.

"We consider society as one of the natural wants with which man has been created; that he has been endowed with faculties and qualities to effect its satisfaction by concurrence of others having the same want; that when, by the exercise of these faculties, he has procured a state of society, it is one of his acquisitions which he has a right to regulate and control, jointly indeed with all those who have concurred in the procurement, whom he cannot exclude from its use or direction more than they him." — Thomas Jefferson[8]

It's all over the foundational works of American Founders from Sam Adams, to Henry, to Franklin, to Jefferson, that our faculties operate under personal freedom. Ours is a liberty society which

---

[8] http://www.let.rug.nl/usa/presidents/thomas-jefferson/letters-of-thomas-jefferson/

established a restricted associational management system termed "government," beneath the commonality of individual freedom for the purpose of diplomacy and trade, that establishes an external force to dangers as an assurance against all external and internal forces threatening our personal liberty.

Though their own disconnect from history led some Founders to believe they were the first to push for real limited government, the truth in observation of the stated purpose of every historical republic from Sparta to Rome has been the same as America's—the redemption, or assertion of personal freedom to do as one wishes and for one to respond to any threat to that ends. From now on if you read the histories of those most cited by the educates of modern society, and the greatest of historical philosophical and liberty-minded political figures (many of whom designed the concept America is faceted upon), you will find the claims of republic having a central authority (government) to determine social behavior are nothing more than fantasies of psychological control artists to gain adherence to organizations that have everything to lose when you know they have no legitimate power over you and your doings.

Keeping this in mind it will be nearly impossible for you to lack understanding in the examples I will furnish you in this book, and when you read them for yourself you will see where the minds and histories referenced are speaking to those who understand freedom systems, versus those who would be threats if too much of the intention of liberty was exposed.

I was taught in my history classes in general education very clearly that the men of the Enlightenment often wrote and spoke in code, or vaguely, for if they were too clear of their intentions of informing the masses that governments are *beneath* the free individual, that their kings, and religions, their governing organizations would surely—and in many cases did—have them killed or ostracized. This bit of material should help clarify and solidify in your mind why we are not taught the true focus of historical republics was to insure the knowledge in the individual of their right to dispatch individually or collectively a threatening group (or person) to secure liberty for the individual and for the society at-large. Thus, the public perception and opinion can be damning.

PART ONE: REPUBLICS

Modern historians are under the impression that republics were trying to better the relationship of individuals through the assurance of groups or institutions to direct social behavior, namely government. In truth, they were individuals assuring the individual *over* groups, or at least this was their intent.

REPUBLIC IN RETROSPECT

It is my endeavor into the past of Republic to discover what it is, how it forms, how it maintains, and how it collapses. We will retrace the history that the Founders of the American Republic once argued over themselves while debating the type of government we should have, only to find we were already a *liberty republic*.

I am not saying in this process there were no wrongdoings—no slavery, servitude, lesser classes, imperfections, or misuses of these systems—as we dismantle the public perception of republic. We are focusing on the aspects that asserted and assured the greatest personal independence and cultural/technical advancements through the use of pre-existing liberty we all share by fact of existing, that was often the basis for the authority of the *citizen*, who historically is seen as a totally-free person in being.

This is the *Encyclopedia Britannica* definition of Republic:

> Republic, form of government in which a state is ruled by representatives of the citizen body. Modern republics are founded on the idea that sovereignty rests with the people, though who is included and excluded from the category of the people has varied across history. Because citizens do not govern the state themselves but through representatives, republics may be distinguished from direct democracy, though modern representative democracies are by and large republics. The term republic may also be applied to any form of government in which the head of state is not a hereditary monarch.

This is the false definition the Aristoi[9] created to bury the freedom society, though you will find there is some truth there. Much is said

---

[9] The Aristoi (Greek: ἄριστοι) was the label given to the noblemen in ancient Greek society, and in particular ancient Athens. The term literally

24

in this one line—"because citizens do not govern the state themselves," yet, America is a republic and was clearly defined by the Founders as a society of self-governed people. In truth, the greatest republics were direct republics, where you are your own representative, wholly empowered to govern your affairs. Thus, the term "self-government" and what the Founders of the American Republic meant by "sovereignty rests with the people." The State is limited in what it can do, and that is the real republic element. And what the State can do is limited to public matters, which Britannica completely ignores. The representatives are used only when the political body is over a larger region. How is a sovereign directly ruling the State, even when using a representative? This is most recognizable in Noah Webster's Majority Response to the Minority Dissent of the Philadelphia Congress, where he wrote:

> Do you not know that in this country almost every farmer is the Lord of his own soil? That instead of suffering under the oppression of a Monarch and Nobles, a class of haughty masters, totally independent of the people, almost every man in America is a Lord himself...

It is important to note that by saying this, Webster was undermining his own push for establishing a federal government through the Constitution that the minority of representatives at the Philadelphia Convention saw as illegal. Many Founders defined in depth the reality that the citizens govern the State, the States governed the Union, and liberty is the primary source of power over all of them.

As Madison says in *Charters*:

---

means "best", with the denotation of best in terms of birth, rank, and nobility, but also usually possessing the connotation of also being the morally best. —https://en.wikipedia.org/wiki/Aristoi

In Europe, charters of liberty have been granted
by power. America has set the example and
France has followed it, of charters of power
granted by liberty.

Jefferson said:

When the Government fears the people there is
liberty...

If the State governs us why would it fear us? If liberty granted the
State power, how can it be over liberty?

REPUBLIC IN FORM

We really need to understand three distinct forms of republic:

1. **Natural Republic** (free involvement/participation = *liberum particeps*): Personal liberation above public matters with authority to be willfully involved. The republic under which all human action/interaction happens freely to which each individual is responsible for the nature-driven (natural) consequences of their actions. Natural Law is the observable maxims that all life presents, and it is the matter all are in.

2. **Direct Republic**: Representing yourself in a public matter. The power of the citizen to exercise their will and directly interact with any public community group claiming organizational operation in an area in addressing an issue or happening; to override, overrule and supersede their group body's authorities when they clash with the individual's authority, morals, and properties. In other words, the retention to opt out of participating with collective action.

3. **Political Republic** (Republican Association of Nations or large bodies): Where public matters are addressed by a political association of the people of the, or a community at-large, under certain limitations (rights) to address public concerns using officials, or happenings over a large region that have solutions which require long-term fixes with short-term involvement that still does not and is not to supersede individual will. It only complements the *natural authorities* of the individual to assure the political agents stay restrained, and individuals amassing power do not abuse the average person. It focuses on travel ways, drainage, sewage,

27

diplomacy, trade protections, contract disputes, and the completion of these projects. This is including warfare on an invading force and punishments for failing to aid fellow members' military assets in skirmishes with a defined enemy. It tends to have power over those who are officers and agents under its power, giving up their general liberty to be public servants. There can be the freedom of the individual to agree to artificial consequences through courts of the republic mixing in the sub-facet of *Legal Republic*[10] for arbitration of disputes, and the personal power to refuse and disregard without reprisal those artificial consequences so long as there has been no physical harm or destruction. Governments are simply axillaries in republics. They and their agents are always beneath the individual, especially individuals of the Liberty Society. Any use of this otherwise is an act of war the individual may respond to and is to be protected from persecution for, accept in acts of invasion or rebellion against the society, but when not against the "government" agencies or its officials.

Most general misunderstanding of the freeman and government in republic streams from the focus on Political Republic, often called "republican government" or the *Political Body*.

Often the Political Body, having its own rules and punishment statutes, warps views into allowing the political to manage the real — a lack of understanding that a bunch of things you can personally do cannot necessarily be done with the political body, including aspects of using civil charges and public courts of record. In other words, people improperly let an artificial construct built on human-contrived

---

[10] *Legal Republic*: The arena where legislative statutes (paper law) are used as guidelines to address disputes over for interpersonal private activity, or punishments for abuse of public means, or constructs. Required to be adhered to by political officials, or willing participants in a "legal being," not by citizens in abstention. (Author)

rules lord over natural outcomes and responses, when the truth is those constructs must work in concert with or beneath *nature*. The politically-bound are processed through the artificial rules of suffrage, because they have chosen to serve and take title that can become perceptually powerful.

Consider this briefly:

> Suffrage, political franchise, or simply franchise is the right to vote in public, political elections (although the term is sometimes used for any right to vote). The right to run for office is sometimes called candidate eligibility, and the combination of both rights is sometimes called full suffrage. In many languages, the right to vote is called the active right to vote and the right to run for office is called the passive right to vote. In English, these are sometimes called active suffrage and passive suffrage.[11]

We now are presented with a public right (voting) extended to real liberated people artificially welcomed into a political organization's authorization to decide on the outcome of a collective agreement, to being a person with an ability to optionally run for a position who will/can hold an office to have a say in said agreement at all. Yet, both are still clearly an authorized, or "permitted" action, not necessarily natural actions, because you naturally do all this managing for yourself, even if you do it poorly. Thus, the Enlightenment realized those of artificial constructs of suffrage cannot direct the organic being. The organic being, being flawed, cannot force others to follow their direction, only appeal for aid, otherwise turmoil and abuse are assured.

In this, the concept of "legal being" tends to improperly overshadow "natural being." In the *legal being* is where external representation exists, and where paper law has "weight" (Political Republic or any political body). So, to say Political Republic has a

---

[11] https://en.wikipedia.org/wiki/Suffrage

representational aspect to it is true. To think any republic requires this is false. A representative re-presents a position of an authorizer, constituent, or voter.

The "representative" in the encyclopedia, and general definition of republic is implied to be a "trustee;" giving it often a democratic oligarchy element, not a republican one, implying this person will decide by position and personal judgement what is best for the State or people... because that is what Lords of Land and Self would do — be subjugated. (I'm being sarcastic.)

This is incorrect, as the representative is in a subservient role and they only ignore the will of the constituent when the constituents are at odds with the common law (social agreement) *under natural law*. In America's case, that means their representative's actions cannot stifle personal liberties. In all other cases, the representative is commanded as to how to vote by their direct community within the confines of the compact that laid out their position's purpose. This is in fact the citizen governing the state. So, in actuality the *Encyclopedia Britannica* definition above is telling us by its improper terms that we live in a totalitarian, party-based, democratic oligarchy that selects leadership amongst itself in a capacity that you are to just "trust them." It is telling you the representative governs that State to action they deem best by majority agreement. That can't be a republic of self-government and is very much *democracy*. It also is admitting a democracy can be monarch-held. However, so can a republic, but the contract dies with that family. You will see this around Alexander the Great. Democratic monarchies just hand off to a new ruler based on a majority vote. Even so, the republic monarchy is strictly for political activity under the permitted activity by the Free People, or Society.

As Jefferson wrote to P.S. Dupont de Nemours Poplar Forest, April 24, 1816, "the people (by which is meant the mass of individuals composing the society)." He also said in many places the individual is always free.

As a side thought, ever notice how openly government agents tell us we both *have* democracy, and are yet *striving* for democracy? Almost like a religious mantra to focus you on only some unobtainable democracy. Don't worry, we most certainly *do* have a democracy at this time, but how is this not just tyranny? I guess because the oligarch could at least be your neighbor, positioned through election? Or so long as it's your tribe in charge?

Throughout many of our historical republics, free individuals whose authority to hold and secure what they gained and what they want and to enforce the "law" by all means available to them, are primary fixtures, along with the common goal of assuring these personal liberties for other participants of the common cause — liberty. The political features that we end up focusing on are of human design and often against liberty while being totally for themselves over others, when they are to be a secondary (or per the list above tertiary) feature, an auxiliary subservient to the primary feature. Throughout the *true* Pax Romana, the Solonian and Spartan Republics, we see liberty offers some of the most stable advancing societies and cultures in man's history.

All which comes to collapse with democracy.

DEMOCRACY

Yet, when speaking of democracies, the amount of excuses for the collapses and rights destructions it has caused is always backed up by the excuse that it was/is evolving as a "philosophy" or "concept." Other tyranny-supporting philosophies get this excuse as well, such as, "That wasn't *real* socialism," or "Crony capitalism isn't *real* capitalism."

While only the collapse of republic, often caused by democratic operations being there from the start or illegally installed later, is noted as "how republics are," this determinative response from the democratic support system is very telling of the true purpose of those in democracy. When speaking of republics, we are told by the professionals of politics (especially poli-sci majors) they've simply failed to work, and prove despotic in their rule of "absolute" law, and they don't evolve, but, they say that demonstrates how central government is needed, even though that is the *opposite* of what the Founders said they were doing with republic in America. They were clear they were evolving it to *not need* government over the people. The claim republic rule of law is absolute is an interesting one when juxtaposed between Draco's absolutism of Written Law left to the ruler's interpretation and the enforcement by its minions, and Solon's absolutism of Natural Law and the dispersed right for natural enforcement of the law by anyone of the land. Examples of interpreted ancient renditions, or modern Socialist and Communist fascisms masquerading as republics, are all that is used now as what a republic is, though those nations regularly fanned democracy, which allowed the despots to takeover.

Multiple pro-republic Founders noted this has been done since before their day. Denmark was called a republic even though it was a council-run democracy. Even England was called a republic just because of the House of Commons (though the Magna Carta at least supports the underpinning of England being for individual "natural rights," supposedly). This was not the case however, because they did not have "absolute" laws which couldn't be interpreted by the governing body.

What I mean by absolute law in purity, means they could not change the laws through legislation or public vote. In Republics these are the maxims of the society. They are what they are and carved into stone. Democracy changes the meaning and use of "law" all the time through majority votes, or legal rulings. Ancients had to end the existing culture to change the "law." The purpose for the maxims and their establishment are what is seen as the "social contract" such as Locke described. When properly observed we find the governing body was usually left powerless to the individual's will, decisions, the individual's liberties of absolute power, and held to the carved "letter of the law." Only when democracy is allowed to interpret these laws and enforce written code law as absolute to the whole public, and, or government's controlling will do, the republics collapse into monarchial or democratic despotism. Per Locke, you have to completely redesign the society and route the system when a political republic is contractually violated by democracy.

CITIZEN

As *Encyclopedia Britannica* stated in the definition of republic earlier, who is a citizen "varied", or "the category of the people has varied." Notice how the encyclopedia makes the statement "citizens do not govern the state themselves" but "through representatives." Yet, this is exactly the opposite of what the Founders described our Republic and society as a whole to be. *We the People* govern the State(s) through our representatives. However, in actual practice we will see there *are* universal standards in republics. Were the Founders lying, or is *Encyclopedia Britannica* wrong?

As Machiavelli warned upon the term republic, which he only used a handful times in *The Prince*, there was generally a warning included to the elite to abstain "from the property of his citizens and subjects and from their women." Do you see the distinction between "citizen" and "subject"? A primary principle we find all throughout republics is *free men own things*, things that are not of the King's registry, or not of the King's ownership. These things are under one's personal dominion, to which Machiavelli warned, "in republics there is more vitality, greater hatred, and more desire for vengeance, which will never permit them to allow the memory of their former liberty to rest." The King is often also under the power of the citizen who can reject and replace him, though tyrants and tools of higher authorities hide this fact. The subject is to accept this condition under the King, for being serfs they cannot know the will of the citizen (free man), and the King technically owns all their stuff.

Another republic commonality we'll see historically when redeeming every one of these societies' dictatorships into republic is usually a leadership out of the middle-class citizenry, almost like a clear beacon that the middle road protects the republic greater than the bottom or the top social tiers.

At the finish of this endeavor it will be clear the true power of republics is in their unfettered citizens, and their perfect state is the common agreement to assure and protect the liberated citizen in freedom, not to simply elect representatives, the/a central authority, and/or participate in civics to direct personal behavior, and not to be in safety from all possible harms. Though the power to personally enforce all levels of civil, common, and natural laws is paramount.

Machiavelli statue near Uffizi, Florence[12]

---

[12] Satdeep Gill, Public domain, via Wikimedia Commons

REPUBLIC FROM THE PERSPECTIVE OF THE FREE INDIVIDUAL:

I see the best example of ancient republic in its prime as the Roman Republic. The Founders make clear in many works Rome was a major inspiration in the style of republic America took on. Founded on the paraphrased oath of Lucius Junius Brutus, "No more kings!" the Romans exiled the king and replaced him with a Consul. I've already discussed the basics of the Consul of Rome. Citizens and their representatives would meet with the Consul and he would advise them on solutions to problems which vexed them, mediated over larger issues that were of the public matter (res publica), took a diplomatic role with foreign bodies, and when of urgency the Consuls gained limited director roles like that of the ancient kings of Sparta over the military and likely some local facilities. However, in order for the oath of Brutus to be true there were "no kings," so the Consul could command no one unwilling to heed their orders when not on the field of battle, or when they *were not* officers of the people.

Rome's senates, magistrates, assemblies, courts, laws, titles of honor were all either limited in their ability to specific actions only (with political/civil requirements to hold them), or simply as a show of accomplishment and trust for addressing certain matters. No free man had to use them. These terms did not take on connotations of authority in the Republic era in the way we think. Often, the misused applications of legal authority that tyrants wielding democracy slowly installed in Rome, using Draconian codes that led to the Empire, are often what are presented as the "Republic" of Rome. Nowadays, only modern dictatorships that use the oligarchical power structure mixed with imperial militarism, strict citizenship, and border controls are pointed to as examples of "republics" to turn the public against the idea and compare it to a modern political party platform. One of the first things your enemy will do is *rebrand* you, from the inside first, if possible.

Instead of building upon this system with our new knowledge, inventions, and education to better the self and liberty society, we continue to degenerate the republic into mob rule through democracy, never learning the lessons of Ancient Greece and Rome, almost as though someone was trying to steer us only to build upon its consolidated failures, hijacked religions, permissioned rights, and not its successes protecting the individual and true liberty.

It is to this misidentification this publication endeavors to correct the record. For despite the too-common public perception, *republics have historically garnered the greatest advancement in human existence,* because the powers of liberty never change. The free being does what it wants and accepts responsibility by nature's consequences for its actions, and the natural consequence of the event that another *free* being may bring upon them for causing destruction. No group may strip a being of their dignity, holdings, or life. To this we present to you the truth about republics throughout history as an example of where we need to head and what course of advancement we were really put on.

PART TWO:
HISTORIES

ATHENS

NESTLED ALONG THE coastline in a natural harbor (called an "acropolis[13]"), along the olive fields of yore sits Athens. Usually, Athens is where people start when discussing citizen-directed government (often democracy), and since it's the generally educated starting point, I'll address its past first. It is often exampled first, because its system of councils and senates are tools a republic can use politically, but it is a poor example independently as it was a democratic city-state overall, and a haven for abusive merchants. A city-state is basically the *polis[14]* condition or the condition of a domestic people. City equals *polis*, state equals *condition*. The other reason it is often a focus is because it leads unified Greece in one of their first confederations, a subject we'll arrive at later. Mainly, Athens was a political state, one that was often taken over by outsiders running it, or one led by a tyrant, not to mention the corrupt regional merchants that ran Athenian trade routes. Though, Athens is often a Natural Republic where the certified historians fail to notice it to be "republican." We can easily define a political state as the close

---

[13] acropolis (ə-krŏp'ə-lĭs) noun, The fortified height or citadel of an ancient Greek city. A raised area holding a building or cluster of buildings, especially in a pre-Columbian city. — *American Heritage Dictionary of the English Language*, 5th Edition.

[14] Polis, ancient Greek social and political organization — Wikipedia

conditions in which a community lives and agrees to generally interact. That's all it really is.

The citizen position in Athens is of the most concern first. Their comparisons to Sparta are highly important, and the United Greece after the Battle of Thermopylae is important to understand for its association with republic. Greek city-states were usually small communities. Citizens knew each other from market, senate, and being about. Facebooking was a skill not an app. This is why Jefferson preached he believed republics needed to be small, for close community and familiar faces. As one city-state began to claim dominance over another due to inequitable agreements thanks to poor ethics, it would faction the populace through propaganda to whittle away at self-reliance and introspection in the name of a greater (group) cause than liberty. Usually, this cause was the disenfranchised people kept from the city-state's internal politics by policies emplaced for its domestic protection and stability, that thing called "political rights," a horror we now over-relate to everything as the Athenians eventually did, as "good." For if you *must*, and you must, suffer under a ruler or group of rules, then you should have a say in their actions. So is the claim according to mainstream politicos. Thus, suffrage rights (voting) and the attitude of, "If you choose having no say, well that's what you get," is how they morally justify mobs violating individual liberties—"consensus" and "welcomed" participation in the consensus which eventually becomes psychologically mandatory.

Athens is believed to have been settled anywhere from five to eight thousand years ago and grew into a massive seaport. They also acquired silver and marble mines that built up some of the ruling families. It is important we understand that despite the insistence of many experts out there, most of these people's freedom societies lasted longer than is either recorded or admitted too in order to assure the perception that majority or alpha rule is necessary for humans. Though, Athens' longevity is probably pretty accurately aged— Remember, religious and social marauders have ransacked many of the world's most successful cultures to bury their knowledge and hide the truth of their histories, liberty, and natural republics, not to mention the effects of geological cataclysms.

Over the course of their being, their harbor bore them a legendary fishing industry. Their successful sea and materials merchants and navy empire have radiating effects even today, with the usurpation of citizen rights through merchant law adapted from the ocean and applied too much too modern law through agreement of unelected merchants and guild leaders via modern "regulation." It was through these installations and usages of their merchant laws that they grew into an empire as a proper democracy does. Yet, this too took time as the sea tends to first birth strong-willed individuals who prefer their autonomy when home. The most successful families of the farming, mining, and sea trades had great wealth, and usually made up local councils that turned into leadership governments. This was the class of the aristocracy, or *aristoi* (best people), proclaimed to be of the highest stock. This tends to diminish the view of the citizen. These were not the only true citizens, though "class" may work as a term in these divisions. It is only when the power of protecting the individual domestic is equal between all "classes" do we have republic, and for individuals to do so we end up with a true form of citizenry. These, however, are the foundational beginnings of people with a semblance of self-rule from the ancient perspective.

The governing operations that allowed and barred this type of behavior from happening, we are told, we know little about. How convenient. Most views on how the Greek governments worked are based on limited writings. So, it is quite impressive the assertions we have that they were democracies and that republics are like democracies, even though we regularly find massive tyrannical rule at place in democracies when they are their most "democratic" in their leadership and politics, and least in liberation in their citizenry. It was this way (we're told), especially under Archon Draco until Archon Solon opened up the positions of government to all with property qualifications (ownership concepts). Yet, this was a political action, not a natural state action. Those were more addressed by some of Solon's maxims.

Portrait of Solon Legislator and Poet of Athenes by Merry Joseph Blondel[15]

Let me back up slightly. Prior to Solon and often repeated in history, once in political council form, these families ruled through an *Areopagus*[16], a council of elders. They'd select three absolute directors

---

[15] https://commons.wikimedia.org/wiki/File:Merry_Joseph_Blondel-Solon.jpg

[16] *Areopagus*, earliest aristocratic council of ancient Athens. The name was taken from the Areopagus ("Ares' Hill"), a low hill northwest of the Acropolis, which was its meeting place. The Areopagite Council probably

called *Archons*, required to be "nobles[17]" by birth, or really to be accurate a term just meaning notable person. That's it. They are notable to the actions they've taken. Doesn't really make them better than anyone else and back then the common community understood this.

The society of Athens was broken into four classes, three of which had seats for voting in the assembly, much of this arranged by respected — and even greedy — families in the "classes" in common agreement (contract). These were the Athenians and freedmen (generally labors) who made up citizens, Metics[18], and slaves. *These are political classes! Artificial bodies to limit foreign influence on the community!* And the class you were in defined whether you could pass laws, vote, or serve in public office. This is not the same as *natural being*.

As I'm about to clarify these classes, let's look at the common perception of a citizen and see how mis-informers have manipulated the term slowly to hide its meaning right before our eyes. As mentioned prior, *citizens* and *subjects* were intentionally and wrongfully intertwined:[19]

subject (1 of 3)

noun

1 : one that is placed under authority or control: such as

    a: VASSAL

---

began as the king's advisers.
(https://www.britannica.com/topic/Areopagus-Greek-council)

[17] *nobles*, belonging to a hereditary class with high social or political status; aristocratic. (Google dictionary)

[18] Metic
Foreign resident of Athens, one who did not have citizen rights in their Greek city-state (polis) of residence

[19] https://www.merriam-webster.com/dictionary/subject

b (1): one subject to a monarch and governed by the monarch's law

(2): one who lives in the territory of, enjoys the protection of, and owes allegiance to a sovereign power or state

c: the mind, ego, or agent of whatever sort that sustains or assumes the form of thought or consciousness

3 a: a department of knowledge or learning

b: MOTIVE, CAUSE

c(1): one that is acted on

(2): an individual whose reactions or responses are studied

(3): a dead body for anatomical study and dissection

(4): a person who has engaged in activity that a federal prosecutor has identified as being within the scope of a federal grand jury investigation

subject (2 of 3)

adjective

1: owing obedience or allegiance to the power or dominion of another

2a: suffering a particular liability or exposure

subject to temptation

b: having a tendency or inclination : PRONE

subject to colds

3: contingent on or under the influence of some later action

the plan is subject to discussion

subject (3 of 3)

verb

1a: to bring under control or dominion : SUBJUGATE

b: to make (someone, such as oneself) amenable to the discipline and control of a superior

2: to make liable : PREDISPOSE

3: to cause or force to undergo or endure (something unpleasant, inconvenient, or trying)

was subjected to constant verbal abuse

As a synonym for subject Merriam-Webster happily guides you to the word citizen.

Let's look at the legal definition of subject too:

SUBJECT, contracts. The thing which is the object of an agreement. This term is used in the laws of Scotland.

SUBJECT, persons, government. An individual member of a nation, who is subject to the laws; this term is used in contradistinction to citizen, which is applied to the same individual when considering his political rights.

2. In monarchical governments, by subject is meant one who owes permanent allegiance to the

monarch. Vide Body politic; Greenl. Ev. Sec. 286;
Phil. & Am. on Ev. 732, n. 1.

I've shared so much in regards to the definition of a subject so you can see it is obvious that a subject is a lesser-than, something beneath any said thing it pertains to. Is a free man ever subject? No.

In regards to contracts it means, "The thing which is an object of an agreement." In America's case, the subject is the "positions and power of the government found in the constitutional contract." These things are all subject to "We the People." Not once is it the actual people of the United States who are subject... Hmm?

In regards to persons and government, "subject" is used in "contradistinction," so contrast when considering an individual's political rights. But, he's not subject to these. He is either able to use them, making them subject to his will in what they have participatory permission to effect, or he cannot, making them distinct and separate from him. So, they are subject to him and his political condition as citizen, or as a subject. As citizen you are still like a free man. When subject you are then reduced to the permission of your political rights while not as the free man — the political body owns you.

The last one is of the most importance. "Meant one who owes permanent allegiance to the monarch." They've just swapped monarchs out for nation/government in most other definitions, and implied subjection onto all people of such things. But it's wrong and evil for them to have done such a thing.

For the definition of citizen, per Merriam-Webster's "simple definition" a citizen is:

:a person who legally belongs to a country and has the rights and protection of that country

: a person who lives in a particular place

Here is the "full definition":

1: an inhabitant of a city or town; especially, one entitled to the rights and privileges of a freeman

2: a: a member of a state b: a native or naturalized person who owes allegiance to a government and is entitled to protection from it

3: a civilian as distinguished from a specialized servant of the state

In an offshoot description Merriam-Webster says, "*Citizen* is preferred for one owing allegiance to a state in which sovereign power is retained by the people and sharing in the political rights of those people."

Why ever the two separate styles of definitions, beyond an "origins" definition? Oh, and by the way, *civilians* are completely different from *citizens*. In fact, a specialized servant is much closer to what a "civilian" is as they are restricted in what they can do and held to a *legal* standard. Also, how is one a freeman who "legally belongs to a country?" Legal and Lawful are different, and means this definition is claiming legal ownership over a living being. Slavery.

Oh, for fun here is Noah Webster's direct definition from 1828 for citizen and freeman:

CITIZEN, noun

1. The native of a city, or an inhabitant who enjoys the freedom and privileges of the city in which he resides; the freeman of a city, as distinguished from a foreigner, or one not entitled to its franchises.

...

5. In the United States, a person, native or naturalized, who has the privilege of exercising the elective franchise, or the qualifications which

enable him to vote for rulers, and to purchase and hold real estate.

FREE'MAN, noun [free and man.]

1. One who enjoys liberty, or who is not subject to the will of another; one not a slave or vassal.

2. One who enjoys or is entitled to a franchise or peculiar privilege; as the freemen of a city or state.

Let's check a few more definitions from him since his definitions will be most accurate to what these words meant when the U.S. was founded.

What is a *naturalized* person?

NATURALIZE, verb transitive [from natural, nature.]

1. To confer on an alien the rights and privileges of a native subject or citizen; to adopt foreigners into a nation or state, and place them in the condition of natural born subjects.

—Webster's Dictionary 1828

So to be *naturalized* is to be permitted equal civic powers to engaging and adjust the political structure as a native.

What's a franchise? Oh, you're going to love this. I do.

FRANCHISE

noun fran'chiz. [See Frank.] Properly, liberty, freedom. Hence,

47

1. A particular privilege or right granted by a prince or sovereign to an individual or to a number of persons; as the right to be a body corporate with perpetual succession; the right to hold a court leet or other court; to have waifs, wrecks, treasure-treve, or forfeitures. So the right to vote for governor, senators and representatives, is a franchise belonging to citizens, and not enjoyed by aliens. The right to establish a bank, is a franchise

2. Exemption from a burden or duty to which others are subject.

3. The district or jurisdiction to which a particular privilege extends; the limits of an immunity."

— Webster's Dictionary 1828

Huh? Notice the disconnect already? We are told the *citizen* is "owned" by the country because they "owe" it allegiance. Yet, the "full definition" tells us clearly the inhabitant is *entitled* to "the rights (community recognized behavior law cannot interfere with) and privileges (permitted political actions) of a freeman (one of natural law free from claims on paper and community standards)." It is also said "sovereign power is retained by the people." So, if you are the *sovereign*, how can you be *subject*? Well, if it is narrowed to a term meaning one of a country, or "particular place" how can the word *citizen* be, as some dictionaries tell us, related to *kosmopolítēs*? Which means people of the world or properly, the universe. They also cross-breed *civilians* which have inalienable rights (which subjects don't "legally" have, unless stated in their statutes) but are restricted from political actions or privileges versus the freeman who is not, often for domestic and cultural security.

It is clear by a read of histories republican citizens are freemen in a culture (or community) that assures their native citizen is at total personal liberty with a full political voice, while minimizing the options of a foreigner's ability to be involved in politics to undermine the domestic tranquility. For they are not necessarily freemen and often serfs (subjects) of their kingdom. You'll see this as we continue.

As an addition it is important to note Greece had their embodiment or persona for liberty in *Eleutheria*. Her name translates to *freedom*. Yet, unlike the Roman *Libertas*, her history as a deity is barely known, almost as though the tyranny in Greece over the years led to the burying of her knowledge when the democrats and foreign invaders would run amuck. I believe this is likely the case, and the only reason we know of her Roman counterpart is because Rome took over the world and deeply embedded their history proudly into everything they touched in a wider area with more control for a longer period of time than the Greeks/Macedonians. Yet, I am very positive her importance to Grecian liberty was as central as Libertas' to Rome and is in the way I define a citizen or individual autonomy in Greek societies as we move forward.

Properly understood, "citizens" are of native-born parents, and in older times needed deep lineage in the area, known as *phyle*, the root for the taxonomy term *phylum*, meaning a citizen is born to, at least, a father who was Athenian-born, and in time two people born in Athens (or Greece) make a child of the city-state (or of Greece), creating a natural-born free citizen. I believe the idea of it only being linked to the father goes back to Rome when at one point in its monarchial form it was heavily male and needed more women for breeding. American Founders build off this principle found in the *Law of Nations* by Emerich de Vattel and based on the histories of Rome and Greece and "noble families." Founding family birthrights were initially gifted as the freest being related to the founders of a community, with natural-born Greeks not of aristoi in a more "civilian" role until later reforms when they would meet public service standards (duties), or at least acquired a sword. We do find our most republican principles in the Athenian citizen's authorities. Any citizen could submit a decree or law proposal, and they could sit in on, speak upon, vote, propose and counter-propose legislation. This is self-government (self-representation) of the public functionaries and the right of individuals of liberty, or direct republic—at least it is when the minority dissent was/is protected. Direct democracy is when majority rules the vote outcome and *all* must comply. How is that freedom? Citizens could also enforce laws and dispatch corrupt officials. Very republic.

Metics[20] are called by some mere inhabitants, but that is partly incorrect. They are actually civilians. Their rights are limited, because they are from outside cultures whose full acceptance into a society/culture could lead to infiltration and collapse without proper restrictions or assimilation. Put simply, they are people without loyalty and ties to the local body. Essentially, they are security threats as anyone with a titled position can be influenced by profits and foreign power.

Slaves were not always what we are taught. Though there were those beaten in battle, contracted into servitude, or bought as property (or in early stages of Athens taken for debt reimbursement). Many "slaves" were poor (or at times landless) people who worshipped a freeman and offered to serve him or her in various ways. Somewhat like indentured servants, more like groupies, and in the worst of times they would be persons who owed their allegiance solely to a free man or person of titled nobility, and be subjects.

The citizen after meeting certain duties while growing up entered a state of "total freedom," one of both natural and political rights. Their political rights—which again, most mainstream politicos fail to understand was not the same as their natural rights—were usually tied to land ownership, because a man with a piece of Athens/Greece under his belt has more to lose than a bunch of non-land owning, often foreign (outside the city-state) workers. In their natural state of total freedom, no authority, including the city, had power over the citizen, their actions, worships, or their property unless they were actively destructive or treasonous (at least in their freest forms and times as real citizens).

Much law in these early republics was taught orally and kept in memory with the key maxims carved into wood or stone. By the time things were written down, many times it was by wealthy members, foreigners with no stake in the culture (just an admiration or disdain), and/or followers who did not obey or understand the tenets or maxims of the society. Often, they were (and are) culturally disconnected elitists who had interests outside of the polis-state that they preferred over the people in their homeland. But people who

---

[20] *Metic*, Foreign resident of Athens, one who did not have citizen rights in their Greek city-state (polis) of residence. —Wikipedia

understood their position made themselves no more important than any other citizen, because often you had to serve in the military and in politics so you would understand the "game of politics" and the reality beyond your culture. You also knew everyone was trained to fight you if you tried to seize power. This made many who had wealth jealous they were not seen as better-men. Furthermore, if you didn't assure all your people's freedom you were not assuring your own. To despots this matters little. God knows the damage a self-loathing influence could do to the historical record when that influence's works are the only known history of a people.

The other factor in being a freeman in Ancient Greece (and Rome) was to own a sword. A man with a sword, or arms, in most republic cultures was a freeman, end of story. Such possession implied/implies one had/has authority to use said armament against oppression.

This factor is the primary relation of Athens to a natural republic and a regular theme in all republics. Including in America's 2nd Amendment.

The historical record finds that after the aristocrat-run Areopagus (elder or ruling family council/senate) became too inept from hedonism they ended their poor judgement by electing Draco[21] as director of Athens, Dictator. Draco's laws were a little republican in one concept. We must understand Statute (written) Law is *dead*. *Statue*, statute. It is a human concept and using the laws Draco wrote assured the violator was often *made dead* to the letter of the law.

---

[21] *Draco* (Δράκων) was the first law scribe of ancient Athens, Greece. The laws, transcribed in 621 BC ... were particularly harsh: the death penalty was the punishment for even minor offenses. Any debtor whose status was lower than that of his creditor was forced into slavery... The stringency of these laws gave rise to expressions such as "draconian punishment", "draconian laws", and more generally, the far-reaching "draconian measures"... Draco was the first to codify Athenian law; contrary to popular belief, however, he was not the creator of those laws... Draco's code of law was superseded by that of Solon in the early 6th century BC. — https://www.hellenicaworld.com/Greece/Person/en/Draco.html

Draco's horrible reign in Athens collapsed into a cesspool of murder and corruption through what we call *Draconian Law*.[22]

> Draconian laws: traditional Athenian law code
> allegedly introduced by Draco c. 621 BCE.
> Aristotle, the chief source for knowledge of Draco,
> claims that his were the first written Athenian
> laws and that Draco established a constitution
> enfranchising hoplites[23], the lower class soldiers.
> The Draconian laws were most noteworthy for
> their harshness; they were said to be written in
> blood, rather than ink. Death was prescribed for
> almost all criminal offenses. Solon, who was the
> archon (magistrate) in 594 BCE, later repealed
> Draco's code and published new laws, retaining
> only Draco's homicide statutes. Modern
> scholarship tends to be skeptical of the Draconian
> tradition.

Skeptical scholars may be, however academia supports end-all be-all-style laws just as those Draco published, and Draco's face sits above the U.S. Supreme Court. So, I'm sure they are "skeptical" because they can't have people disliking their preferred method of enslavement. Important here also is the notation that Draco "enfranchised the hoplites." Basically, he made them a direct, instituted arm of the government as opposed to a militia of the people, creating a prior non-existing protected "law enforcement" class out of the military.

---

[22] https://www.britannica.com/topic/Draconian-laws

[23] *hoplite*, heavily armed ancient Greek foot soldier whose function was to fight in close formation. Until his appearance, probably in the late 8th century BCE, individual combat predominated in warfare. At that time, new and heavier armour now gave the foot soldier stronger protection: he wore a metal helmet, breastplate, and greaves; on his left forearm he carried a shield that replaced one hung around the neck; and he carried a sword and a six-foot (almost two metre)-long thrusting, instead of throwing, spear. —https://www.britannica.com/topic/hoplite

The Great Lawmaker, Solon the Lawgiver, was tasked with fixing the laws of Draco. During his rule, he retracted the death laws, and instituted laws of "forced" liberty, and equally distributed the power of enforcing the laws that wield death (which were limited and clear) into the whole citizenry's hands regardless of class. Forced liberty seems counterintuitive to restoring people to "freedom" so we need to remember these people were heavily mentally abused. Dropping them right back into unstructured liberty without personal confidence wouldn't have worked out well.

To hold office, Solon designated four financial classes as opposed to heretical requirements, along with a pre-existing requirement of two years of military service. This allowed any citizen to work up into the law-making *Ecclesia* (like Congress) where any Athenian could participate. Generally, it is said that democracy was invented at this time with the election of leadership (and later Solon's institution of a political representation for commoners), but this activity was already in place and if democracy was the order of the day, why is it called "Solon's Republic"? Why is it said also that, "Solon appears to have established the foundations of a true republic?" (Wikipedia) Elections then, can't be a feature of republic or democracy as much as simply a tool for local public appointments. In order for Draco to take power a small ruling minority picked him through vote and ruled as a mob. *Democracy is mob rule.* Doesn't have to be through the public body at-large. We tend to call this *oligarchy*, and today they try to relate this false impression of "popularly elected leaders" upon so-called "democratic republics." The inclusion of the fourth class, the *Thetai*, receiving a seat in the senate is the big reason for my relation of it to political republic, because all classes became representatively equal in the "leader's" election and public matters. Put another/proper way, the minority gained an official assurance and say. Republics protect minorities. However, it is highly incorrect to call *that* democracy. Mob rule (democracy) did not necessarily have a say in the rules Solon dictated either, just his election by the ruling class and later popular elections of officers. The political bodies were still officially (contractually) limited in their power and scope, while in a *pure democracy* they are only limited by public will/perception. Also, Solon's rule created a power for the minority to defend itself against any abusive majority taking control.

Solon's rules are brilliant in their purpose, but historically become confused to the non-liberty-minded. His maxims (yes, I'm finally getting to them) were to reach specific psychological goals of *ownership, self-worth* and *self-responsibility* into the citizenry, so they would take care of their problems directly, and thus return the Athenian back into self-government rather than being dependent on a central ruler. On the outset, it doesn't seem this way, but these ideals were not there before it became a republic, or more accurately were reestablished when it returned to be a more natural one.

The key maxims of Solon were:

1. The citizen could not sell their land. They could lease it, but they had to retain holding it. This taught them the importance of property and kept elitists and foreigners from buying up Athens. Also, you could move up in political class as you acquired wealth and land; a precursor to the removal of any land requirement to hold office at all in future republics.

2. Fellow citizens who owed on loans could no longer be placed into slavery until their debt was paid. Prior, any Athenian citizen who owed a loan was owned by the financier and required to give their life if directed to do so by the lienholder, much like some today when they're told to come into work in dangerous conditions or having to be unarmed while working. So, when the Spartans attacked some rich politician would make you, a fellow Athenian, go die for him. No longer under Solon was this so. Athens and any state-of-being's goal needs to be self-preservation. As such it is easy to understand why the rulings and edicts of these rulers/city-states only applies to *their* citizens.

3. Every Athenian was to enforce the law personally. As I said, this power was "distributed to the whole citizenry," all classes. No police as we know it, and there was a disempowering of the enfranchised hoplite Draco had created. It is the only thing that explains Socrates, Aristotle, and other writs of the time's relation of the free Athens of Solon and United Greece to the pit of foreign-influenced corruption that was killing their enlightenment during their lifetimes. This rule and others were very similar to the Spartan Constitution, meaning Solon was likely influenced heavily by Lycurgus[24] the Lawgiver.

This, due to the redemption of the natural liberties of the citizen was Solon's Republic. I see none of this personal authority in democracies. For instance, secondary and tertiary police enforcement is almost a requirement in democracy to carry out the claimed majority's will, and a similar force selected out of the soldier hoplites class is how Draco enforced his murderous laws, and how Peisistratus[25] later seizes control.

Enfranchisement, or specializing, is done to turn the hoplite (or any field "professional") into a state police force and build generations of government-loyal subjects indebted to the political body over the people. In fact, the style of "democratic republic" that we're told was established at this time is disproved when Solon leaves Athens after having the political system and people swear an oath to his laws, which only he can overturn. Then he left on a ten-year journey, though in truth it appears this was to allow the laws to settle in, and so he would not be influenced. Even so, officials violated these

---

[24] *Lycurgus*, (flourished 7th century BC?), traditionally, the lawgiver who founded most of the institutions of ancient Sparta. — https://www.britannica.com/topic/Lycurgus-Spartan-lawgiver

[25] *Peisistratus*, also known as *Pisistratus*, was a tyrant of ancient Athens who ruled from 546 BC until his death in 527 BCE. His unification of Attica, the triangular peninsula of Greece containing Athens, along with economic and cultural improvements laid the groundwork for the later pre-eminence of Athens in ancient Greece. — https://en.wikipedia.org/wiki/Pisistratus

laws, refused to leave office, and caused much general trouble. We can bet citizens upheld Solon's reforms and rebelled often. One day Peisistratus, Solon's cousin, implemented a takeover of Athens. Solon was replaced by the Tyrant (or *tyrannos*: one who took power by force) Peisistratus, who kept many of Solons reformations in place. Solon returned after 10 years and over time vocally resisted the Tyrant, even to the point of regularly standing outside his own estate as an old man in full armor, but Peisistratus succeeded in gaining and holding autocratic power.

Peisistratus unified the "poor" (this tends to mean non-landowners) and external people of the lands—those living in the hills—who were self-sufficient but "disenfranchised" through democratic votes. So, he used those people living outside of Athens who were upset they weren't being allowed to influence Athens to get him into power over Athens. Thus enfranchising them into the Athenian legal system and under its legal power. In a true and confident republic he would have been dead quickly, and not just as a titled person overstepping their limitations, but for running a mob over the local populace, which was something Romans managed to stave off many times, and Sparta greatly succeeded at preventing for most of its existence. It is different when you invite surrounding regions to join the republic.

We see in his action not just the tyranny of one man killing and oppressing, but real democracy, just like in Nazi-elected Germany and even in the current U.S. party-based democratic system, or in the U.N. under the new "ruling houses" (nation states) who vote on international "policy." Even under mob pressure some Middle Eastern religious groups are using such oppression to get their way as their agents did in ancient Greece. At the time of this writing, there were reports of Muslims literally storming European cities as "civilians" on foot, just stampeding through homes like animals. True or not, a perfect example of democracy in action.

When we grasp republic, we see with no uncertainty that democracy equals tyranny; that tyranny always uses force and leadership, but this does not necessarily mean a ruling person is alone in holding power. *Democracy* made the leadership easy pickings by Peisistratus's ability to hobble together some outside disenfranchised populations who created the real pressure that allowed his control, but he needed a public mob. Many times the reverse happens and the mob places rulers they can change at will, but this is always done with the most un-republican goal of *forcing* their social ideal(s) over individual actions and those wanting no part in the activities. In short, abuse of the minority (individual).

Yet, some of the Tyrant's reforms were massively republican:

- He cut taxes on the poor. (In republic there should be no taxes, and taxes may not even be the right associated term to describe these "fees.")
- He sent out roving judges as arbiters to help settle disputes—not necessarily dispense "justice."
- He created a monies system tied to silver (hard asset).
- He created cultural programs that helped usher in a Greek Enlightenment, though in real republic this isn't in the government's authority to make happen, only to encourage.

These are things Peisistratus could and should have encouraged and taught—on a personal level as well as in political and public knowledge—in a public education system like Sparta had, and all through an accessible Halls of Record. And, maybe he did. Maybe jealousy of his actions has skewed what really happened, though I doubt that, only because of the claims of Solon's resistance to him.

Solon's and Peisistratus's reformations did help define the *Seven Sages of Greece*[26] during a Greek Enlightenment, and bred the likes of Socrates, Plato, Xenophon, and Epicurus. What we end up with from Solon until Hippias (Peisistratus's descendent) is the "Grecian Republic," a type of cultural republic and a close resemblance in

---

[26] The Seven Sages were renowned wise men of seventh and sixth century Greece. The earliest list of the Seven Sages, in Plato's Protagoras (circa 387 b.c.e.), includes Thales, Pittacus, Bias, Solon, Cleobolus, Myson, and Chilon... Many of the maxims that appear at Delphi are attributed to the Seven Sages, including Meden Agan ("Nothing In Excess") and Gnothi Sauton ("Know Thyself). The sages were known for wisdom in its most general sense, encompassing everything from poetry and politics to predicting eclipses. —https://www.encyclopedia.com/history/news-wires-white-papers-and-books/seven-sages

many ways to, and a stepping stone from a good republic, but still under too much central control to really be a true republic. These Athenians were a people advancing in the sciences with very minimal intrusion by their council and with simple laws directly enforced by the individual citizen, when these societies were in their most successful condition.

According to academia, the governing operations that both allowed and barred this type of progress we know little about (how convenient). Most views on how the Greek governments worked are based on limited writings. Today it is asserted that they were democracies, and that republics are just like democracies, even though, again, we find massive tyrannical rule in democracies when they are their most "democratic" in their leadership (ruling minority), and least in liberation of their citizens (living majority/free individuals).

The perceived branches of government, which I believe were separate functionaries, that did have power in their freest forms to "check and balance" others, were, over time, brought together to centralize power. It just seems more logical to use these branches to have each self-governing "class" work in agreement for mutual protection. Otherwise they are enslaved to each other. Where is the liberty in that? Often, mutual protection is the original intention of the Greek Confederations. To think Solon didn't see this seems disingenuous, and an underestimation of the man's intellect.

I will share *branches* of various governments/societies in each chapter as I can, but I can't stress enough these are auxiliaries and facilities that can take many forms as the freemen establishing them choose. Their reach is regularly expanded by usurpers over time, centralizing the body's power. The purpose of their foundation is to assure a community or an individual's liberties be retained as the primary purpose beneath the collective or leadership's desires. In other words, they really aren't important because they aren't to supersede the individual. However, they often reveal their purpose of assuring personal liberty throughout their early operations. My concern is for you to not get lost in the minutiae or false idea that these bodies are the pinnacle of civilization, or that the cooperative function of the collective will over individual will is the goal and purpose of mankind, for as noted, *civilians* (people of civilization or under civic laws) are not free people.

THE BRANCHES

These "branches" in Athens were:

THE ECCLESIA[27] [28]

Unlike a parliament, the Assembly's members were not elected, but attended by right when they chose. Greek democracy created at Athens was direct, rather than representative: any adult male citizen over the age of 20 could take part, and it was a duty to do so. The officials of the democracy were in part elected by the Assembly and in large part chosen by lottery in a process called sortition. (Basically, sortition is a lot selection process because political education was general, not professionalized/compartmentalized… imagine that!)

The Assembly had four main functions: it made executive pronouncements (decrees, such as deciding to go to war or granting citizenship to a foreigner), elected some officials, legislated, and tried political crimes. As the system evolved, the last function was shifted to the law courts. The standard format was that of speakers making speeches for and against a position, followed by a

---

[27] *ecclesia* (ĭ-klē′zhē-ə, -zē-ə) noun, The political assembly of citizens of an ancient Greek state. —The American Heritage® Dictionary of the English Language, 5th Edition.

[28] https://en.wikipedia.org/wiki/Athenian_democrac

general vote (usually by show of hands) of yes or no.

Though there might be blocs of opinion on important matters, sometimes enduring, there were no political parties and likewise no government or opposition. Voting was by simple majority. In the 5th century at least, there were scarcely any limits on the power exercised by the Assembly. If the Assembly broke the law, it would punish those who made the (illegal) proposal that it had agreed to. If a mistake had been made, from the Assembly's viewpoint it could only be because it had been misled."

In short, it was the House of Representatives where the reps were the freemen of Athens directly involved as they wished to be. In other words, a congress of the people for dealing with issues within Athens and setting civic standards. This isn't really democracy though they imply simple majority, which means they didn't need a 60 percent majority to codify a decision, only 51 percent. At least, it was not a democracy so long as the minority was protected from any majority act violating their natural liberty and birthrights as Athenians. It was a direct republic because the entry and historians admit all can/could equally enforce the law, were informed of the law, and one could likely abstain from activities the majority wanted to engage in that one disagreed with. Otherwise how were they free men? I'm excluding rules that might exist by any league they were in agreement with for regional defense purposes to an extent, but much of that come closer to the end of the 4th century B.C. I believe this ability to abstain was the case after Solon's reforms and the democracy and collective adherence to it that educates, and politicos speak of, came later. The Republic is what Socrates and ilk were lamenting about as the Athenian Golden Era. It is also what Cicero later focused on in his studies of their society while researching Rome's past.

Note: "As the system evolved, the last function was shifted to the law courts." Did it evolve, or was it corrupted, and the courts used to undermine the people's authority through perceived judicial powers?

Since sortition was done because all were educated in politics it makes one wonder why anyone would want to steal that knowledge from the public and put it in the hands of the few. Often it seems the claim was because of population growth, but that has a simple fix of starting a new "forum" or political body to handle similar affairs in freer matters. Unless of course one is a power monger wanting to centralize authority instead of allowing for dispersed power, dispersed power being the goal of Solon's reforms. Also, note there were not political parties. This isn't totally accurate as each tribe was its own political party, but the goal should have been the stability of Athens and the maintaining of its principals.

When it eventually became a democracy the people were as easy to sway and manipulate as today:[29]

> The public opinion of voters could be influenced
> by the political satires written by the comic poets
> and performed in the city theaters.

Meaning men of wealth and people of influence used media to direct the public opinion to format the law, which would lead to free-minded individuals not buying parlor tricks or trusting the shadows on the walls to being outcast and attacked, ostracized, as occurred against Socrates and others. A democracy allows one holding an office to be the supreme director who can overstep their position, unless his actions anger the people. As long has he prosecutes those the public hates, his position is safe and he is no different than a king over his little precious office. This is unlike a republic where one is to only do the job they were hired for, directed by a set of a rules he is not to diverge from, and to which any violation of the private citizen's liberty is an act of war on the whole body. Oh, democracies set rules for positions, and the mob will indignantly riot on the city as whole, but the system is run by majority perceived rule. As long as the majority in power find overstepping the rules to be okay, then it is okay. How often have you heard it said that when a party takes over, they make the laws? They say this ignorant crap in the U.S. often. It is

---

[29] https://en.wikipedia.org/wiki/Classical_Athens

not true. We're a republic with a contractually limited government. Yet, we see majority abuse of the law all the time when presidents, congressmen, and judges do things that violate the permitted power of their positions, while their public supporters cheer and excuse the acts as necessary, or use some childish relation of how it's okay cause the other guys were doing it.

THE BOULE[30] [31]

In 594 B.C., Solon is said to have created a boule of 400 to guide the work of the assembly. After the reforms of Cleisthenes, the Athenian Boule was expanded to 500 and was elected by lot every year. Each of Cleisthenes's 10 tribes provided 50 councilors who were at least 30 years old. The Boule's roles in public affairs included finance, maintaining the military's cavalry and fleet of ships, advising the generals, approving of newly elected magistrates, and receiving ambassadors. Most importantly, the Boule would draft probouleumata, or deliberations for the Ecclesia to discuss and approve on. During emergencies, the Ecclesia would also grant special temporary powers to the Boule.

Cleisthenes restricted the Boule's membership to those of zeugitai[32] status and above, presumably because these classes' financial interests gave them an incentive towards effective governance. A

---

[30] *boule*, noun, a legislative council of ancient Greece consisting first of an aristocratic advisory body and later of a representative senate — https://www.merriam-webster.com/dictionary/boule

[31] https://en.wikipedia.org/wiki/Athenian_democracy

[32] *Zeugitai* (from zeugos, 'yoke'), at Athens, Solon's third property class, said to comprise men whose land yielded between 200 and 300 medimnoi of corn or the equivalent in other produce (the other three classes were *pentakosiomedimnoi, *hippeis, *thētes). — https://oxfordre.com/classics/

member had to be approved by his deme[33], each of which would have an incentive to select those with experience in local politics and the greatest likelihood at effective participation in government.

The members from each of the ten tribes in the Boule took it in turn to act as a standing committee (the prytaneis) of the Boule for a period of 36 days. All 50 members of the prytaneis on duty were housed and fed in the tholos of the Prytaneion, a building adjacent to the bouleuterion, where the boule met. A chairman for each tribe was chosen by lot each day, who was required to stay in the tholos for the next 24 hours, presiding over meetings of the Boule and Assembly.

The boule also served as an executive committee for the assembly and oversaw the activities of certain other magistrates. The Boule coordinated the activities of the various boards and magistrates that carried out the administrative functions of Athens and provided from its own membership randomly selected boards of ten responsible for areas ranging from naval affairs to religious observances. Altogether, the boule was responsible for a great portion of the administration of the state, but was granted relatively little latitude for initiative; the boule's control over policy was executed in its probouleutic, rather than its executive function; in the former, it prepared measures for deliberation

---

[33] *deme*, Greek Dēmos, in ancient Greece, country district or village, as distinct from a polis, or city-state. Dēmos also meant the common people (like the Latin plebs). In Cleisthenes' democratic reform at Athens (508/507 BCE), the demes of Attica (the area around Athens) were given status in local and state administration. Males 18 years of age were registered in their local demes, thereby acquiring civic status and rights. — https://www.britannica.com/topic/deme-ancient-Greek-government

by the assembly, in the latter, it merely executed
the wishes of the assembly."

This was a council to check and balance the Assembly which
could be overtaken by outside influences, protecting and allocating
the city's finances to local concerns and military equipment upkeep,
verifying elected officials and punishing them, and to make decisions
regarding trade relations between members and foreign bodies to
secure domestic interests—much like the U.S. Congress. They would
become the leadership during emergencies to minimize confusion
when addressing an immediate threat. Though there was always
council on sight for the Boule I do not really believe the Boule or the
Ecclesia were active every day. The U.S. Founders, in fact, intended
for representatives and senators to be home more often than not.
These people are really to have very little to do much of the time.

Oh, and I will regularly contend a free man was defined in Greece
and Rome as anyone who owned a sword. To the class called zeugitai
Wikipedia says:

> The term appears to have come from the Greek
> word for "yoke", which has led modern scholars
> to conclude that zeugitai were either men who
> could afford a yoke of oxen or men who were
> "yoked together" in the phalanx—that is, men
> who could afford their own hoplite armor.

Meaning men who owned swords and could fight. The last
definition is likely the true definition for the Solon Reforms focused
on assuring the right of *every* Athenian to be able to physically enforce
the law. In school you should have learned (as I did) the common
knowledge that free men needed only own a sword. Seems odd that
modern scholars need to imply it was tied to wealth, to affording a
bovine. Yet, it is likely true one would have to have producing land
to be on the Council as Solon was placing Athens back into the hands
of the local Athenian and removing the foreign influence which had
been buying up and selling out the local people.

THE DIKASTERIA

Athens had an elaborate legal system centered on full citizen rights. The age limit of 30 or older, the same as that for office holders but ten years older than that required for participation in the assembly, gave the courts a certain standing in relation to the assembly. Jurors were required to be under oath, which was not required for attendance at the assembly. The authority exercised by the courts had the same basis as that of the assembly: both were regarded as expressing the direct will of the people. Unlike office holders (magistrates), who could be impeached and prosecuted for misconduct, the jurors could not be censured, for they, in effect, were the people and no authority could be higher than that.

My favorite part:

The system showed a marked anti-professionalism. No judges presided over the courts, nor did anyone give legal direction to the jurors. Magistrates had only an administrative function and were laymen. Most of the annual magistracies in Athens could only be held once in a lifetime. There were no lawyers as such; litigants acted solely in their capacity as citizens. Whatever professionalism there was tended to disguise itself; it was possible to pay for the services of a speechwriter or logographer (logographos), but this may not have been advertised in court. Jurors would likely be more impressed if it seemed as though litigants were speaking for themselves."

First off, "full citizen rights" does not mean *everybody*! "The people" means everybody. The citizen has both natural liberties and local permission to partake in the local political matters. If you really grasp why outsiders can't have a say in enactments of internal affairs this is the book for you. I will explain succinctly now. The Public Assemblies of any republic mentioned here, generally, are formed so that the populace domiciled and residing (meaning living as permanent and temporary inhabitants) can meet and proclaim their position on legislation that may affect *everyone*. The private assemblies keep the public assembly from affecting the native community and culture which is to *always* take precedence. Not every society is freedom-based, and thus, *cannot be involved* in the local affairs of a liberty-based people.

To the section I noted as "My favorite part," when the legal system is professionalized the citizen is treated as uneducated and ignorant. The professionals can then conspire and the influential can begin to manipulate the "law" to suit their desires and protect them. Of course, good luck getting the mainstream law professionals, politicians, and historical scholars to generally admit this. Why would they give up power over the mass's perception? I also find it interesting they claim it was "elaborate." Often it is professionalization that complicates processes so there is a reason to have professionals over a field who are the only ones who can possibly understand the intricacies of "law." Else it is simple, and anyone can understand it. That would be how *all* Athenians were educated in their customs. They had to be simple. Which would be most likely how it was as the people were the true judges (jury).

As Jefferson noted in his writings:[34]

> Laws are made for men of ordinary understanding
> and should, therefore, be construed by the ordinary
> rules of common sense.

Or put another way, the law is written commonly for common men. It is not meant to direct them, but be so that they can understand

---

[34] https://founders.archives.gov/documents/Jefferson/98-01-02-3562

and direct it themselves. The U.S. system is based on this fact, but the professionals lie about the power of the juror who can supersede any lesser law (code or statute) when making their ruling, a process known as *jury nullification*. In a jury trial in America as well as many other ancient republics, the magistrate is only a referee to be sure the process is moving forward and is completed. The jury is the sovereign who make the decisions. A judge is an arbiter in which a jury is not involved.

I beg you, as you move forward in this book, to not lose sight of this quote:

> The jurors could not be censured, for they, in
> effect, were the people and no authority could be
> higher than that.

Meaning the Archons (or kings) did not overrule the freemen nor did judges or magistrates. This is the truest fact of all republics. It is what the Founders put in motion with the Declaration of Independence, the Articles of Confederation, and the Preamble of the U.S. Constitution. Elitists manipulate this fact to imply a group is the highest authority, especially a group's perception of what is—often that being "accepted" law. That is a lie. It has *always* meant "the people" as persons, persons as individuals.

You are the highest authority over any artificial construct or human rule. So long as you have not physically harmed.

In the case of Solon's laws his predecessor Peisistratus kept modified forms of the law, but because they were modified technically the Republic of Solon was undermined and practically over with at that point, if it ever was one in the first place. It becomes obvious how laws remaining common and agreed upon paramount to security and stability, but the issue we will see that befalls these republics in history is the idea that the government enforcing the laws is as absolute and irresistible as the maxims that authorize it, especially over the personal liberties the people were regularly trying to assure. Maxims like Solon's were not to be altered, or it's not the same concept. This ideal was applied in Rome as well.

Though I have laid out for you the lack of republic in the concept of voting, the dictator Cleisthenes shows us why voting and representatives are *not* synonymous with republics. Cleisthenes, who overthrew Hippias, son of Peisistratus, replaced the four classes with ten, but he removed class bias and made them "electorates," trustees who would choose the leader by *majority* vote. Essentially, he created tribal districts; another dangerous democratic feature, and only a useful *tool* when under republic. The removal of class bias is a major republican feature and the lack of the need for official class recognitions is useful to it. Poor or rich, if you are in a district (which really should be seen like townships) it is hoped you would be more of your community then political class. What matters is we're natives and men of liberty, not how wealthy we are or aren't. However, Cleisthenes is the "Father of Democracy" as this increase in districts is used to create more majority rule over the auxiliaries we today call "government." Lords of influential wealth buy off other admiring locals and their status becomes why they are elected and not their ability to make decisions, nor loyalty to the purposes of the society. Playing the majority to a cause gets the public will behind it and leads to majority will overthrowing the limitations on the political body, which does not make the alteration lawful or acceptable, though modern politicos and *judicites* will argue otherwise.

It's clear to me the ploy that drops us into democratic tyranny is constantly the attempt to assure equal "representation" into central power hubs in the cities through trustees as opposed to through self-"representation" (representatives). No matter the claim of collective will being at work, some handful of manipulators are at the helm for validation of their egos and right to direct the masses. Rural and suburban areas seem to unify more easily in respect for each other's personal property and selves but are easily divided by charismatic personalities. I wonder, could this consolidation of power in cities be a result of all those external trade influences which amass where industrial activity is high?

Another possible rule Cleisthenes may have introduced was *ostracism*, whereby a vote by the citizens could exile a person for 10 years. Generally, this was a citizen deemed a threat to the "democracy" attempting to be a tyrant. However, soon after, any citizen judged to have too much power in the city tended to be targeted for exile. In my view this is only natural as lawmakers tend to hide knowledge and abuse power. Under this system, the exiled man's property was maintained, but he was not physically in the city where he could risk creating a new tyranny. This is very republican, to an extent. They respected the man's property, maybe because subconsciously they understood they were just scapegoating some people at times. This activity was long practiced in the land of Britannia too, well before the Roman Empire arrived.

Today's largest misstep in liberty ideology is the lack of understanding when one can and can't destroy a servant, and or their property. In this case, these were not necessarily civil servants as we understand them. These were supposedly full citizens which is kind of a problem with democracy. Your dislike for another's understanding of the law may have been reason enough to assault and drive one out with enough "public" (mob) support, but not to kill and dismember them, something generally seen as a last resort, even back then. Being democratic over republic, using these rules the influential magistrates and titled could sit comfortably while directing blame for issues they likely caused on some underling or unsuspecting citizen. In America, however, because we set up a government under the Constitution of the People, and not one of directed operation *over* the People, the elected official enters into serfdom like a proper republic. Though we respect agents' Natural Rights, We the People are in a state of total citizen freedom and they, reduced into *civilian-ship*. As such their right to punish the citizen for behavior they dislike where no one is hurt is removed; their ability to pass laws over these social and moral activities, taken away. Their right to wage war, reduced to specific actions per conditions. They are only to assure our trade and domestic tranquility in a perfect, personal state of freedom.

Anything outside these permissions places them beneath the citizen and under that citizen's personal authority to dispatch for treachery. Note: This *is* the extreme fact of your authority. It does not mean courts, arbitration, or exile through mob isn't "legal" or acceptable. However, the first thing a mental abuser will do is tell you, *you* can't hit *them*. Simply not true and a proven deterrent. For an additional consideration keep in mind imprisonment is technically theft of a man. Do you have the right to steal and keep away a freeman, often one who if found guilty of a minor crime was placed into servitude to the wronged until they were repaid? Prison wasn't generally a concept in liberty-leaning societies. It's the creation of despots who see the people as property.

Expansions of Democracy like Cleisthenes' continued to weaken and destroy what aspects of republic Solon had recovered. Cleisthenes was actually in charge of Athens at about the time Rome rebelled against the monarchy and as we'll get to about 40 years later, they sent representatives to learn of the Greek system built on Solon (and in my opinion Sparta's Lycurgus). He is also claimed to have referred to his reforms as "isonomia" and not "demokratia" which in Wikipedia's entry is described as:

> Isonomia (ἰσονομία "equality of political rights,"[1][2] from the Greek ἴσος isos, "equal," and νόμος nomos, "usage, custom, law,") was a word used by ancient Greek writers such as Herodotus and Thucydidesto refer to some kind of popular government. It was subsequently eclipsed until brought back into English as isonomy ("equality of law").

And...

> Mogens Herman Hansen has argued that, although often translated as "equality of law," isonomia was in fact something else. Along with isonomia, the Athenians used several terms for equality all compounds beginning with iso-: isegoria (equal right to address the political assemblies), isopsephos polis (one man one vote) and isokratia (equality of power).

When Herodotus invents a debate among the Persians over what sort of government they should have, he has Otanes speak in favor of isonomia when, based on his description of it, we might expect him to call the form of government he favors "democracy":

70

> The rule of the people has the fairest name of all,
> equality (isonomia), and does none of the things
> that a monarch does. The lot determines offices,
> power is held accountable, and deliberation is
> conducted in public

This description seems to fall more toward republic, which is again, a Roman term and would explain why it seems to have some experts confused.

> Thucydides used isonomia as an alternative to
> dynastic oligarchy and moderate aristocracy. In
> time the word ceased to refer to a particular
> political regime; Plato uses it to refer to simply
> equal rights and Aristotle does not use the word
> at all.

The suffix -onomy or -nomy does not always mean law. It is used mostly to imply an area of study, or a knowledge based in a specific field. If you do a search through Google for onomy you get this:[35]

> The suffix -logy means a branch of learning, or
> study of a particular subject. The suffix -nomy
> means a system of rules or laws, or body of
> knowledge of a particular subject."

Being Cleisthenes is still close to the Solonian reformation it seems likely this was still a republic system under this term. Especially, since the words demos (many or village) and poli (city) are completely devoid from the term. So, it could mean equal under the law, or more accurately *all are equal under the law*, but it's more likely that it means

---

[35] https://english.stackexchange.com/questions/.../meaning-of-onomy-ology-and-ography

"all use/know the law" or "equal knowledge." By Wikipedia's own notation it possibly just means *equal usage*. Mix that with what you will learn about what Rome built as their republic and it makes sense—that's what an *isonomia* is. The line "The lot determines offices, power is held accountable, and deliberation is conducted in public," is the major tell as the action of agreement would have to occur on the public record, and by Solon's reforms "power" being held accountable for violating the law would automatically be that of armed citizen's authority, let alone the equal applicability of general civil punishment. Also, my position that republic is often used to imply oligarchy, isonomia is the same as republic by the claim it's "an alternative to dynastic oligarchy," as such claims, I will continue to note throughout the work, are a bastardization that ignore the fact that republics were originally to assure the local native peoples their dominion over the political body of their culture. They further note Plato uses this to refer to equal rights and Aristotle doesn't use it at all. Since republic was fading this would make sense. It had been nearly 200 years since Cleisthenes and would be why Plato failed to title *Politeia* as *Isonomia*. Three hundred years after that, Cicero titles *Politeia* as *Res Publica*.

If you are the tyrant lawgiver whom law does not apply to (the *anarchist supreme*) you can damn well bet you want everyone under you to understand the law still applies to *them*. However, in his use of political representation too much power in the hands of a political majority with a disempowered individual will and did assure mob rule by the wealthy. The disempowerment of the individual as the primary law enforcer over and against *all* "state" agents gave way to democracy. Eventually, democracy poisoned the entire Greek Confederation. Athens' Solonian Golden Era was horribly disfigured by the 3rd century B.C., though there was an interesting development around Socrates's era.

THE THIRTY TYRANTS

In this event, which occurs nearly 200 years after Cleisthenes' rule, Sparta defeated Athens in the Peloponnesian War. The Tyrants are put in charge to root out the democratic elements of Athens and restore the "Ancient Constitution." What could this "Ancient Constitution" be? Well of course, republic, which Sparta had maintained for hundreds of years by this point, and under the claimed first Constitution ever by the sage Lycurgus. Athens had already once squelched its return to this concept after Solon. Now they were being directed by an oligarchy of natives placed by foreigners.

Keep in mind *oligarchy* just means few rules/rulers and thus political rule by a few or few rules, but Athens was long screwed up in understanding the separation of political rights from natural liberty(ies) by this point. Even so, this incident still maintains a theme in which the power was reduced back to a few, because mob rule (democracy) had been out of control. Being oligarchical wasn't the problem. Young fools lacking honor was. Mainstream historians sympathetic to democracy in our modern democratic-leaning societies make it seem this was an oligarchical rebellion like Peisistratus' seizure, but we must note a student of Socrates, Critias, is the leader of the Thirty Tyrants; a young man who unlike his counterpart Theramenes, didn't seem to understand Socrates' teachings. It is also believed by some that Xenophon, the historian, was a commander under the Thirty and due to his apparent Spartan sympathies, this may be true. The Senate was still intact, but the Thirty were dictating the magistrates and creating laws at will.

That aside, I surmise the intention was a return to republic based on this line in Xenophon's history, *Hellenica*, where he states:

> "Besides," he (Theramenes) said, "we are undertaking, in my opinion, two absolutely inconsistent things — to rig up our government on the basis of force and at the same time to make it weaker than its subjects."

The prior is his concern that with their tyrannical tactics against people, that they will rally too great a group who oppose their actions, and the latter is him noting the actual reason for their placement. If the new government is to be weaker than its "subjects" this would not be a democracy or an oligarchy as we're taught in how they later operate, or how the prior is ignored to truly be, as this history shows us. He is also likely describing the position of *citizen* as it was under that action being taken against fellow Athenians. They were being treated as subjects. It is likely not an accurate description of what the citizen was, for as constantly noted, citizens are historically treated as free men, persons of the cosmos, especially free Greeks who are *kosmopolítēs*, citizens of the universe

We're taught the Thirty slaughtered thousands, many without a trial, and in later cases clearly out of greed and vengeance. The lack of a trial is troublesome, though not always wrong. The initial routing of democrats was welcomed as Xenophon notes many knew those initially prosecuted were commonly understood as enemies to the aristocracy, and as already noted in this work this means political ruling families that were natural-born citizens of Athens (generally). So, the Thirty were routing Democrats, supporters of mob rule over the city-state by many insiders and outsiders.

Well, if the sitting political leadership of Athens is criminal (operating against the community standards) which is what the 30 were established against, and these Tyrants were freemen of Athens and aware of the corruption they were under, they would have also then been under no requirement to provide a trial to anyone and have lot of political (civic/legal) power to do so as well, bestowed by the winner of the war that put them in charge and per their birthright. The problem with the Thirty is they were to establish a new constitution by the ancient standard, and as Xenophon notes:

> Although chosen, however, for the purpose of
> framing a constitution under which to conduct the
> government, they continually delayed framing
> and publishing this constitution.

Yet, the egos of Athenian heritage, long soaked in a mob-rule mentality (thanks to Peisistratus) saw this as an opportunity to seize control themselves, some of whom tried using democracy to seize control in other areas around Greece. Theramenes, when being accused by Critias of treason against the Thirty, noted Critias was:[36]

> establishing a democracy in Thessaly along with Prometheus and arming the serfs against their masters.

I dare say this line sure does support this writing's position on what democracy is used for, doesn't it?

The worst act was the Thirty disarming the public, which is unacceptable in any freedom/liberty society, especially considering the quote about Critias' democratic endeavor. Many of these men lacked the ethics the Spartans had in duty to liberty. However, the failed war against the republic of Sparta was an opportunity to vanquish the actual tyrants who over 150 years seized control of Athens and were directly responsible for the erosion of the Enlightened society Socrates and others of his time were lamenting about. Had the Spartans been listened to, and the aristoi's brainless ego-driven youth simply focused on the task, the efforts to bring about the strong return of Athenian democracy that overthrew the Tyrannical Thirty would have been non-existent, and republic in Greece could have flourished against the encroaching powers that sank the area into despotism in the coming centuries and beyond.

---

[36] www.perseus.tufts.edu/hopper/

The Death of Socrates, by Jacques-Louis David (1787)[37]

If you look over the Britannica links I provided you'll notice it is at least honest when it often states/phrases, "It is likely that…" — at least more than most excepted sources in the field of Ancient Greece tend too. I contend that claims of inaccuracy in my interpretations will come from people who knowingly are making assumptions on information that is only "likely." Though I have similar positions, they look at the cultures through the lens that believes the structure of today comes from the seemingly pro-authoritarian parts of these old republics (presented as collective agreement in democracy), necessary to keep the masses from being barbaric, not from the actual individual expanding powers and "policies" as a despot overthrowing the republic by democracy for gain and glory. What I am taking you through is some of what our Founders realized in their studies. The over-focus on political rights and structure leads one to the conclusion of government being the identity of these cultures. The Men of the Enlightenment read past that information to the key concepts of personal liberty and assurance of personal freedom. This

---

[37] https://commons.wikimedia.org/wiki/File:David_-_The_Death_of_Socrates.jpg

is the hardest part of understanding liberty a student can go through, and most people fail at it, misconstrue/manipulate it, or run from it. However, with this information under your belt it will become a more likely possibility that freedom will be the focus and not the appeal to authority to shirk self-responsibility, as so many currently strive to do.

The implications of political and natural rights that date back to antiquity can be found in Xenophon's *Hiero*, where Hiero is relating the differences of the private citizen in liberty from that of the despot, who clearly has "power," a "throne," and political adversaries.

Something well imbodied in the action of Alexander the Great.

THE GREATEST MACEDONIAN:

Alexander the Great in Skopje, Macedonia[38]

Let us start by knowing Alexander the III was tutored by Aristotle, himself a student of Plato, and thus basically a student of Socrates and

---

the Socratic Methodology. This means Athenian thinkers had serious influence in a foreign land. Also, tying Aristotle to the 30 Tyrants by way of some being Socrates' students we can bet Alexander understood how such persons behaved. It is claimed that Socrates did not support the action of the Tyrants, but it seems to me Socrates was and would be in support of the Spartan direction over Athens in returning to the old Constitution, which for Socrates would be the Solonian Reforms, and thus an influence of Lycurgus the Lawgiver of Sparta. Lycurgus was so influential in the area we can bet the Macedonians had their system of politics influenced by his reforms as well.

Alexander took control of Greece through alliances his father forged, under his father's plan to invade and pacify Persia which had been a regular nuisance since long before the Battle of Thermopylae. Basically, Alexander headed up a *confederation*. He had no personal power over the members in ruling their domestic political activities. How do I know this? It is the cornerstone of the term *confederation*. Also, there is the oath of the League of Corinth, which he gained his throne by and which tells us this kingship, or imperial position, was only for a military purpose and enforcement of the agreement. Does this mean there was no oppression by the body of this League? Of course not. This is what the term means and what the intention of such a construct is. That is all I am saying. Since each side of a conflict or ideal has their own perception, I am sharing that some of these events under the narrative that these people of title often claim to be overstepping their position, might be in fact in accordance with the agreement of the title overall, and what that means in a liberty perspective. To the League of Corinth, the agreement was:[39]

> Oath. I swear by Zeus, Gaia, Helios, Poseidon and all the gods and goddesses. I will abide by the common peace and I will neither break the agreement with Philip, nor take up arms on land or sea, harming any of those abiding by the oaths. Nor shall I take any city, or fortress, nor harbour by craft or contrivance, with intent of war against

---

[39] https://en.wikipedia.org/wiki/League_of_Corinth

the participants of the war. Nor shall I depose the kingship of Philip or his descendants, nor the constitutions existing in each state, when they swore the oaths of the peace. Nor shall I do anything contrary to these agreements, nor shall I allow anyone else as far as possible. But if anyone does commit any breach of the treaty, I shall go in support as called by those who need and I shall fight the transgressors of the common peace, as decided (by the council) and called on by the hegemon and I shall not abandon (the listed members)"

Broken down by Livius.org:[40]

The provisions of the treaty were:

1.   that the constitutions of the member states would remain unchanged;

2.   that violence between the member states was no longer permitted;

3.   that, in case of the overthrow of a government, a congress of representatives was to meet at Corinth;

4.   that it (the League) would establish the facts and declare war;

5.   that the league's army was to be commanded by Philip;

6.   that the league's member states would send a number of soldiers to the league's army in proportion to their size.

There is a common suggestion in academia that Alexander was conquering members for wanting "freedom" from his rule. What seems more accurate is that he had to use force on the members who were trying to weasel out of the compact before the Persians had been dealt with. A review of this League and its purpose makes that rather clear, though other sources try to misrepresent that. What I have noted is basically iterated by Wikipedia and Britannica:

> The decision for the Destruction of Thebes as transgressor of the above oath was taken by the council of the League of Corinth by a large majority. Beyond the violation of the oath, the council judged that with this way, Thebeans were finally punished after a long time because they betrayed the Greeks during the Persian Wars.

And:

> the league's major action seems to have been the condemnation of the Thebans to slavery and the distribution of their territory among neighboring states following their revolts (336 and 335 bce).

Yet, as an example of how this action is abused by historians generally as Alexander conquering a Greek nation for imperial control as a central government, as opposed to just a military league for defense, the website History of Macedonia.org says:

> The city where Alexander's father was kept as hostage for three years, was plundered, sacked, burned, and razed to the ground, just like Philip acted with Methone, Olynthus, and the rest of the Greek cities in Chalcidice. Only the temples and the house of the poet Pindar were spared from

destruction. This was to be an example to the rest
of Greece and Athens and the other Greek city-
states quickly rethought their quest for freedom.
Greece remained under Macedonian rule.

Do you see the implication that *all* of Greece was under
Macedonian rule? This kind of poor interpretation is rampant in
general education and a prime example of how historians and
scholars can skew a historical narrative. Despite the clarifications by
Wikipedia and Britannica above they still imply some of this
misnomer. Even the broader article on the League by Wikipedia
defines the League improperly (in my view) as a federation, not a
confederation, just as the History of Macedonia page seems to imply a
rulership. A move to imply a single political body was formed by
idealism and influence, not direct intensions with a limited purpose.

With Macedonia we have another society conveniently lacking in
documentation of the system occurring under the general king(s),
even though letter-based writing existed in Greece for nearly 500
years by this point. As Wikipedia so kindly notes for us after defining
some of the titled positions with the king, it says:[41]

> Evidence is lacking for the extent to which each of
> these groups shared authority with the king or if
> their existence had a basis in a formal
> constitutional framework. Before the reign of
> Philip II, the only institution supported by textual
> evidence is the monarchy."

Oh look! Conveniently, the only surviving documented history on
a position of power was that of the monarchy, and then the existing
history beyond that is based around a centralized, authoritarian
regime, presumably. The historians often cited in determining the
culture and governing styles of many of these ancient peoples are
generally German or social progressives of Europe (many from

---

[41] https://en.wikipedia.org/wiki/Government_of_Macedonia

nations that fell to the Roman Empire). Why is this important? Because most Germans during the time period when current history establishes norms for the Antiquity were of the socialist mentality of the late 19th to 20th century. Socialist progressivism and the Germanic Counter-Enlightenment are in full swing in academia during that time, through to today, let alone any earlier histories transcribed and interpreted by pro-centralist Catholics. Meaning the perception, the more modern German and "progressive" (socialist) historian is going to give these past histories, will lean towards duty to community, leadership and *need* for government, not toward personal freedom and liberty — the focus of the Enlightenment and the ideals of ancient Greece and Rome according to the American and English Enlightenists. Current interpretation is a complete farce as to these ancient republics, of which I contend Macedonia can be counted. For the idea the king could leave on a world-conquering campaign and have little rebellion, if it is a centralized system, seems unlikely. Not that there weren't skirmishes at home. Misinterpretation gets worse when we understand that many of the cited ancient written works about most of Macedonia (and early Greece) are all long after the fact, but for a handful, and generally by foreigners. Many of which are Roman like Titus Livius (Livy), and Plutarch living during and after the transition from B.C.E to C.E (or B.C. to A.D.).

Also, as Wikipedia notes:

> Following the Roman victory in the Third Macedonian War and house arrest of Perseus of Macedon in 168 BC, the Macedonian monarchy was abolished and replaced by four client state republics.

Now, by this point in time (long after Alexander), Rome was far more imperial. The deal here was still likely more tributary as a "client"-style relationship, like latter free Roman cities, these states likely managed themselves in most or all domestic matters, leaving defense and trade to Rome Prime. We're also told:

It is unclear if there was a formally established constitution dictating the laws, organization, and divisions of power in ancient Macedonia's government, although some tangential evidence suggests this.

Well, since Lycurgus was the father of constitutional government, they, just as Solon's Athens, were likely set up similarly, as we'll discuss later with Sparta's kings, who were not necessarily rulers over the People, except when in battle. Thus, why Alexander went off on campaign. It would assure he could keep commanding the confederation. So, there is a good chance that Macedonia which was founded around 700 B.C. likely adopted similar branches since the cities of Sparta (established somewhere around 1200 to 850 B.C.), and Athens which again reformed in 650 B.C. were extremely probable influences.[42]

We're pretty well affirmed in this point as:

Kings served as the chief judges of the kingdom, although little is known about Macedonia's judiciary. The kings were also expected to serve as high priests of the nation, using their wealth to sponsor various religious cults. The Macedonian kings had command over certain natural resources such as gold from mining and timber from logging. The right to mint gold, silver, and bronze coins was shared by the central and local governments.

These are almost exactly the same powers as the Spartan kings had when at home, except money was banned from Spartan usage. As "chief judge" they would be consuls like in the early Roman

---

[42] https://en.wikipedia.org/wiki/Government_of_Macedonia_(ancient_kingdom

Republic, and this seems to be well after consuls were used in Rome, making a relation likely. These regions aren't all that far apart and Rome invented their first "Great Road" in 312, meaning they were using lesser roads for some time prior. Intercultural influence is not only likely, but this is assured as the Republic of Rome *did* study the Solonian Reforms in Greece. As was noted earlier consuls do not command. They give an opinion. The participants in the issue do not have to take their advice, at least not in a real republic based on liberty/freedom. Maybe in Athens, and Macedonia this wasn't the case. Maybe the king's ruling was to be absolute, but that wouldn't be freedom or liberty, and "little is known about Macedonia's judiciary."

The Spartan kings also oversaw certain rituals as "high priests," which is a likely modern relation of the position to something more recent under the Vatican's rule, and not necessarily a direct correlation. So, we again have the king of Macedonia taking on a similar role to another major city-state. Additionally, these relations do not mean they got along.

The distribution of power in Macedonia we're told:

> From at least the reign of Philip II the king was
> assisted by the royal pages (basilikoi paides),
> bodyguards (somatophylakes), companions
> (hetairoi), friends (philoi), an assembly that
> included members of the military, and magistrates
> during the Hellenistic period.

That is, setting aside the military as something the King surely commanded and usually something all citizens served in. None of these positions are known to have carried any real lawful weight or power. Pages, bodyguards, companions, friends are all entourages that may have enjoyed some type of preference from the King, but that doesn't mean real lawful authority over the citizen. Magistrates would be less powerful than the chief judge, and more like arbiters then "judges" as we think of them today.

Putting these concepts forward let's examine Alexander briefly. For the most part, there need be no interest in his military campaigns, but for the resulting political condition. Focusing on his conquering and military maneuvering is how he and most all historical figures are deified and used as examples as to the—false—claim that man naturally desires central control, or to centrally control. Instead, the relation of how he left the areas he overtook tells us the general concept his culture leaned towards. Though I do not deny that as he had victories, his head/ego and his need to dictate versus liberate grew in proportion to each other.

Yet, when Alexander took a nation, he placed a general in charge of security, but not to command the local culture. If and when they were found to be abusing the locals, Alexander would send another general to remove the current one by force and take over. The locals still determined their political leaders and style, but were to have a foundation similar to Greek liberty whereby the generals were not to violate personal liberties. I get this sense from the realities of what I've already noted about the fact his campaign was occurring by permission of the League to wage a war on Persia and eventually other threats, and not to command the legal style of Greece, or the nations he came across. Thebes was a member who betrayed the League, so it was liquidated—not overruled or altered, straight-up beaten and *ended*. Proper warfare. To add, the concept of Greek liberty by some may be considered of a different people than those of Macedonia, but it was arguably *all* Hellenistic at the end of the day.

Most Persian-held prefectures Alexander went into on campaign had simply gotten the treatment by the Persians we saw played out in the movie *300* from Persia, as in the scene when Xerxes' envoy arrives in Sparta and demands tribute of earth and water from their land. This act represents submission and means they assumed ownership over them. But Alexander was taking the position and then releasing them from the servitude, so there was no need to liquidate most of them, like Thebes. Even Xerxes generally "claimed" he would leave them free to govern themselves. His actions were always to commandeer the people to the expansion of his empire and their submission to *his* law, whereas it could be argued that though Alexander would require men able to fight needed to join his campaign, out of debt due to his men's losses in freeing them, the law implemented was that of respecting national (city-state) and personal liberties, or Natural Law. Some of these areas seem to have been under Persian control so long they suffered a form of Stockholm

Syndrome with Persia, but like a beaten dog they sided with their new master quickly.[43]

> Throughout all these campaigns, Alexander spread the culture of Greece while allowing the people of the various regions to continue worshipping the gods of their choice and conducting themselves as they pleased – as long as they caused him no trouble and kept his supply lines open – while simultaneously investigating and recording the culture and other aspects of each land.

The historical website also notes that "scholar Ian Worthington comments:

> Homer was Alexander's bible and he took Aristotle's edition with him to Asia...During his campaigns Alexander was always intent on finding out everything he could about the areas through which he passed. He took with him an entourage of scientists to record and analyse this information, from botany, biology, zoology and meteorology, to topography. His desire to learn, and to have information recorded as scientifically as possible, probably stemmed from Aristotle's teachings and enthusiasm. (34-35)

When I was in school this was taught in World History class. I am always astounded by the people who do not know these things. Much of what I am discussing with you comes from my experience in those classes, the rudimentary information we all should have gotten in our

---

[43] https://www.ancient.eu/article/94/the-hellenistic-world-the-world-of-alexander-the-g/

general education. It's general knowledge, should need no citations, and yet most of the populace seems totally oblivious to these small facts.

Alexander then cross-bred the Greek and Persian cultures with each other. One cannot blame the Greeks for being angry at this act, but it appears more so that he was trying to unify the region in knowledge of each other and hoping the best of their cultures would be taken on, though it's also thought he was suffering from syphilis and may have not been in the same state of mind he began in.

Some claim when he got to India he left because his men threatened to mutiny after their battle against King Porus. However, it is also said that between his interaction with Porus and in seeing the unity of the Indians in amassing to confront him, Alexander believed they knew who they and their culture were, and left because India appeared to be a confident, stable land. This would make sense if he was rather consistent in his Socratic roots, though his soldiers may have just been sick of being away from home too.

When Alexander died the so-called Empire was split among his four generals, but it was just a league. They had no power to seize control of the league simply because the "king" had died. As we'll understand by Locke's observations of these types of bodies (in a later chapter) the league was, as of that time, without an heir apparent. For what did the Oath of the League state?

> Nor shall I depose the kingship of Philip or his descendants, nor the constitutions existing in each state, when they swore the oaths of the peace.

The generals were none of these. The body was dissolved naturally. The tyranny of the generals leads to the misunderstanding that Alexander owned these lands that were pacified and freed.

SPARTA

Through Sparta I will try to narrow the detail of the similarities with other republics down, while expanding on the areas that were either more republican or that added to the republic of Greece that Sparta and Athens' relationship helped form as we examine Sparta. I will try to keep it brief as there are general similarities when these cultures were their freest. You will likely see most of which are found in Athens under Solon's reforms.

Sparta, unlike Athens, is a republic filled with freemen and women and a far more accurate representation of republic. It sits along a river and is protected by two mountains that provide narrow access to the area, resulting in Sparta never being sacked.

Though the common attributes focused upon by usurpers of its traditions are its militantism and requirements to "serve," when we go back far enough with these initial republics, we find the use of the term *mythological* to imply these are stories with no physical proof, leaving us with, again, that oh so unreliable verbal history *according to the experts*. As Encyclopedia Britannica states:

> In the light of the conflicting opinions about
> Lycurgus held by writers before 400 b.c., some
> modern scholars have concluded that Lycurgus
> was not a real person. They point out that the
> Greeks tended to discuss the origins of political

and social institutions in terms of the personal
intentions of a single founder.

So, the lack of ancient proof that can easily be hidden beneath ancient cataclysms and personal biases or conquering enemies overrules the verbal histories of the native people, apparently. Yet, I shall note this claim is exactly what this work is doing, or at least in this case where it suits the establishment that studies such histories. Looking at the *intentions* of the societies, we see the focus on liberty…

Hmm?

Odd, their position when examinations of Native American tribes and their verbal histories were often found to be accurate, and if modern experts and professional historians tend to lie about more recent histories as some European or American historians did about certain cultures they considered less civilized then the ancient people must of too…

Hmm?

They are also telling us in this quote that Greece was focused on the intention of the foundation, and primary position I am postulating to you in this examination. Interesting isn't it? However, historians argue against the scholars so they can't even agree in their studies. So, it is with the commonly accepted view I'll review Lycurgus and the great republic he designed. Though I must add, Plutarch notes:[44]

> Timaeus conjectures that there were two Lycurgus
> at Sparta, at different times, and that to one of
> them the achievements of both were ascribed,
> owing to his greater fame; he thinks also that the
> elder of the two lived not far from the times of
> Homer"

---

[44] http://penelope.uchicago.edu/Thayer/E/Roman/Texts
/Plutarch/Lives/Lycurgus*.html

Though generally Homer is thought to have been born in 850 B.C. more and more, scholars are thinking the eldest lived in 1200 B.C. If true, and if Lycurgus the Lawgiver lived in that era Sparta could have been a 1,500-year-old city before the common era. In addition, Rome may well have been a nearly 1,000-year-old republic in my view.

Lycurgus the Lawgiver[45]

Sparta had been much like a micro-Athens hundreds of years before the Athens I just described in the last chapter. There were constant fights between founding (ruling) families, mob insurrections and invasions by outsiders trying to seize power. Some of this is due to claimed Spartan ancestors, the Dorians, and their forceful entrance and seizure of the Peloponnese native peoples. Though the Spartans often implied they spoke in the true Greek laconic style of the native language, which would make them related to Laconians, the mainstream narrative is rather clear that the dark ages which surround the Dorian invasion (Dorians actually being Macedonians) do not have enough information to ascertain what really occurred and

---

[45] https://en.wikipedia.org/wiki/Spartiate#/media/File:Lycurgus.jpg

that Sparta was hard to physically access. Thus, Dorians were most likely one of the peoples who sparked the mob-led insurrections, but it doesn't mean they ever became the people of Sparta. Sparta also had this issue with the Messenians. The agreement Sparta struck with Lacedaemon could be seen as the first real republic, if we knew all the information. Of what we do know there is a pretty strong argument for this dissertation's assertions.

Lacedaemon is the man who founded the nation he named after himself, and Sparta is a city named after his wife. So, the relation that Sparta was/is the region seems rather incorrect. The nation and the city created a relationship as a protectorate as the peoples of Laconia for political-military control of the region, while leaving many of the communities and people in total freedom of local governance. Again, a situation that gets confused with the abilities to hold office verses the direct powers over faculties, interactions, and assets often by much later events. Basically, the city opted to become the military might for the region. My guess is because the Dorians really had a tough time getting into the city, and the Laconian Spartans ran them out of the greater region and had that success to build on in the deal. However, popular opinion, religious authoritarians, and senate influence still allowed for democracy, to leave the political structure of Sparta weak to tyrannies and despots.

To fix this defect of constant usurpations, Lycurgus, brother to the king, had taken power, but the brother had borne a son. Due to internal jealously, and fearing he'd be framed for an unfortunate event upon the boy, Lycurgus gave up the throne and traveled to Crete. At least this is what we're taught. He researched "governments," or I believe societies of Crete, to Ionia to Egypt. Lycurgus is said to have fashioned Sparta after Crete and Ionia— Crete for discipline, and Ionia for arts and passions. This later point disproves claims they had no arts and no architectural ability. It is also claimed he traveled to Egypt where he devised the plan to separate the military from the laborers. He was begged by many to reclaim the throne and when he did, they received the Lycurgus Reforms.

Lycurgus then implements the *first constitution*. ALL OTHER constitutional societies note him in their histories. All constitutions are sure not to meet his standards, but what do his standards—which many of the historians of antiquity considered nearly perfect — tell us about the purpose of a constitution?

- It is a promise of service by the titled, and entrusted by the/a people.
- An equality in assests among the whole State as family.
- Based on harsh life realities.
- Dissuaded wealth, lethargy, and lavishness.
- Funded the military through public donation and limited crop tithes to feed the tightly regulated food and health-oriented military.
- Equalized political power among the freeman (Lacedemonians/Spartans), soldiers (Spartiates/military), and the Political Body.

Key to understanding is he separates (politically) the military from the laborers, but as you'll learn, or may already know, the native Spartan laborers were completely free "Greeks," possibly even more so thanks to Lycurgus' regionally known political structure.

Xenophon writes this about his initial impression of Sparta:

> It occurred to me one day that Sparta, though among the most thinly populated of states, was evidently the most powerful and most celebrated city in Greece; and I fell to wondering how this could have happened. But when I considered the institutions of the Spartans, I wondered no longer.
>
> Lycurgus, who gave them the laws that they obey, and to which they owe their prosperity, I do regard with wonder; and I think that he reached the utmost limit of wisdom. For it was not by imitating other states, but by devising a system utterly different from that of most others, that he made his country pre-eminently prosperous.

Xenophon starts his examples of Lycurgus's crafting around the raising of children:

> First, to begin at the beginning, I will take the begetting of children. In other states the girls who are destined to become mothers and are brought up in the approved fashion, live on the very plainest fare, with a most meagre allowance of delicacies. Wine is either withheld altogether, or, if allowed them, is diluted with water. The rest of the Greeks expect their girls to imitate the sedentary life that is typical of handicraftsmen — to keep quiet and do wool-work. How, then, is it to be expected that women so brought up will bear fine children?

Paramount to breeding children, but also essential to a strong native culture, Xenophon says of Lycurgus,

> He believed motherhood to be the most important function of freeborn women.

Interesting, "freeborn" women? Meaning that concept of women politically being property was completely discarded? He continues that he... "insisted on physical training for the female no less than for the male sex," and thus, *both* parents being strong bettered the offspring. Women had to be as free as men and as strong for the times when the men were off to war, a similarity shared by the Nordic Vikings. (There are in fact many similarities with the Vikings or Norse society.)

The women of Sparta were openly educated and done so through a public system as with the men, with activities suited to their skills. This is said to be unusual for Greeks. Usually, we're told, women were seen as inheritable property. A legal claim (human law) propagated by politics of the era and something, which again, is different than natural being. It is also something we see in recorded histories later on, religious historians of misogynistic orders, foreigners, religious cults, and not necessarily something that was the case in the truly early and freest points of Greek/Athenian cultures. In other words, Sparta carried this tradition long enough to be noticed as different from cultures who's observing historians may not have known that their culture was that same way two to three hundred years prior.

The translations lead us to believe that Lycurgus "ordered" stiff restrictions in personal relations, specifically marriage which was also encouraged to be open so women who found men of strong genetics could assure those traits for their children while maintaining their family unit. We tend to forget that people in ancient (or "classical") times were literalists with virtue. These are equivalent to small town moral people. Some of the rituals of Sparta were to aid in this tight-knit community way. Something I believe gets lost in translation is that because they had virtue, these were more likely maxims which Lycurgus tied to oaths that people actually took seriously back then, or at least he cultivated a people who did through their trust in him. Also, keep in mind this seems to have been a city regularly run by tyrants, so his edicts are probably like Solon's. They are to establish a parameter for a people with no understanding of freedom to operate in at first, and then to expand from. I say this as his marital rules seem to allow for a lot of malleability.

There is also the matter of how he designated rivalry which also plays into their ethics and morals. The purpose is to teach the men to observe other's character and to proclaim openly when they have violated their honor. Of this process Xenophon tells us this:

> Here then you find that kind of strife that is
> dearest to the gods, and in the highest sense
> political — the strife that sets the standard of a
> brave man's conduct; and in which either party
> exerts itself to the end that it may never fall below
> its best, and that, when the time comes, every
> member of it may support the state with all his
> might.

In other words, by calling out another you aid him in staying honest and thus strengthening the culture against political predators preying on low morals and weak wills. Others are then used to such action and don't get emotionally degraded by that action, unlike many tend to do in today's weak culture. Yet, jeering your fellow soldier was to cease upon his request, else he could righteously exact wrath. It is important to note this calling out is *personal authority* as freemen. They don't go whining to the state or making it "official police business" that another is of weak character.

In education, the boys were trained in warfare and survival and regularly had a leader or mentor. For the record, contrary to the claims, there was no boy loving beyond that of the plutonic. All citizen children were taught to read, make art, music, and athletics. Art was useful. For example, the warrior cup of the Spartan was known for its design and how it held back sediment from dirty water. The technology was useful. This factor of education leads to a key factor in any quality republic: defused knowledge.

Today we're being made to think of an "open society" as one where no one should hide anything from anyone, especially of personal nature before the State. False. Rather, governments, leadership, manufacturers, and educators are not to hide anything *from citizens*. All public-funded/official actions and all finances must be disclosed and accessible to everyone. This can even be said to apply to technologies invented with public funds or by publicly-licensed companies, not in the sense that someone may make an inventor expose how his creation works, but that anyone who figures out how it works is free to, and encouraged to tell others without fear of legal repercussion, political oppression, or robbery of their non-monetary gains.

In child-rearing in Sparta, any citizen could reprimand another's child for misbehavior, and likewise any troublesome fellow citizen as noted earlier. Once the child is a man Xenophon is clear:

> When a boy ceases to be a child, and begins to be a
> lad, others release him from his moral tutor and
> his schoolmaster: he is then no longer under a
> ruler and is allowed to go his own way. Here

again Lycurgus introduced a wholly different
system.

Thus, the Spartan is fully self-governed being in his affairs,
especially, because knowledge was defused. Yet, there were still
manners in which the youths were taught and duties of the military
that were structured into them to keep them from becoming lethargic
and hedonistic. Should they freely choose to be lechers, winos, or
slackers, they would be shunned from military activities. This doesn't
mean they were no longer freemen, but being a freeman does not
equate to having to be tolerated in an area of security where you may
become a danger.

Militarily, Kings of Sparta were not as we think of kings today.
These were more of the councilor (consul) position than of ruler, for
as already clarified, once you were a man you were in government of
yourself and as such, a keeper of your community. Kings were the
statewide representatives for animal "sacrifices" (religious rituals)
and to lead in war campaigns. As again Xenophon tells us:

> These then are the honors that are bestowed on
> the King at home during his lifetime; and they do
> not greatly exceed those of private persons.

Again, "do not greatly exceed those of private persons."
Interesting.

Xenophon's *Hiero* dialogue alludes to this important distinction,
in which the poet Simonides of Ceos is asking Hiero I of Syracuse
what it's like to be a despot. Hiero refers to the common man as
"private persons" and "private individuals." He notes their ability to
go anywhere they wish, whereas he, the despot, is clearly a public
figure to whom people show false attitudes too, and who risks all his
things being stolen by adversaries if he leaves his home for travel—a
metaphor for how a titled official can't just leave the kingdom
unguarded. As this is the same writer of one of the tellings of the

Spartan Constitution, he must be using this term "private person" with the same meanings.

Wikipedia states:

> Isocrates refers to the Spartans as 'subject to an oligarchy at home, to a kingship on campaign.'

Which is a quote found in many other sources on Sparta. There is truly too much restriction upon the Spartans when conditioning them to the culture to call it a perfect republic, but it was a republic nonetheless, as the "oligarchy" (lifetime Senate) and the kings, not to mention all citizens, were pledged to superior maxims that the individuals could equally enforce when a violation by the titles occurs.

Rome's Polybius[46] says of Sparta:[47]

> Lycurgus ...combined together all the excellences
> and distinctive features of the best constitutions,
> that no part should become unduly predominant,
> and be perverted into its kindred vice; and that,
> each power being checked by the others, no one
> part should turn the scale or decisively out-
> balance the others; but that, by being accurately
> adjusted and in exact equilibrium, the whole
> might remain long steady like a ship sailing close
> to the wind. The royal power was prevented from
> growing insolent by fear of the people, which had
> also assigned to it an adequate share in the
> constitution. The people in their turn were
> restrained from a bold contempt of the kings by
> fear of the Gerusia: the members of which, being

---

[46] *Polybius*, (born c. 200 BCE, Megalopolis, Arcadia, Greece — died c. 118), Greek statesman and historian who wrote of the rise of Rome to world prominence. — https://www.britannica.com/biography/Polybius

[47] http://www.perseus.tufts.edu/hopper/

selected on grounds of merit, were certain to
throw their influence on the side of justice in
every question that arose; and thus the party
placed at a disadvantage by its conservative
tendency was always strengthened and supported
by the weight and influence of the Gerusia. The
result of this combination has been that the
Lacedaemonians retained their freedom for the
longest period of any people with which we are
acquainted.

*Jean-Jacques-François Le Barbier (1738–1826), The Magnanimity of
Lycurgus (1791)*[48]

---

[48] https://commons.wikimedia.org/w/index.php?search=Jean-
Jacques-
Fran%C3%A7ois+Le+Barbier+%281738%E2%80%931826%29%2C+The+Ma
gnanimity+of+Lycurgus+%281791%29&title=Special:MediaSearch&go=Go
&type=image

THE POLITICAL BODY

The political body of Sparta was made up of:

- **Kings**: There were only two, and whose only power over others was on the battlefield. They would participate in diplomacy, but were primarily heads of rituals for the people of Sparta. The kings swore an oath to themselves, basically, putting their name on the line with their honor, which mattered in those days.

- **Gerousia**: Which was the Senate made up of Elders appointed for life because they were old men. However, two of the 30 members had to be the two kings, who could be of any age. They would hear the motions that would go before the assembly and arbitrate the trials of Spartans. It is believed they could overturn any motion passed by the assembly.

- **Apella**: The Spartan Assembly was the House of Commons. The place where all citizens could debate and vote upon a motion. Most importantly it was the body that elected the Senators and Councilmen (Ephors). It was managed by the Kings at first and then the Ephors.

- **Ephors**: Were a Council of five elected every year, early on. They were not to be a perpetual leadership. They swore an oath to the city. The Ephor could file charges for crimes, aid in managing judicial hearings, and oversaw city operations.

There were, at times, consultations with the religious head at Delphi. Though this did impact the political body it will not be a focus in this work as the Pantheon was wide and Gods over cities often changed. Also, much of the interaction in asking Delphi's input is subject to speculation, and interpretation like much in history. Views on how religion influenced Sparta can be left to the theocrats. Though impactful, it is not as important as understanding the reason for the local political bodies existing in the first place, or the purpose and spirit in which the natives came together.

It's vastly important we understand the Spartans were the military stronghold, or city of the military for Lacedaemon. They were just an organization in Lacedaemon. The citizen of Lacedaemon was not the same thing as the Spartan which was not necessarily the same thing as the *Spartiate*. The Spartiate, the "Spartan," the Lacedaemonian, the *Perioikoi* and many within Lacedaemon were all free Greeks. They did a lot of what they wanted to within their local, cultural (including religious), and natural rights. The Perioikoi were like Metics in Athens when in Sparta because they were foreign to the city, but not necessarily foreign to Lacedaemon.

In monies, we are told by the contemporaries that the Spartan was believed to use iron bars for currency, but these have not been found in archeological digs. So, it is thought they just used another culture's currency. I surmise they probably used no currency. I base this on the recognition that many things from child correction, hunting equipment, and livestock like horses, were the property of or at least openly available for anyone to use or handle, so long as they used it carefully and returned it to the private owner quickly and in good condition. Xenophon tells us:

> The result of this method of going shares with one
> another is that even those who have but little
> receives a share of all that the country yields
> whenever they want anything.

He also basically says they didn't use money by pointing out why they wouldn't need it:

Indeed, how should wealth be a serious object
there, when he [Lycurgus] insisted on equal
contributions to the food supply and on the same
standard of living for all, and thus cut off the
attraction of money for indulgence' sake? Why,
there is not even any need of money to spend on
cloaks: for their adornment is due not to the price
of their clothes, but to the excellent condition of
their bodies.

So the masses of wealth that we will see the Perioikoi had have
more to do with foreign trade, businesses, and professions, while the
mass farming of rural peoples which would be considered a need is
done for the benefit of the whole, under Spartan protection (now
described as ownership over, but was more likely as an assigned
arbiter and security guard agency); and for their professional security
services the Spartiates, who have a limited eating regimen, are at
liberty in property usages/gains without need to pay via money. This
applies to any citizen of Sparta, mind you. If the food supply was to
be equally contributed to, it means the Spartans personally had to
grow food in some capacity too. For a man cannot be free if he cannot
provide his own food and raiment.

"But at Sparta Lycurgus forbade freeborn citizens
to have anything to do with business affairs. He
insisted on their regarding as their own concern
only those activities that make for civic freedom."

— Xenophon

Wherein "civic freedom" is the liberty of Sparta. In fact, Lycurgus
made having money unbearable. If someone suspected you were
carrying it a Spartan citizen could demand to search you. If you were
carrying excessive amounts you could be imprisoned. Why? I surmise
because of what was depicted in the movie *300* when the Senator is
revealed to have foreign gold, suggesting (the threat that) you are
bought or may be paying off officials. If one had money they would

have to carry it in iron and in large amounts as for it to be seen by all, a metaphor for how material wealth weighs you down. I am also quite sure Lycurgus saw the corruption that merchants and financiers can easily spread, this being a primary reason competent U.S. Founders opposed centralized banking and unsupervised mercantile exchanges.

I'll now focus quickly on the classes as I see them, designed after Lycurgus's rules began to weaken, though you should retain that his rules created such a successful society for what could have been easily 600 to 800 years even before the latter half of the 835–ish years that academics officially ascribe to Sparta's existence, based on limited writings. It is clearly in the history works that the Sparta of the time of the antiquity writers is not the same Sparta that garnered fame and respect in most cases. Early Sparta was a humbler society, as it was with almost all republics. In discussing its later forms, it cannot be attributed to being as much republic as it was corrupted by this point.

THE CLASSES

SPARTIATES

Spartiates were professional warriors and essentially stationed in the military city Sparta as the center in charge of diplomacy and war, but if we're really looking at the freedoms of the people of Sparta we realize the "classes" of Sparta (which tend to encompass the whole region as a term) didn't change the fact they were all free Lacedaemonians, and that this political layout simply applies to the Spartiates of Sparta, also known as "men of equal status." They are the people who stay in the military concept after becoming self-governed men. Artifacts are said to reveal military operations and defenses were their main training, they were highly literate, and creative in potteries and other such arts.

SPARTAN

A *Spartan* was one born in Sparta, but not necessarily still in the professional military establishment, people who were not "active duty." Some of these persons were referred to as *mothakes*; offspring of one Spartan parent and one outsider. These were professionals in domestic arts, agriculture, technologies, and infrastructure. I must note it makes no sense for Lycurgus to understand the importance of Sparta being a self-sufficient people but thinking they should be relying on outsiders and "slaves" for imperative infrastructure and equipment. Why would they have potential enemies forging their weapons or planting their crops, for instance? That's dependency. It only makes sense that this is the reason there is a distinction between the Spartan and the Spartiate in many historical observations. Both of whom would have the same basic skills from their general education, one of which staying the course of being regulars for the military.

PERIOIKOI

Perioikoi were artisans, architects, businessmen, professionals, tradesmen, and merchants, fellow Lacedaemonians as well as migrants. The Lacedaemonians were totally free in their activities, except when inside Sparta or in conducting war and diplomacy, which they did through Sparta. As citizens of Lacedaemon they were expected to join military campaigns lead by the Spartiates. Many seem to wonder why, and figure it must be due to a cast system, then a social compact, but the surrounding territories needed to have some skin in the game and not just expect the small populace of Sparta to supply the full regiment against forces like Athens or Messina, or Persia. In the American Revolution people like Spartiates were called "Regulars," professional soldiers who relieve, or back up the local militia. These Lacedaemonians were also fellow countrymen! So, they needed to help assure the culture of their people. The migrants would have likely been acknowledged in their natural freedom, but any attempt to gain political power or to insult a Spartan would likely not end well.

HELOTS

Helots were people of a neighboring region beaten in war, placed into serfdom, and retained certain autonomy of their cultural identity. Historically, we're made to think they were just suppressed and enslaved, but the actions of the early Spartan Republic seem to imply they were required to supply a percentage of their harvest (more than any Lacedemonian would be asked too), but unlike actual slaves throughout Greece, they could marry and conduct most of their own affairs.

The general narrative described in Wikipedia says:

> The helots (/ˈhɛləts, ˈhiːləts/; Ancient Greek: εἵλωτες, heílotes) were a subjugated population group that formed the main population of Laconia and Messenia, the territory controlled by Sparta. Their exact status was already disputed in antiquity: according to Critias, they were "slaves to the utmost," whereas according to Pollux, they occupied a status "between free men and slaves." Tied to the land, they primarily worked in agriculture as a majority and economically supported the Spartan citizens.

It would do a reader well to also know that Critias is the scumbag democrat who ignored the Spartan's order to his Thirty Tyrants to reinstate the Constitution of Solon, and that Pollux lived in 2 AD and most his work has been lost. Not exactly direct sources to be trusted, though Pollux's observations meet the general consensus that helots were basically serfs. They were to be involved in the wars no matter what, and usually served the soldiers as caddies. Though we are told the Spartan waged war on them to make them know their place, this seems to be more in the later years and even so could have been, and in some cases served as the suppression of democratic revolts being planned by despots or tyrants attempting to do in Sparta what Peisistratus and others did in Athens, which appears to have eventually happened as their population declined. There is also a high probability many Helots in Sparta were willing serfs, poor people who wanted to aid a greater (stronger) people. As I pointed out above, they were of beaten nations (cities) but they were also foreign workers and tradesmen. As outsiders and former enemies, they could not have the same political rights as the citizens of Sparta or they would infect the government and make it susceptible to foreign corruption and infiltration. Thus, the Helots were more like foreign *civilians* as opposed to *citizens*.

Here is a great example of the failures to apply the term civilian to a Metic-type class in modern writing, using the helots:[49]

Laborers

Greek society included a significantly larger proportion of laborers than slaves. These were semi-free workers, wholly dependent on their employer (many were foreigners). The most famous example is the helot class of Sparta. These dependents were not the property of a particular citizen – they could not be sold as a slave could (which can be seen as a protection of them) - and they often lived with their families. Generally, they formed arrangements with their "employer" such as giving a quantity of their produce to the farm owner and keeping the rest for themselves. Sometimes the quota required may have been high or low, and there may also have been some extra benefits to the serfs such as protection and safety in numbers. However, the serf-class or helots could never achieve any real security as they were given little or no legal status and harshly treated, even killed in regular purges, in order to instill a fear which would ensure continued subordination to the ruling class. In certain periods such as war, helots were required to serve in the armed forces and, fighting well,

---

[49] http://www.ancient.eu/article/483/

they could even earn an escape from their lot and join the intermediary social groups which existed below the level of full-citizen and included such individuals as children with parents of mixed status (e.g.: father-citizen, mother-helot).

"Semi-free" because, again, they were from foreign nations, beaten nations, or put more simply from outside the city-state. They had plenty of security just as the Spartan did. They had a sword and could defend themselves, just not necessarily against a full-citizen, without repercussions. They had Natural Law protection, but not Human Legal protections, much like a civilian today who may be arrested for harming a police officer who violated their natural rights. You might be in the right, but his buddies in the legal system will do something about it. They would also have been likely to have to defend their actions in court, whereas a full citizen could state their reason for a publicly-witnessed destructive act against a foreigner without necessarily *having* to be arraigned in court. For again, what they did not have was *legal protection*. "They were given little or no legal status." In other words, political rights, because they were not natives.

That is what most historians nowadays mean by a description like that. Giving such people those rights is why Athens, and as you'll soon read Rome, was collapsed, though I highly doubt they lacked protection for the assurances of contracts. Any legal protection "laborers" lacked is directly due to the fact they were a security risk that could undermine Sparta (or Greece). They likely had legal protection in their homeland, though from time-to-time the Spartan had enough actionable threats from the helots to pacify any possible insurrection upon that region, too. Possibility is enough to act on when you are a freeman, not when you are an agent for the State or a foreign state. However, remember the Helots were from an already-conquered region known for being a problem and under Spartan authority. It is not the same as Sparta believing Athens is up to something and preemptively sacking them with an official army.

Additionally, "even killed in regular purges..." When? At what point? Was this really the case from Sparta's inception in 1200 B.C. all through to their fall to Rome in 149 B.C. or was it only the case after the quake when they needed to secure their small population? Most accounts are so long after the fact can we really be sure as to why and when? Just food for thought.

There is of course the true slave class, but it falls into the same point as above. When? Most importantly can we be positive that we have a proper translation on the term's usage when so many people nowadays throw the word around for any position in which one served another and accepted that leader's authority to punish? For instance, the difference between an indentured servant who still has legal protection and assurance for their basic rights and contracted services versus a slave who has none. We all have a good grasp of what a slave is, and there likely were many, but there is also a good chance even the helots had slaves. So, what's the point in degrading the Spartan or any particular culture being discussed if it was that widespread? It's bad either way, but that does not change the attempt at erasing it over one's own people when that opportunity is taken. Often it was a trade taught to a region by others.

Many do not know American slavery was legalized when a black man demanded another black be made his property in a British colonial court. The construct of slavery had no legal protection here prior and was by and large a Muslim and African tribal activity. Most Africans brought to America were already enslaved by a conquering tribe of Africans who sold them off. Human trafficking continues even today, but the rebirth of Ancient Republic in America forced it into the shadows in most first-world societies. The goal should be furthering the respect and empowering the free being to defend their liberty so those enslaved can escape and feel safe to dispatch their captors. As we're seeing this must be primarily respected as a personal power in total. Imagine arresting a person being trafficked for murder of a man who imprisoned them because they didn't try taking him to court. That is the type of elitism and democracy that has been used to subvert true self-government and personal enforcement for over 3,000 years.

LEAGUES

Sparta was influential in creating and running some of Greece's first Leagues, or United Nations. Much of its operations are still used in today's international leagues. As Wikipedia claims of the Peloponnesian League:[50]

> The league was organized with Sparta as the hegemon, and was controlled by the council of allies which was composed of two bodies: the assembly of Spartiates and the Congress of Allies. Each allied state had one vote in the Congress, regardless of that state's size or geopolitical power. No tribute was paid except in times of war, when one third of the military of a state could be requested. Only Sparta could call a Congress of the League. All alliances were made with Sparta only, so if they so wished, member states had to form separate alliances with each other. And although each state had one vote, League resolutions were not binding on Sparta. Thus, the Peloponnesian League was not an "alliance" in the strictest sense of the word (nor was it wholly Peloponnesian for the entirety of its existence).
>
> The league provided protection and security to its members. It was a conservative alliance which supported Oligarchies and opposed tyrannies and democracies.

How convenient that again we are given the term *oligarch* in comparison to *tyrannies* and *democracies*, even though the term *republic* is applicable to some of the governments they were in league with. Also, why are tyrannies in the same category as democracies? I say

---

[50] https://en.wikipedia.org/wiki/Peloponnesian_League

that because the socialist-minded narrative defines any culture that keeps leadership local as oligarchical, as we see democratic usually implies a political say by all communities in a region, which kills native identity and eventually individualism all together. Put another way, it becomes clearer upon study that democracy isn't about equal say in political activity but centralized control over all participants. How is there freedom in that?

We see admission of the interaction with the military organization of the Spartiates, and a Congress of their allies limited in their ability to damage the Spartan in the league Sparta established—a clear republican protection of sovereignty. This includes not being able to call forth the Congress without the Spartans present—a protection against democratic coup d'état. Sparta also was not the government of the members, or their people. It was the diplomatic leadership for management or tribal engagements because "the league provided protection and security to its members," which supports the claim of this work that a republic is a trade protectorate at heart, which assures the free actions of the individual when it was founded under liberty.

What is often left out when discussing these leagues are the agreements of each member's citizen being treated equally within each other nation's borders, as was the early intention of the U.S. Constitution. This wasn't always the case, but it is how an alliance best meets the needs of its members and can assure an equivalence across the union.

What we really had in Sparta is lost to the whims of big-government-loving idealists who think history is a big compilation of large authorities run amuck while man just tries to find the perfect supreme governor that balances itself, all needing to make it sound like their solutions to freedom are unique to their activities, but equal in their international behavioral standards. In this, they constantly overlook and disregard successful republics as independent barbarous warring regions. The fact that they were peaceful escapes any possibility in their mind, or the fact their wars were external against jealous principalities, or internal revolts against overreaching democrats. Not always, but generally. This is seen every time the House of Sparta's legal operations are mentioned. From their senate (Gerousia), to the Ephors, to their kings, it is ignored that a limited scope power is how Sparta conducted its diplomatic business and that is why the Perioikoi had no representation — they were too likely to use the power of military might and legal perception to enslave *everyone*.

It is ignored that Sparta secured all of Lacedaemon so the people and villages could all operate in their own way. Sparta did not control their governments; Sparta was a service society in Lacedaemon's diplomacy, a trade protectorate, and their defense from invasion, as was how the Roman Republic operated during the actual Pax Roman (pax means *peace* in Latin) which was the 500 years preceding the rule of Augustus and Imperial Rome, in my view. The claims of the Helots being some oppressed people misses the greater reality that they were a defeated enemy the Spartans spared either because they were fellow Greeks, or because they needed to make an example of them. As we saw with Alexander the Great, proper warfare was to annihilate the enemy and the Spartan knew this well yet did not waste the Helots. This class of the "Helot" wasn't necessarily existent until about the 5th century B.C. (some claim 8th century, but that comes from a source in 2 A.D.). Even in their "slave" position, unlike other Classical Greece slaves, they could marry and they retained 50 percent of their productions. Despite throwing around the word "slave," mainstream historians still admit the Helot was rather autonomous. They just had some required duties, and because they had raised a sword against Sparta they faced a stiff punishment and fines for criminal activity in a lesser position than that of a free citizen.

These slaver interpretations come from the view of outside peoples like Athenians, often, and the Spartans that existed by Plutarch's day are clearly a great leap from that which Xenophon speaks of. Even Xenophon was 500 years disconnected from the heights of what he is discussing.

Though historically we are told they warred themselves out of existence, I believe it important to note Sparta suffered a landslide in 464 B.C. Otherwise, their population loss is generally attributed to *wars* over the following 100 years. However, that landslide contributed to a loss of a large portion of the city. It was likely the biggest factor in their later decline in population and loss of native-born Spartans to outsiders granted citizenship in an effort to save their culture, which became the basis for the slave-driving egotists from the near end of the B.C. era.[51] [52]

[51] https://en.wikipedia.org/wiki/Peloponnesian_League
[52] http://www.perseus.tufts.edu/hopper/text?doc=xen.+const.+lac.+1.1

UNIFIED GREECE: HELLENISTIC PERIOD

From Athens and Sparta's repellence of Persia and propelled by Alexander the Great's conquering of the known world, Greece set the standard for the western world and spread its influence to the front doors of India. In my research this area of information is where more proof to the mixing of natural and political republic can be found. Yet, let it be understood there was already a thriving Roman Republic.

The histories of such can begin with the different leagues which sprang up from this repulsion.

> The Hellenistic period lasted from 323 BC, which marked the end of the Wars of Alexander the Great, to the annexation of Greece by the Roman Republic (more likely already in an Imperial status) in 146 BC. Although the establishment of Roman rule did not break the continuity of Hellenistic society and culture, which remained essentially unchanged until the advent of Christianity, it did mark the end of Greek political independence.[53]

---

[53] https://en.wikipedia.org/wiki/Ancient_Greece

"Greek political independence" is not the same thing as personal independence, a centerpiece of both Greek and Roman cultural understandings of liberty. This was the local intention of assuring Greeks were leaving the city-states independent from foreign entanglements caused by strife between their domestic operations. It also was to create agreement that protected the personal liberty of each Greek when visiting between different regions while keeping foreign traders in check. Unifying with Rome as the head of the union was joining a nation that would entangle you in affairs you had nothing to do with, which was more Rome's style by 146 B.C., but not in their prime republican state.

ROME:
NO MORE KINGS

In Rome, nearly at the same time as Sparta and Athens, we find the product of two brothers supposedly raised by wolves. Some speculate they were orphans from the fall of Troy. At least that's the myth which starts us with a hereditary monarchy. So, it's not that important. The truth is, Rome was possibly one of several tribal settlements in the area. What's important about that is it's said Rome was cultivated by people who were outsiders from their homelands, people claimed by others to be murders and thieves, general dis-reputables. Yet, if we consider the tendencies of monarchies to bastardized anyone and anything that seems a threat to themselves or their rule, it is quite logical to conclude many of these people may have been folks who simply enforced their natural rights, such as to defend themselves, personally recover property, and deal with a community threat that held power. This would explain the people's tendencies of self-government in most matters. Many older societies were better about understanding the use of exile and ostracism than most democratic tyrannies tend to.

Rome sits atop Seven Hills and took in outcasts from all over. As with Greece, to make an absolute claim of these laws and operations is tough as it was all *spoken history* centuries before the Empire came to be. Many general laws were in favor of Romulus and Remus, but it can be expected such a culture left lots of power in personal hands, more likely to have a people pledged to the kingship for trade, security, and external political matters, than over most interpersonal matters. They served as imperial kings till Romulus killed Remus.

Succession of kings continued until the King's bloodline was taking from the soldiers' too often. The general activity of Rome in its early inception was very similar to Greece, and the actual creation of Rome's Republic maybe closer to the same time period as Lycurgus's rising of Sparta or Solon's Republic in Athens. Much of the information we get on Rome is from latter historical sources like Livy, well after Rome was sacked, its libraries burned, and the Empire growing over the Republic.

Rome goes from a monarch to what is termed as "classical republic," a term by which mainstream academics imply that even though the Roman Republic was "a state where sovereignty rested with the people rather than a ruler or monarch," and that the words Cicero used to describe their republic "res publica" mean a "public matter," we're told its modern usage would be "body politic" or "commonwealth."

Wikipedia on Classical Republic:[54]

> Classical republicanism, also known as civic republicanism or civic humanism, is a form of republicanism developed in the Renaissance inspired by the governmental forms and writings of classical antiquity, especially such classical writers as Aristotle, Polybius, and Cicero. Classical republicanism is built around concepts such as civil society, civic virtue and mixed government.

(An interesting factoid: The well-historically-researched *Civilization* video game series identifies mercantile skills and influence tightly with the Classical Republic Era. Interesting?)

Wikipedia mangles their definition in the end as *libertas* was the status quo, thus the Enlightenment's ideals of free speech, freedom of religion, personal liberty, and property rights were all part of Roman civil society. Not to mention the absolute power of Natural Law via

---

[54] https://en.wikipedia.org/wiki/Classical_republicanism

the fact the individual citizen was the sovereign whereas in democracy the collective government is the sovereign, seeking compromises from public vote. "Republicanism" however, is a falsehood which implies a belief system, which is why I often write *republic* and try to limit using the term *republican*. *Commonwealth* as a term is not too far off, though we have been led for the longest time to think *republic* has something to do with *representation*, it does not mean "a matter of representation" nor does it require a group of political organizations intermingling. So, it must be something different then a government structure.

Via Definitions.net:[55]

Classical Republic

A classical republic, according to certain modern political theorists, is a state of Classical Antiquity that is considered to have a republican form of government, a state where sovereignty rested with the people rather than a ruler or monarch. These include states like the Roman Republic. The Romans used the term res publica to describe their state, but the most common sense of that term is closer to body politic or commonwealth. The phrase was coined, it seems, to distinguish the post-Tarquin political system with the previous monarchy, the res privata. The idea of republicanism was a creation of the Renaissance. The Renaissance scholars, most prominent among them being Niccolò Machiavelli, looked back on the ancient period with great interest and reverence. They defined republic as any state that was not headed by a monarch - thus including the Roman res publica. The Italians, themselves living in Republics like Florence and Venice, looked back on these states as models of social organization.

---

[55] https://www.definitions.net/definition/
Classical+republic

They looked to the history of the classical
republics and attempted to emulate their model.

Did you catch it? "A state (political body) where sovereignty
rested with the people rather than a ruler or monarch." This is why
political science majors play up the claim that republics are like
democracies, but this in no way means the people directed the
individuals, or that individual freemen ruled over the people's
authorized powers, which would be *res privata* (national matters
being the say of individual as though it is their property) in this
definitions usage. The general term was *res privatus*:[56]

Privatus

In Roman law, the Latin adjective privatus makes
a legal distinction between that which is "private"
and that which is publicus, "public" in the sense
of pertaining to the Roman people (populus
Romanus).

Used as a substantive, the term privatus refers to a
citizen who is not a public official or a member of
the military. Increasingly throughout the Middle
and Late Republic, the privatus was nevertheless
sometimes granted imperium during a crisis; the
definition of crisis was elastic, and the amassing of
power by unelected individuals (privati)
contributed to the breakdown of the checks and
balances of the republican system.

Legal terms

Res privatae, private property, or "things
belonging to individuals," in contrast to res
publica.

---

[56] https://en.wikipedia.org/wiki/Privatus

Res privata Caesaris, the property of the emperor
that was purely private."

If you understand this definition, you'll find it nearly totally justifies this work's position:

A legal distinction… the term privatus refers to a
citizen who is not a public official or a member of
the military.

One who is not a servant *to* the people, a freeman. It then goes on to show there was a weakening of restraint on property usage during war when the citizen became "imperium." However, I think this is an error in their understanding and translation since *imperium* means *sovereign* and that is what every Roman was considered, just as in Sparta. The definitions all even admit that but want you to think that "collective sovereignty" only in the political or legal usage, when it is a definitive of *all individual Romans*. Shortly, you will read the problem in Rome was title worship or over-trust in honored persons, not necessarily the freedom of the individual in their property usage.

Even Oxford is honest that we don't really know much about these things:[57]

Patrimonium and res privata were divisions of the
property of the Roman emperors, whose precise
nature and interrelation remain obscure.

And that's just *res pirvata*, a power of the Emperor. They should have some decent understanding of his rights and powers because of the egos that would assure a written history of their exploits, however, these powers of personal property of the emperor are

---

57 https://oxfordre.com/classics/

"obscure." Yet, we should trust the absolute statements on *res privatae* and *res publica*, right?

Notice the Definitions.net claim the corruption was due to unelected officials? Yet, unelected doesn't mean "not publicly employed" and war was the cause for the change they mention. So, they were likely officials (ranked officers in the war for example), or even more likely, they were merchants since it was a republic by which every servant of the people fell into a lower category from the citizen. If they were dangerously amassing power they could be equally dispatched by any citizen at any time, which I surmise happened often in the early Republic, because even this Wiki entry admits the corruption was a problem in the "Middle and Late Republic," a point by when the population would have surely increased. A fellow citizen could be dealt with in private and public ways. It was *government* that created standards protecting the pirate degenerates amassing wealth for power's sake regardless of being elected or not, but often as government preferred persons above the *imperium civis* (sovereign citizen).

On *imperium* Wikipedia first says:

> In ancient Rome, Imperium was a form of
> authority held by a citizen to control a military or
> governmental entity.

But—I argue—not a single elected citizen's authority, but *all* citizens'! Which is still alluded to in the further description:[58]

> In ancient Rome, imperium could be used as a
> term indicating a characteristic of people, the
> wealth held in items, or the measure of formal
> power they had. This qualification could be used
> in a rather loose context (for example, poets used
> it, not necessarily writing about state officials).

---

[58] https://en.wikipedia.org/wiki/Imperium

However, in Roman society it was also a more formal concept of legal authority.

Unlike many other titles this one had a very imperative meaning. It can be imbodied in the term, *"Imperium Est Civis"* (Sovereign is the Citizen). You can find any Ancient Latin to English translator (except for Google) and find the term *imperium* means sovereign, at least when I was writing this book you could. But once codified in the terminology of legal authority it is centralized to only those "officially" (formally) titled. So, what must that mean when a people are *imperium*? Who can command of a sovereign when every person is a sovereign? Yet, how do they spit on the term, and misapply it? For example, some sources say poets used it while not necessarily writing about state officials. So, they admit truth and then imply that it was used by some small minority of artists, though we can clearly see it applies to "the people" and thus the free individual.

Even the libertarians who trumpet some relation to Classical Liberalism can't manage to not be taken in by the lies when describing classical republics that their very own pre-19th centuries heroes adored:[59]

> Nonetheless, the liberty of the classical republicans is in some ways an ancestor of the modern libertarian tradition. At the same time, ironically, it also has played a role in shaping modern collectivist ideologies. *(Wrong!)*
>
> ...
>
> Classical republicans did not emphasize or even write often about the natural rights of individuals."

---

[59] https://www.libertarianism.org/encyclopedia/republicanism-classical

THE INFORMED REPUBLIC

(Completely wrong as you will learn in the American Section.)

I am trying to save you some reading time. The longer definition from Libertarianism.org has much right, but when you read it for yourself their fundamental flaw is in thinking classical republicanism supported the idea of government being good or necessary, and in republic being an ancestor to "classical liberalism." They construe strong community activity and involvement with required participation, as most who want a government around do, and that is the libertarian's weak point. They can talk of freedom all they want; libertarianism requires the existence of a government to some degree. Republics simply provide a place for the individual to manage their own affairs on record, encourages auxiliaries for solving disputes, and offers some guidelines for public awareness where group power ends that is enforceable by any interested citizen. That simple. They fail to understand their own teaching from classical liberalism in having to hide truth with falsehood to spread the ideal of freedom when under despotism, such as men like Locke or even Machiavelli defending "government" in order to inform the freeman of his right to kill authority and live without it.

Republics are comprised of voluntary auxiliary systems that we get once people comprehend limiting or removing government and living by one's (personal) honor.

Republic is the evolution of proper classical liberal (or libertarian) thinking, evident in many U.S. Founders' writings when discussing liberal thought. The so-called classical republican authors — many of whom were stewards of the Roman Republic we're discussing in this section — were bringing the fact of republic forward to ease us into liberal thought so we'd fall back into the pinnacle of free society, *republics*.

Libertarian thinking also implies:

> No classical republican would view the collapse of
> a republic as surprising; for them, republics
> tended to do just that.

This is a religious flaw in the thinking of the libertarian of Libertarianism in the belief they have a superior ideal. The fact is, the old writers knew republics would be regularly infiltrated, obstructed, and dissolved by tyrants, for freedom means danger exists. Libertarians think the exalting of liberty simply converts serfs that may undermine the domestic body into freemen by virtue of its use, a highly naive belief. It is not "collapse of republics is expected," but regular rebellion against insurrection by infected auxiliaries and dishonorable agents trying to seize power that is to be expected. Jefferson would often relay it as, "the animated contest of liberty," evident in Machiavelli's warning in *The Prince* for the principality to leave republics alone in their things and dealings.

Yet, we see the classical republic which led to the creation of the United States is directly tied to the Roman Res Publica. The term is erroneously defined in English as *respublica: government*, an intentional manipulation since the term "public matter" in itself means anything of a private, personal, or social matters (like interpersonal behavior or religious rites) is off limits. Especially, preemptive government — a sin in republic, something like decorum falls into the power of the people as individuals, not the government, to shun and ostracize. Public matters are limited:

- infrastructure projects for common (shared) use,
- roads,
- goods and persons being attacked by bandits and pirates (other nations or domestic criminals),
- and natural disasters.

This, all under the fact it often only applied to the city only, as it was a center of commerce, negotiations, and trade. Today's terminology does all it can to wrap in a myriad of non-sanctioned social and moral laws and societal ideals that collapsed real "classical" or antiquity republics, bundling up as many domestic cultures for implementation of democratic imperialism.

Lucius Junius Brutus[60]

---

[60]
https://commons.wikimedia.org/wiki/File:Lucius_Junius_Brutus_MAN_Napoli_Inv6178.jpg

The proof modern political science is wrong about republic is in the Roman Republic's rise. When Lucius Junius Brutus rebelled against the corrupt King Tarquinius Superbus he supposedly declared resoundingly, "No more Kings":

> By this guiltless blood before the kingly injustice I swear – you and the gods as my witnesses – I make myself the one who will prosecute, by what force I am able, Lucius Tarquinius Superbus along with his wicked wife and the whole house of his freeborn children by sword, by fire, by any means hence, so that neither they nor any one else be suffered to rule Rome.[61]

Another translation by one George Baker reads:

> By this blood, most chaste until injured by royal insolence, I swear, and call you, O ye gods, to witness, that I will prosecute to destruction, by sword, fire, and every forcible means in my power, both Lucius Tarquinius the Proud, and his impious wife, together with their entire race, and never will suffer one of them, nor any other person whatsoever, to be king in Rome.[62]

If this oath did occur it is quite the thing for those who want us to believe republic is the ancestor of modern government when considering this statement, "neither they nor anyone else be suffered to rule (or be king in) Rome," especially in light of the fact they still had "governing" councils, and publicly supported officials. Though I think Livy's history is spot on overall, certain wording under an

---

[61] https://en.wikipedia.org/wiki/Lucius_Junius_Brutus
[62] https://oll.libertyfund.org/titles/livy-the-history-of-rome-vol-1

imperial tyranny like, "No more Kings" could get him killed and is suspect to being placed under a softer meaning as to protect his neck.

Nevertheless, "No more Kings" was the foundation of the entire Roman Republic. It's odd we should think the goal after this was to design a council that would act as a king over everybody's actions since that didn't work to an equal legal advantage of the free individual at all. Though bear in mind the communities and representational bodies were much smaller than what we are used to today. There is a mindset the Senate directed personal authority as though Romans were so simple back then they wouldn't understand a group can be as corrupt as a king. Even American Founders like Benjamin Franklin were clear, 500 kings were as deadly as a single king. The safest route in a society where everyone was a trained soldier is an ability to equally self-enforce the law and manage one's own disputes — a rule from the Solon Republic and Sparta — especially when our historical scholars love noting how important being educated and civil was to the Roman even in the days of the Tarquins.

The historians try to tell us Brutus was vying for kingship before the revolt. The story is that he and another candidate were told by The Oracle at Delphi that the first to kiss their mother would be King. The worse of the two was closest to Rome at the moment, and would have to beat Brutus to their birth mother, so Brutus "tripped," hit the ground with his lip, and proclaimed he was first to kiss his mother as Earth was understood to be the mother of us all. Yet, to say he was vying for kingship just because some corrupt men were making it into such a scheme is as accurate as saying he was happy the kings were there until they raped his niece, which history tells us he was not. He found his uncle the King to be a terrible blight. If that were the case, he would have been for replacing the Kingship, not deposing it. Just seems like taking an oath against kings is a harsh stance to tell hardened soldiers who are your neighbors, and then just go on to be king like they'll do nothing about it.

After the revolt Brutus acted as a consultant in an amicable agreement, but in order for his oath to hold true he could not command a happening, unless it protected liberty, and the action could not make a Roman subservient to his title or that would make one another's king. As I said earlier, only a public matter of maximum

126

endangerment could be reason to subvert the individual rule of the citizen, such as war, or he'd have been more than a consul.

THE REPUBLIC

La liberté, Nanine Vallain (1794)[63]

---

[63]
https://commons.wikimedia.org/w/index.php?search=La+libert%C3%A9

We're taught the Roman Republic was "governed" by a complex constitution, which centered on the principles of a separation of powers with checks and balances. The Constitution of the Roman Republic, we're told, was an informal, unwritten set of guidelines and principles passed down mainly through "precedence," uncodified, and supposedly constantly evolving. So why would it be complex if it was spoken? If it is to keep titled men from running amuck why wouldn't it be informal (common)? Formal would mean those men could change it upon their whim, like through *precedence*. Also, can it evolve beyond the maxim of its purpose, which *was* usually carved in stone or wood (written down)? Doubtful, as that would mean precedence would still fall to the carved maxim.

Rome is guided by virtues, basically their primary maxims, often expressed in the forms of gods. The highest embodiment of all the virtues combined was Libertas. Romans were born into this Goddess's blessing. The process of entering liberty when one was not a natural-born "Roman" or was a Roman civilian under legal care (under contract) of a Free Roman was through *Manumission*. Today the related ritual is called *Knighting*. Examining this ritual exposes the rights of *all* free Romans. A person to be freed was taken before a priest or priestess of Libertas who themselves were imbued with liberty through a staff of liberty (*vindicta*), turned to the doorway of the temple, and then are shoved by a witness, advocate or master there to free them as a testament in public support and affirmation the admonished are worthy of freedom. The harder the shove and the closer they were to the ground the stronger in freedom they would be seen. The emancipated were not to be helped up or this was an insult and destruction to their and Rome's liberty. The freed was then, with a bald head, to place a red cap (a *pileus*). How can this not expose the driving factor in their republic? All republics? How is it not a proof the political bodies were to have no power over the individual, as another was not to interrupt one entering into liberty? How is serfdom to the state the goal when the entire purpose of the removal of the kings was individual liberty for *all Romans*?

What's that? You say it didn't apply to women? I know some buy the interpretations women were legal property of men or lesser-

---

beings, but nothing says women couldn't be "mancipated" into liberty or "emancipated" in the actual Republic era. Hell, the scepter bearers were often female, as was Libertas herself. This is probably another mangling of political rights with natural rights to a degree. As we see with Sparta, feminine inequality wasn't the case and it begs to reason that this is probably similar with Rome as well. Though it is true that early in Rome's history a party was held to invite neighboring regions to which the end result was Roman men basically kidnapping those people's daughters, mind you, this was because the neighbors were forbidding the daughters from inter-mingling with the Roman men for fear of damage to their population and power. This was before the Republic, though, and does not mean they were generally mistreated.

You can read some of the descriptions in the links in the footnotes below [64] [65] where Tufts University has a great compilation of Greek and Roman writings. However, some of their examples lead me to think they are more focusing on the operations of Roman Law after the Republic had already collapsed, which the mainstream points to when they note Caesar went to seize control. In truth, the collapse of the Republic was well before Caesar, and so these comparisons are of different cultures. What is of the artificial Laws of Man is not of the Natural Law Republic the lesser codes were intended to be maxim-ed under. A detailed read clarifies that slaves of that time were not as thought of as today and being under someone's authority didn't necessarily mean the person was in servitude or restriction of natural authority.

If you think I'm incorrect about the intention of *all* Romans to be free over the state, then let me jam this tasty morsel from Oxford Dictionary of the Oxford University down your throat:

---

[64]

http://www.perseus.tufts.edu/hopper/text?doc=Perseus%3Atext%3A199
9.04.0062%3Aentry%3Dmanumissio-harpers

[65]

http://www.perseus.tufts.edu/hopper/text?doc=Perseus%3Atext%3A199
9.04.0063%3Aalphabetic+letter%3DM%3Aentry+group%3D1%3Aentry%3
Dmancipii-causa-cn

"Libertas, 'freedom', personified deity at Rome, linked with Jupiter in the cult of Jupiter Libertas and the censors' headquarters, the Atrium Libertatis; worshipped alone on the Aventine in a temple built by Ti. Sempronius Gracchus (Livy 24. 16. 9, 238 bce). Her ideological connection with the freedoms of the ordinary citizen is apparent: freedom opposed both to the state of slavery and to dominatio by the powerful. The term was often used in the late republic and early empire to designate the liberty of the politician to develop his career without interference, and so came to focus various types of resistance to the more autocratic aspects of the early Principate. But Augustus had made a point of restoring the temples of both Libertas and Jupiter Libertas, and the slogan libertas Augusta (Mattingly–Sydenham, RIC, Claudius 97) was the final response."

— Nicholas Purcell on the subject of Roman Myth and Religion, Oxford Dictionary[66]

Notice how they are clear Libertas was hijacked by the political class in the late republic?

---

[66]

http://www.oxfordre.com/classics/view/10.1093/acrefore/978019938113 5.001.0001/acrefore-9780199381135-e-3680

THE LAW:
THE TWELVE TABLES DRAFTING, DEVELOPMENT, AND PURPOSE:

The *Twelve Tables of Rome* were said by the Roman historians to have come about as a result of the long social struggle between patricians (citizens) and plebeians (civilians), especially after the fall of the Kingship. After the expulsion of Tarquinius Superbus, the Republic was governed by a hierarchy of magistrates. However, this tradition cannot be verified, and the drafting of the Twelve Tables may have been fomented by a desire for self-regulation (civil laws) by the citizens (natives).

The interpretations by the mainstream historians again unveil this truth:

> The Twelve Tables are sufficiently comprehensive that their substance has been described as a 'code' *(again meaning not equal to natural or common law)*, although modern scholars consider this characterization exaggerated *(likely because they lack enforce of power through the State)*. The Tables were a sequence of definitions of various private rights and procedures. They generally took for granted such things as the institutions of the family and various rituals for formal transactions. The provisions were often highly specific and diverse, and lack an intelligible system or order.

It's usually viewed that when such rules are unintelligible or disordered that the people making them were dumb or unprofessional. It's rarely, if ever, considered that this is intentional, to limit the overreach of such conditions and external institutions for as the description notes:

> They generally took for granted such things as the institutions of the family and various rituals for formal transactions.

Meaning family power over family members goes without saying as does personal religious participation, and such things are not a public matter. As you read in the Twelve Tables you will find that the law protected private religious activities. It couldn't truly command of them. The line "and lack an intelligible system or order" is a scree of the authoritarian to a missing central control scheme. Further the factor that they described the rules as "private" means they were likely self-enforced. Thus, the reason for the structure of the First Table that I will shortly present to you.

Around 451 BC, nearly 100 years after Brutus's rebellion, the first *decemviri* (decemvirate – board of "Ten Men") were appointed to draw up the first ten tablets. According to Livy, they sent an envoy to Greece to study the legislative system of Athens, known as the Solonian Constitution (Republic), but also to find out about the legislation of other Greek cities. Scholars dispute the veracity of any claim that the Romans imitated the Greeks in this respect suggesting that they visited the Greek cities of Southern Italy, and did not travel all the way to Greece—because what would Livy know? His information only matters when it fits the mainstream narrative, right?

Titus Livius statue at the Austrian Parliament Building in Vienna, Austria[67]

---

[67]
https://commons.wikimedia.org/w/index.php?search=Titus+Livius+stat

The first decemvirate completed the first ten codes in 450 BC. Here is how Livy describes the Tables creation:

> "...every citizen should quietly consider each point, then talk it over with his friends, and, finally, bring forward for public discussion any additions or subtractions which seemed desirable." —cf. Liv. III.34

By noting that the points are discussed with friends we again find a public matter and not a private matter. How and why would a man in Libertas give away personal power?

Interesting that it was known as the "Solonian Constitution" considering that the Tyrant Peisistratus had done his number, as did many others up to that point. Is it possible Brutus' rebellion had happened further back than estimated? Or is it likely Solon's reforms were so effective even tyrants couldn't break the back of their quality quickly? Either way it's clear his and Lycurgus's concepts influenced a very large region beyond Greece. Thus, the Hellenistic period and the term Greco-Roman.

The bias of historians in such matters to imply the elite were doing this for themselves is all over the place. For example, despite a proper introduction of noting the Tables were "a first step which would allow the protection of the rights of all citizens and permit wrongs to be redressed through precisely-worded written laws known to everybody," Mark Cartwright (a contributor to Ancient.eu, whose background screams "soaked in socialism!" to me) in defining the Twelve Tables presents his personal opinion that:[68]

> Perhaps more realistically, the composition of the Tables was an attempt by the elite to better govern

---

ue+at+the+Austrian+Parliament+Building+in+Vienna%2C+Austria&title= Special:MediaSearch&go=Go&type=image

[68] https://www.ancient.eu/Twelve_Tables/

themselves and prevent abuses within their own social group.

The contributor's "About" page defends his poor ability to route bias as professional by quoting Dickens' preface to *Bleak House*:

> I have no need to observe that I do not wilfully or negligently mislead my readers, and that before I wrote that description I took pains to investigate the subject.

Au contraire, mon frere! You who are degreed and seem to believe that makes your opinion something of a master's understanding must absolutely observe and doublecheck what you write. Not doing so constantly leads to missing basic questions that will alter an improper statement that spreads false notions into the narrative by such "credentialed" writers. Questions like: Who were the elite at this time? Native Romans? Citizens? He undermines his own definition to present and arrogant bias to undermine the term *republic*. He is the type of educate that huddles the citizen with the civilian as anyone residing within a political body.

Let us continue.

In 449 BC, the second decemvirate also completed the last two codes, and after a *secessio plebis* (a refusal to participate or a rejection of the motion) to force the Senate to consider them, the Law of the Twelve Tables was formally disseminated. This refusal of the plebs to participate makes clear this was about the native securing their culture of Libertas from external political influence. Livy (AUC 3.57.10) claims the Twelve Tables were inscribed on bronze, and posted publicly, so all Romans could read and know them. Though some scholars think this never happened and all twelve were developed at once.

The Twelve Tables no longer exist although they remained an important source through the Republic, they gradually became obsolete, eventually being only of historical interest, so we're told, but was this before or after they had been sacked and the original Tables destroyed? It's obvious the answer is after. Some believe that the original Tablets must have been destroyed when the Senones burnt Rome in 387 BC. Cicero claimed that he learned them by heart as a boy in school, but that no one "did so any longer." This is nearly 340 years after the Senones. Cicero was from a rural area where the old ways were far more prevalent and the people far more aware of their natural freedom and *libertas* than in the hubris of Rome Prime. Though he likely still learned from the redrafted Tables.

Cicero In Senate Pronouncing His First Oration Against Catiline In The Roman Senate In 64 B.C. Mural Painting By Cesare Maccari[69]

(When this section was first drafted Constitution.org had a really good translation and notations on the Roman Tables, but has since removed that section. Regardless, I have decided to keep the section built around their information. It is similar to other sources.)

---

[69]
https://commons.wikimedia.org/w/index.php?search=Cicero+In+Senate&title=Special:MediaSearch&go=Go&type=image

Below I share with you the First Table translation shared at Constitution.org. The rest you may research on your own.

THE LAWS OF THE TWELVE TABLES: TABLE I

Concerning the summons to court.

Law I.

When anyone summons another before the tribunal of a judge, the latter must, without hesitation, immediately appear.[1]

Law II.

If, after having been summoned, he does not appear, or refuses to come before the tribunal of the judge, let the party who summoned him call upon any citizens who are present to bear witness.[2] Then let him seize his reluctant adversary; so that he may be brought into court, as a captive, by apparent force.

Law III.

When anyone who has been summoned to court is guilty of evasion, or attempts to flee, let him be arrested by the plaintiff.

Law IV.

If bodily infirmity or advanced age should prevent the party summoned to court from appearing, let him who summoned him furnish him with an animal, as a means of transport. If he is unwilling to accept it, the plaintiff cannot legally be compelled to provide the defendant with a vehicle constructed of boards, or a covered litter.

Law V.

If he who is summoned has either a sponsor or a defender, let him be dismissed, and his representative can take his place in court.[1]

Law VI.

The defender, or the surety of a wealthy man, must himself be rich; but anyone who desires to do so can come to the assistance of a person who is poor, and occupy his place.

Law VII.

When litigants wish to settle their dispute among themselves, even while they are on their way to appear before the Prætor, they shall have the right to make peace; and whatever agreement they enter into, it shall be considered just, and shall be confirmed.

Law VIII.

If the plaintiff and defendant do not settle their dispute, as above mentioned, let them state their cases either in the Comitium or the Forum, by making a brief statement in the presence of the judge, between the rising of the sun and noon; and, both of them being present, let them speak so that each party may hear.

Law IX.

In the afternoon, let the judge grant the right to bring the action, and render his decision in the presence of the plaintiff and the defendant.

Law X.

The setting of the sun shall be the extreme limit of time within which a judge must render his decision.

---

[1] Under the Roman method of procedure, until the thorough organization of the judicial system by the emperors, service of summons was always made by the plaintiff in the action. This was even sometimes done after the custom of regularly appointing court officials for that purpose had been established. — Ed.

[2] Notification of the bystanders was made to show that the arrest of the defendant was to compel his appearance before the tribunal, a proceeding authorized by law; and not to insult him, or forcibly restrain him of his liberty, which might form the ground of prosecution for an illegal act. — Ed.

So what do we have here?

Well, we first have an official construct for public record and an arbitration system for settling disputes. The other Tables follow an order of operation, meaning anything listed in them as statutory laws are only enforceable when a person is summoned to court for a claim of accusation, by another person (not the State). That is why I am not going to share all of them in this work. That, and the fact we don't know which version of the Tables we're getting—the true Republic Table or the redrafting after the Senones (Gauls/Celts) invaded (which is most likely). It requires for the process of statute law to begin with *you* making a statement on *your* honor, on the record of a disreputable act by someone. *You* voice the grievance before a *judge* (public magistrate/arbiter), or the *public* (fellow citizens) in Forum. In this *you* are *summoning the accused* to confront *your* allegation. So, *you* must then go bring the *accused* before the *public*. The claim is legally protected by a statute that the *accused* can be made to appear.

However, it is clear they do not have to appear because they are free men. *You* have to get them, personally. It is claimed that with the magistrate's agreement the accuser could ask to take the accused's property. However, Wikipedia mangles this power with the term *Praetor* which they admit to a lack of information as to when the title was created, but for the creation of the *praetura*; a judicial body that came after the sacking. So, it is likely if the accused did not show the case couldn't move forward. Modern tyrants and despotic officials think they can have a near indefinite timescale or immediate gathering of compulsory agents to go use collective violence to force compliance, that one not showing up for an accusation is carte blanche to find in favor the plaintiff, especially when it is the State itself making the complaint, which is a conflict of interest. This isn't freedom. It is slavery to the communal government. Your village does not get to own you. Your accuser is not to be found honest without your defense available. That is why it is the *accuser's* responsibility to make the accused appear.

Now, how do you think a person who thinks themselves above another feels about the fact a lesser can make them appear? They aren't going to like it, are they? So, let us now pay attention to the description's notation:

> Under the Roman method of procedure, until the thorough organization of the judicial system by the emperors, service of summons was always made by the plaintiff in the action.

Again, take careful note of the first notation on the First Table, please notice — "until the thorough organization of the judicial system by the emperors." We have serious focus on a rule implying prior to Emperors you got your hands dirty as noted above. In fact, it's clear the citizen didn't accept this demotion willingly for, "This was even sometimes done after the custom of regularly appointing court officials for that purpose had been established." This also means a class was institutionalized for the purpose of sending *government agents* to seize freemen to protect those who abused the statutes or wielded too much influence, thus demoting the freeman and emboldening the public servant, just as was done with the Hoplites in Athens.

What emperors were there in the Republic? None. So, this is a process of the later Empire for the elitists so as to not be endangered by having to show up before the people, because they matter so much more than your common ass. Does it behoove the Emperor, or the dictator, or even the senator who thinks himself a trustee (as opposed to being a representative or servant) to send others to make a person they accuse come before *their* handpicked judges, or is it better for them to do the deed themselves? How different is the mindset when the judge is a regular citizen in all powers, taking a limited role beneath the parties involved, versus being a specialist trained in a vacuum and station of privy? When even the Emperor must stand before the court with you, equal in all ways, how does that look? Then, what if he must endanger himself personally in acquiring you to be present? In fact, as an officer they're probably beneath you in that regard as Polybius implies when discussing the Roman Constitution:

> The people then are the only court to decide
> matters of life and death; and even in-cases where
> the penalty is money, if the sum to be assessed is
> sufficiently serious, and especially when the
> accused have held the higher magistracies.

And...

> Again, it is the people who bestow offices on the
> deserving, which are the most honorable rewards
> of virtue.

This position is echoed by Walter Raleigh, designer of the American Experiment. We'll get to that later.

Meanwhile, if the *accused* does not arrive when summoned, before going to get them *you* are to call out to other *citizens* to hear the claim and *then you* make the detainment/compulsory appearance. You could also take off-duty legionnaires or additional citizens willing to help, known to us as a *posse*. The capture of the *accused* by force was still not a public observance of guilt. As notation [2] clearly states, the notification of the witnesses (fellow freemen) was:

> to compel his appearance before the tribunal, a
> proceeding authorized by law; and not to insult
> him, or forcibly restrain him of his liberty, which
> might form the ground of prosecution for an
> illegal act.

In other words, it would be an act of war to violate another man's freedom without notifying the public on record why you chained him, and to violate it still after notifying the public, to which you could be killed, and the accused left un-arrested for defending themselves, a power the Second Amendment technically retains for you when a modern law enforcement officer violates your liberty and rights. If you took the accused and did not tell the People of Rome (or the community) why you were dragging a Roman through the streets in bondage beaten and tattered, even they could consider you a threat and act, let alone the power to respond with force of the other freeman you assaulted. This is then mutual combat or self-defense. Natural powers above the Tables.

The trial is then held before *all* at either the Forum *Romanum*, which was a locale for such proceedings (or a place of "Public Record"), described as:[70]

---

[70] https://en.wikipedia.org/wiki/Roman_Forum

the center of day-to-day life in Rome: the site of
triumphal processions and elections; the venue for
public speeches, criminal trials, and gladiatorial
matches; and the nucleus of commercial affairs.

Or they could do it at the *Comitium* which was a public arena for
being vocal about issues before the citizenry to make your issue a
public matter. Thus, again, *res publica*, a public matter. This public
court was the norm in Rome, and even the intention of America's
political system until elitists believing the commoner could not
understand their intellectual genius, use of words and operations
(which is their way of saying "people weren't accepting our illegal
actions") decided the people needed to have less influence and access
to hearings. And so, things were taken "inside," as it were, and legal
field protectionism began to kill the virtue and purity of the court
system, both then, and as is the practice today.

A procedure that at least somewhat survived was that the trials
were to be speedy, and the accuser needed to get things accomplished
quickly. Why? Because per notation [2] one's liberty was not to be
impeded. Think about what happens when government officers stop
you for a government-based claim under a lesser law (code) in which
no one was harmed. Are you in freedom as you wait for them to think
about how they are going to fine (steal from) you, or is your liberty in
pause? How would that go over in the laws (which America is based
on) that you read above?

The worst part about having to use the Twelve Tables is how,
much like the Magna Carta (which was really to assert the rights of
the Lords who were landholders) they don't matter against the
natural rights of free people. The Tables were to protect the people in
Rome Prime from usurpation in their artificial internal diplomatic (or
civil) process, which all senates and houses really are, artificial bodies.
The Tables are a political doctrine. They're to guide an auxiliary you
can choose to use, or deny participation in. So, I have shared with you
the First Table which sets the standard and stage. The others contain
a grouping of other infractions and offenses, or statutes, and even
some regulations by which some things are to be done by community
standards. Yet, it is the First Table that sets the standard in which the
individual must file any accusation to the violation of following

statutes. It is not the power of the courts, its agents, or the separate body of the general government and its officials who are beneath the Roman Citizen to enforce.

Now, because we have been fed the lie for centuries that the American Republic was built on the idea of Roman Checks and Balances, or General Government (falsely defined as Federal Government which is more of an imperial power) over the freedom of the Citizen, we have to take a basic look at that style. To be precise we need to observe the branches of Roman "government."

THE ROMAN POLITICAL BRANCHES:

ROMAN SENATE

For definition of these things I'm going to simply use Polybius as the closet historian to the Original Republic after Gaul sacked Rome, since that's about the earliest historical work we'll get on the subject. On his own work, the father of cryptography, in his description said:

> I am fully conscious that to those who actually live under this constitution I shall appear to give an inadequate account of it by the omission of certain details.
>
> Knowing accurately every portion of it from personal experience, and from having been bred up in its customs and laws from childhood, they will not be struck so much by the accuracy of the description, as annoyed by its omissions; nor will they believe that the historian has purposely omitted unimportant distinctions, but will attribute his silence upon the origin of existing institutions or other important facts to ignorance. What is told they depreciate as insignificant or

beside the purpose; what is omitted they
desiderate as vital to the question: their object
being to appear to know more than the writers.
But a good critic should not judge a writer by
what he leaves unsaid, but from what he says: if
he detects mis-statement in the latter, he may then
feel certain that ignorance accounts for the former;
but if what he says is accurate, his omissions
ought to be attributed to deliberate judgment and
not to ignorance. So much for those whose
criticisms are prompted by personal ambition
rather than by justice. . . .

Another requisite for obtaining a judicious
approval for an historical disquisition, is that it
should be germane to the matter in hand; if this is
not observed, though its style may be excellent
and its matter irreproachable, it will seem out of
place, and disgust rather than please. . . .

Meaning he has focused the subject to the field of the Roman Constitution and its limitations, not what is being done by government at the time, per se, nor the behaviors of the populace at large. Which would include religious aspects.

The Senate was originally a small body of elders who advised the Monarchy, and then did similarly with the Consul, but generally managed the community treasury, managed the public trusts and facilities, and gained additional powers to solve disputes. Of Senate Polybius says:

The Senate has first of all the control of the
treasury, and regulates the receipts and
disbursements alike. For the Quaestors cannot
issue any public money for the various
departments of the state without a decree of the
Senate, except for the service of the Consuls. The
Senate controls also what is by far the largest and

145

most important expenditure, that, namely, which is made by the censors every lustrum (every 5 years) for the repair or construction of public buildings; this money cannot be obtained by the censors except by the grant of the Senate. Similarly, all crimes committed in Italy requiring a public investigation, such as treason, conspiracy, poisoning, or willful murder, are in the hands of the Senate. Besides, if any individual or state among the Italian allies requires a controversy to be settled, a penalty to be assessed, help or protection to be afforded, – all this is the province of the Senate. Or again, outside Italy, if it is necessary to send an embassy to reconcile warring communities, or to remind them of their duty, or sometimes to impose requisitions upon them, or to receive their submission, or finally to proclaim war against them, – this too is the business of the Senate. In like manner the reception to be given to foreign ambassadors in Rome, and the answers to be returned to them, are decided by the Senate. With such business the people have nothing to do. Consequently, if one were staying at Rome when the Consuls were not in town, one would imagine the constitution to be a complete aristocracy: and this has been the idea entertained by many Greeks, and by many kings as well, from the fact that nearly all the business they had with Rome was settled by the Senate.

The Roman Senate would issue edicts which were to be carried out by the magistrates and had powers over executives. Though, the Senate was comprised of natives of Rome basically double-checking public initiatives to make sure they didn't overreach, especially in favor of domestic and foreign laborers and merchants. They verified spending was occurring by the permitted purpose for which funds were dispersed to. The buildings are also denoted as "public buildings," not "government" buildings, because again, in all republics that which the public treasury funds is to be accessible by the whole public.

There are a few reasons I doubt the claims of these orders and rulings had power over the citizens, not *only* the titled or influential of Rome in the republic, namely two reasons:

1. If the Senate was commanding citizens in their behavior it was in the era of the Empire like with the Triumvirate who would have been illegally using the Senate. This is long after the Republic was in collapse.

2. It is the fallout of this Triumvirate that would lead to writings of the history of Rome while it was being altered into an empire, so that serf society is unlikely to know much about its long-lived ancient predecessor, especially from its authors living in the political life under despotism. I'm sure the insane Caesars, and the Moreish invasions have nothing to do with any improper interpretations of Senate authority though (sarcasm). Brutus's oath and the facts of the Goddess Libertas teach all we need to know to understand the truth of why Rome was a republic regardless of late historical claims.

Senate could only command of the magistrates, local official, and other connected governments and their officials because they were civil servants (serfs to the citizenry). It mentions individuals who need controversies to be settled, because an individual could ask senate to solve a controversy. This does not imply Senate could arbitrarily involve themselves in individual (private) matters. Notice also when it came to crimes, Senate oversaw *public investigations* where it was required and those crimes included:

- treason
- conspiracy

- poisoning
- or willful murder.

If one considers the body politics in any of the lands under imperialism of Rome, and often the spill-over into the monarchies Rome placed in the North European countries, these are all actions political opponents tend to take on each other far more often than with the average citizen and would require an investigation by this general body. A crime of citizen-on-citizen violence would be of no business of the Senate as it is not a—that's right, a *public matter*. This doesn't mean they prosecuted anything whatsoever either, as prosecution is the power of the people as we'll read. The acts issued from the Senate were limited, but from a group made up of long-standing Romans. Only when the Senate began to take on meaningless issues to assert *familia*/tribal dominion to hold office perpetually, and enforcing illegal social laws did the system get overburdened with magistrates too big for their britches, who were empowered to carry out the over-burdened Senate's orders over issues beyond its intended scope, turning the magistrates into mob bosses for tyrants.

This leads to one of the other imperative understandings of the republic. *If* there is going to be governing from the protectorate it is the officers of the protectorate who are to be governed and obey the statute codes preemptively, not the free citizen.

Any attempt to place the free citizen under the protectorate's statues and lesser law is slavery and an act of war against personal liberty.

For as we now understand from the Twelve Tables, to restrain a man from his liberty is itself a crime. Even if the citizens wish not to war for the usurpation of their freedom it is an abolition of the social agreement and the people are free to go their own way. This is taught in John Locke's work on social contracting and he learned this by studying Roman and Greek liberty. This is also another reason we're told specifically by the Founding Republicans of America to keep the districts small. In truth, we need multiple "general" capitols (different than state capitols) beyond D.C. with the size of the system we have now in order for it to work to secure freedoms of local communities better. Even then, if the central meeting districts or the "state" capitols

148

don't fear the power of the individual what reason do they have to not centralize power? Especially, in Senates with special interests and courts with interpretable powers.

Polybius defines the impressive background of Rome by its relation to Lycurgus' Constitution for Sparta. The Consul he notes as related to the Spartan kings, something we've already discussed is no higher in status than any other citizen when not at war.

THE CONSULS

The Consuls, before leading out the legions, remain in Rome and are supreme masters of the administration. All other magistrates, except the Tribunes, are under them and take their orders. They introduce foreign ambassadors to the Senate, bring matters requiring deliberation before it, and see to the execution of its decrees. If, again, there are any matters of state which require the authorization of the people, it is their business to see to them, to summon the popular meetings, to bring the proposals before them, and to carry out the decrees of the majority. In the preparations for war also, and in a word in the entire administration of a campaign, they have all but absolute power. It is competent to them to impose on the allies such levies as they think good, to appoint the Military Tribunes, to make up the roll for soldiers and select those that are suitable. Besides, they have absolute power of inflicting punishment on all who are under their command while on active service, and they have authority to expend as much of the public money as they choose, being accompanied by a quaestor who is entirely at their orders. A survey of these powers would in fact justify our describing the Constitution as despotic — a clear case of royal government. Nor will it affect the truth of my

description, if any of the institutions I have
described are changed in our time, or in that of
our posterity, and the same remarks apply to what
follows.

What followed were his thoughts on the Senate that we just read, and sections on "the People," which comes next. To the Consul however, we must note they, "are supreme masters of the administration." Thus, the heads over the agencies of the Roman People. That makes them servants and him their headmaster under public permission. Both the Senate and the Consul are imbued by their power via the People. It is overwhelmingly clear the Consul only had power over non-tribunal magistrates (because consuls could face tribunal) when in peace, and over citizens *only* during war and only in matters having to do with addressing the war. It likely is limited to those in service too and not necessarily the whole. They also enforce the laws against *agents* failing to obey Senate! They must also make sure the public stays informed of any issue which does not fall to the power of Senate or their self. The U.S. President is almost no different. He simply manages the offices/officers/agents (magistrates) in the departments and is to charge them when they are derelict in their duties or commit treason against the *spirit and purpose* of the Constitution. He then directs the armed forces during war which Congress is to authorize. He is not *our* leader. The Consul can spend what they want from the treasury however, Polybius clearly told us where his power was limited to. So, his spending has to occur in that branch and limitation *only*.

The People were the power by which decisions on war were to unfold, and to which honor (positions) was bestowed or when someone was to be put to death. So even where the Consul has war powers in action, the People have to proclaim the war "on" or make the call to action. It seems the Consul can personally punish a soldier who has violated their duty, but that does not necessarily mean he can punish any citizen during a war as he wishes.

POLYBIUS ON THE PEOPLE:

THE PEOPLE

After this one would naturally be inclined to ask what part is left for the people in the constitution, when the Senate has these various functions, especially the control of the receipts and expenditure of the exchequer; and when the Consuls, again, have absolute power over the details of military preparation, and an absolute authority in the field? There is, however, a part left the people, and it is a most important one. For the people is the sole fountain of honor and of punishment; and it is by these two things and these alone that dynasties and constitutions and, in a word, human society are held together: for where the distinction between them is not sharply drawn both in theory and practice, there no undertaking can be properly administered, — as indeed we might expect when good and bad are held in exactly the same honor. The people then are the only court to decide matters of life and death; and even in-cases where the penalty is money, if the sum to be assessed is sufficiently serious, and especially when the accused have held the higher magistracies. And in regard to this arrangement there is one point deserving especial commendation and record. Men who are on trial for their lives at Rome, while sentence is in process of being voted, — if even only one of the tribes whose votes are needed to ratify the sentence has not voted, — have the privilege at Rome of openly departing and condemning themselves to a voluntary exile. Such men are safe at Naples or Praeneste or at Tibur, and at other

towns with which this arrangement has been duly
ratified on oath.

Again, it is the people who bestow offices on the deserving, which
are the most honorable rewards of virtue. Put another way, it is how
one receives a title. By this point, in my opinion, we already have
people improperly letting honor overrule sensible public policy. The
People also have the absolute power of passing or repealing laws, and
most important of all, it is the People who deliberate on the question
of peace or war. And when provisional terms are made for alliance,
suspension of hostilities, or treaties, it is the People who ratify them
or the reverse. By the time of the Empire this is all theater and the
orders for going to war start coming from Senate and the Tyrant
Consuls, or Emperors.

These considerations again would lead one to say that the chief
power in the state was the People's, and that the constitution was a
democracy.

In modern times we find the continual need to relate voting and
government to republic, and yet, the fact is Romans didn't need to
vote to be free men, *they simply were free*. Voting would be more
dangerous of a journey than just fighting the legionnaires for many,
as they are just as well-trained (because you were one at some point,
generally). This would also be a right of theirs *for they were also free*.
The relation is similar to Greece, Athens, and Sparta. Mainstream
narratives still define the voting in assembly in Rome as *direct
democracy*, but it wasn't. Rather, it was *direct republic*, because the
Constitution of Rome under the Republic's purpose which is to assure
personal liberty, automatically nullifies any democratic action which
would undermine it, to which the free man can respond in defense of
his freedom. As such, the individual had every right to self-represent
and abstain from public agreements. Voting was for activity in the
Branches and to show consensus. Consensus is not compromise and
no dissenter in a consensus is required to partake. The votes in Rome
were to only affect Rome, and its diplomacy, not the free citizen and
not all membered areas of the republic, for the membered cities and
external individuals had equal power in their actions to the Roman
Republic Capitol as by being in the Republic they gained equal
freedom to the Roman to determine their own actions. It was when in

conflict with foreign bodies aggressing upon liberty they would need to supply aid to the military action, a feature of Alexander's Greek Empire. The later similar relationship is known as *Roman Imperial Cities*. This was because Rome couldn't easily control the areas directly, which is why the Republic never tried to and the Empire overextended itself in an attempt to. Mind you Polybius is telling us clearly The People's Assembly was not staying within these boundaries.

The citizens would meet in an Assembly of the People, be jury in criminal claims, vote on who would hold office, who would be removed, who were granted titles of honor, create or end laws, and the other actions Polybius mentions above. Oh, and did you notice? We actually get Polybius' opinion:

> Put another way, it is how one receives a title. By this point in my opinion we already have people improperly letting honor over rule sensible public policy.

He tells us clearly people with honors were being allowed to make law out of trust over common sense against the public policy, and the policy in Rome was personal liberty. The People did use representatives for their Tribes though a vote, based on the region in which they resided to issue vote, but as in Athens, nothing kept a man from representing himself on the record. The individual would be placing their view on record which in turn was a protection for him in his lawful dissention when he voted against or abstained. How do I know this? The combination of what it means to be free and the use of public records which is what the political branches were using in doing their business.

A tell on the position this book is taking on republics:

> Men who are on trial for their lives at Rome, while
> sentence is in process of being voted, — if even
> only one of the tribes whose votes are needed to

ratify the sentence has not voted, — have the
privilege at Rome of openly departing and
condemning themselves to a voluntary exile.

A man on trial for his life can just leave. Is this not telling of the
realities of freedom and liberty in republic? Yet, we can also tell
Polybius is discussing a political function and not the Natural People
of Rome for he refers to them as "it" not "us" or "we," for it is the
Assembly of the People. A thing. It is also most likely the man is a
government agent and not just some person. Why would the whole
body be involved in deciding the sentence for a common criminal
when that can be done by a smaller jury in the Forum Romanum?

Polybius writes this in 240 something B.C., right after a sacking
that would change Rome. So, where we may not think these powers
were using Tribunals to stop Consuls and Senate actions, maybe it
really was those free individuals of Rome in "congress" and "court"
and common agreement in their true equivalence as Romans that
forced Senate, and the Executive under them.

Polybius also states as to the Consul, which he defines as the
Greek Kings who only on a battlefield by command have power over
the private citizen. He says:

> As for the people, the Consuls are pre-eminently
> obliged to court their favor, however distant from
> home may be the field of their operations; for it is
> the people, as I have said before, that ratifies, or
> refuses to ratify, terms of peace and treaties; but
> most of all because when laying down their office
> they have to give an account of their
> administration before it.

So essentially, we are not being told of "people" as in the free
private citizen of Rome, but of the House of Commons or *Comitia
Tributa* (Tribunal Committee) or Tribunes, where popular vote is held
upon public matters for, again, a consensus in a *public* matter. Yet,

people are persons. Persons are individuals and individuals are always free. So, this is a meeting of the free individuals for limited reasons. Let me again note, it is before Polybius writes of this that Gaul had already sacked Rome and smashed the original Twelve Tables, burned buildings and any preexisting writings, and the *Concilium Plebis* (The Council of the Plebs) began to have power equal to the *Comitia Tributa* in Rome. A problem, because they were foreigners and residents (which are not the same as domestics or locals) allowed to manage a domestic body with equal power to the native people which really had no power over the political bodies of the foreigners, but for when they were in and working for Rome (residents) and in refusing their ability to direct the local "state." This work is after the political corruptions that had been there for a good 100 years or so. Even then, the Roman system is built on the Greek concepts where the citizen was free to meet their reps, submit legislation, address the legislative body of The People, vote on legislation, and abstain.

It is clarified by history that our main culprit against free citizens is indeed constant external breaking down of the interior protector through the Plebians:

> Shortly after the founding of the Roman Republic (traditionally dated to 509 BC), the principal legislative authority shifted to two new assemblies, the Tribal Assembly ("Citizen's Assembly") and the Centuriate Assembly (Assembly of 100 men). Eventually, most legislative powers were transferred to another assembly, the Plebeian Council ("Assembly of the Commoners"). Ultimately, it was the Plebeian Council that disrupted the balance between the senate, the legislative branch, and the executive branch. This led to the collapse of the republic, and the founding of the Roman Empire in 27 BC

> — Wikipedia

Let us remember the dates we're told of for all these events are suspect as most of these histories were verbal and probably had more longevity than implied. In the case of the Assembly of Commoners, how long did this really take? The Plebs of Brutus' era seem a little more democrat-oriented by 27 B.C., doesn't it?

The Assembly of the Commoners is where the civilians (Plebs, which, as we covered were not free Romans, and were often foreigners) had the ability to influence law. Mind you, many natural-born Romans were reduced to this position of Pleb by the elite, but over time it is where the foreign infiltrates used the power of the Senate to bleed down influence and uphold alteration to the protective laws of the domestic Roman. Through title or honor worship they convinced the Roman citizen to their cause, and through this the outside collectivist hijacked the Roman Republic and reduced it from the inside out. Today we cannot fix America, because America does not even know itself, due to these same tactics by religites, monocrats, and socialists alike.

Okay, like right here:

> The rights available to individual citizens of Rome
> varied over time, according to their place of
> origin, and their service to the state.
>
> — Wikipedia

Of course they did! "Rights" always vary with malleable laws. When they are static Maxims they don't vary, and they aren't rights. They are liberties, or authorizations. So, for a good 200 years from the official perspective before the Senones sacked Rome, Romans had the regular liberties that were intended.

What was the deal with these "privileges and protections" then? Well, first a main protection is always the right of the citizen to be involved in the State's operation. From there, it is all in the claims of "citizens" having "privileges and protections." Privileges and protections were political limitations on the government of Rome and specifically its (en)titled offices/officers, and to what extents a citizen could alter those things. These were not the powers of being a *freeman*, not simply a "citizen." More accurately, officers and agents become a civilian with "given permissions" that then limit their power and "protections" to do their specialized activity without being accused of violating a liberty which would be cause to put the agent to death. Yet, all Romans can still do these activities personally without limitation, thus, their being in liberty. So, in this we then get the line "their service to the state." In other words, their service to the condition of Rome limited the personal power they had due to security of the society from abuse by "power."

This is a paramount tell in the misidentification of rights against liberties, and the intentional skewing of Republics from Democracies.

I would recommend reading Polybius while understanding the separation we discuss in this book, and many will see the separations made in the purpose of the American Republic and why the House, Senate, President, and Supreme Court are separated out like they are. They overstep these boundaries regularly mind you, via interpretation of implied terms with unimplied authority as they eventually did in Rome, made worse by their political pirate parties, so they further claim that such acts are lawful, even after years of complaining in the past such were in fact not lawful, which I'm sure was also happening in Rome.

Furthermore, to the point the People, which in this case is a political body, he separately talks about the citizenry:

> Consequently, all citizens are much at its mercy;
> and being alarmed at the uncertainty as to when
> they may need its aid, are cautious about resisting
> or actively opposing its will.

The Citizenry is thus clearly different than the Consul, Senate, or Tribune (People) and the body, at this point, carrying too much power, likely a result of egos and infiltration.

Again, recall we are at a collapse of the initial Republic of Brutus as is noted here:

"Nay, even when these external alarms are past,
and the people are enjoying their good fortune
and the fruits of their victories, and, as usually
happens, growing corrupted by flattery and
idleness, show a tendency to violence and
arrogance."

Well, this was a period of flattery and idleness where officials and stations were running rampant over a citizenry "cautious about resisting or actively opposing its will." This doesn't mean they never did this, for that is how it became a republic. They were failing to do this when needed, to stay comfortable.

As we in America today are doing.

I think it is also very important when reading Polybius that he doesn't discuss Libertas despite being a central Goddess in Roman culture. Something we do get from Cicero over 100 years later. Why? After all, it's fundamental to being Roman and free. Likely, because of how Romans were failing to oppose government's will. So, though he presents the relation to *checks and balances* which are an executive, a judicial, legislator, and a House of Commons for reviewing and authorizing the other's action—remembering the Citizen was empowered to take any violator before the forum for violating the law and limitations of official powers—there is still no fundamental notice to freedom or even liberty that the society was based on.

This could be a translational issue. It could be that it went without saying as a norm of their culture, that it was secondary to the general topic of the Roman Constitution's operation. This could also be a tendency of any society corrupted by centralized power to omit where personal freedom overrules the "government," too. It could even be Polybius' people had been in government overreach so long even he was ignorant to the reality of personal freedom of the private citizen over the doctrines being issued from the auxiliary. Likely, in my view it's a situational error where, as with the American Founders who opposed the Bill of Rights, felt the reality that government shouldn't be managing anything outside of where it was authored, went without saying. Yet as noted already, he was also focusing on the political structure, and libertas was a social and natural power above such a body. It's also likely that it was like in the whole of European oppression at the time of the Enlightenment, where he would have been killed for being too clear about just how criminal the authority was being. So, he focused on the purpose and avoid dissenting too much. We as freemen really must stop conflating Constituted powers. If a Constitution was necessarily the same as republic, the U.S. Constitution wouldn't need to specify our republican form.

STATE RIGHTS

Another key element the U.S. Founders saw in Rome was "State's Rights," the right of another society's political condition which has joined the Republic to govern themselves has they've always been, a concept inherited from Alexander's "conquest." However, they are to respect all external customs and laws including personal liberty of the outsider when within their "State's" borders. That's because their relation is general protection, unlike the league of Corinth which I've already noted had to do with agreeing to a central leader having power to use all members' military force to defeat a *specified* enemy. This is because a state is just a political condition permitted to operate on participants' behalf. It is artificial. The Romans and U.S. Founders knew this, to which in Rome Senate and the Consul addressed as a diplomatic process—not one of Master Government over Servant Governments. By the republic they are all beneath the free individual person. This is done in the U.S. Constitution, as we will later read.

In most historical republics this is how it would play out, but wars would also happen because it is important to respect other's social and personal ideals. If Texas were *not* membered with the Republic of the United States, it would then be a sovereign political body and can wholly undermine people's personal ideologies, but again, there is still a risk of war and the individual's natural right to violently resist persecution of a natural liberty by an artificial body.

FALL OF ROME

In the rise of the Empire of Rome the Triumvirate comes from the *Optimate* (again, meaning *best men*) or "ruling class," trying to keep the Populares from instituting … take a guess? Right! Democracy! Do you see the problem now with the terms "ruling class," oligarchy, and aristocracy? Over time they've been warped and eventually applied to the power-mongering democratic (mob inciting) dictators, and no longer applied to the natural-born citizens, simply securing their local community, as would be the case in a small region. You'll notice this every time a republic is sieged. For example, from the website WorldHistory.org we are told:

> The ruling class called themselves Optimates (the best men) while the lower classes, or those who sympathized with them, were known as the Populares (the people). These names were applied simply to those who held a certain political ideology; they were not strict political parties nor were all of the ruling class Optimates nor all of the lower classes Populares. In general, the Optimates held with traditional political and social values which favored the power of the Senate of Rome (patricians/founding families/Natural Born Romans) and the prestige and superiority of the ruling class. The Populares, again generally speaking, favored reform and democratization of the Roman Republic. These opposing ideologies would famously clash in the form of three men who would, unwittingly, bring about the end of the Roman Republic.

So the issue isn't class-based, it is ideological. Are we Romans or globalists? Are we a republic protectorate assuring the natural liberty of all those who live in our lands and those bodies who member with us for protection of their way of life, or are we the police of global social equality to be focused by the majority will of those in charge?

What scenario do you know of like this today? We again have no full relation of the timeline the quote is discussing, but the description implied is closer to Julius Caesar's time. Meaning further mangling of the already dead Republic with the Empire the vultures are vying to be king of it.

Note: The Triumvirate may have come from the Optimate, yet these were not real Romans, but democratic power mongers like some of the Thirty Tyrants. The Republican Optimates I'm referring to above are few and far-between by the time of the Triumvirate of Caesar, Pompey, and Crassus.

As it was at the founding of the U.S., in the Roman Republic we see pro-Romans, born of Rome, Loyal to Rome, also called the *Patricians* (patriots?), and a worker and foreign class (or class loyal to a foreign, employing, or central entity, like the federalists) adherent to different style systems, what we know as the Plebeians. In this case, it is most likely the exact same culture that collapsed both Athens and Rome through democracy, the excerpt itself even noting the Populares wanting to democratize Rome; meaning populate with an amalgam of outsiders, and ruling the political body by the predominate view of the time, and not by the limitation upon the governance system.

We see the continued theme of republics trying to keep out foreign tyrannical systems of popular assimilation be accused of oligarchy and tyranny by the very same despotic mob agitating tyrants trying to overtake them. This is why often bleeding hearts suggest open borders. Yet, if they actually study the record they would find the liberty society's creature comforts tend to be the primary reason the locals did not force the foreigners out, and that those societies often had no problem with the foreign ideals so long as they weren't being domestically implemented through the body politic. As already noted, most outside cultural customs were already protected as the political body had no power over them in the first place. In other words, republics are more tolerant and assure a connected cultural is autonomous in its way of life. The fact is, democracies by their nature require all involved in the democracy to obey the majority "will." Thus, it kills culturally-independent identities, and protects only the one it prefers at any given time.

Our reason to distrust the official claim of what a ruling class is comes to a comfortable conclusion in this statement from Wikipedia on Plebeians:

> The 19th-century historian Barthold Georg Niebuhr held that plebeians began to appear at Rome during the reign of Ancus Marcius (reigned 642–617 BC) and were possibly foreigners settling in Rome as naturalized citizens. In any case, at the outset of the Roman Republic, the patricians had a near monopoly on political and social institutions. Plebeians were excluded from magistracies and religious colleges, and they were not permitted to know the laws by which they were governed. Plebeians served in the army, but rarely became military leaders.

The point on not knowing the law ties in well as to why *all* Romans would have the Twelve Tables accessible in the forum and why Romans would aid each other in knowing it.

The fact is admitted above that this class of Plebeian grew out of an immigrant class, with equal rights to the Roman early in Roman history due to monarchial expansion, principalities, and migration to the successful region to be part of it, not to simply partake of it. Clearly, migrant tendencies to their old mentality of serfdom were a concern for any burgeoning or solidified culture and made them the perfect tool to have as irate mobs for any elitist, self-believed to be above the common law, who recognized these migrants were used to such a system. Yet, so long as they wanted real independence that the native had, they conformed to local customs and banned together with local freeman over the despots, which is something migrants do not do. Migrants keep allegiance to where they were from and are only in a place to work. Immigrants arrive to be a part of the new culture. Everywhere peoples with no wish to unite started to swell, there went the city-state. Natives would eventually have to run them out or fall to mob rule. In Rome's case, it appears the leadership pissed the legionnaires off first during Brutus' day, but the tight relations

162

built in killing the kings dwindled in time, giving the power monger sway with the Plebs. In time, this happened with every sovereign state, and every sovereign state was destroyed not by simple immigrants, but by migrants who would not convert to the local ways and who rather converted the center of power to the subservient, dependent authoritarian concepts of their homeland, often out jealousy. The claim the Plebs were not taught the laws they were governed by is a lie. They needed only learn the language of Rome, and ask questions of the natives, as the laws were on display at the Forum. At least by the 5th century B.C. they were. And, the duty of the Roman was to assure anyone trying to engage the Forum's use was properly informed, so the process wasn't damaged, or their own liberty endangered.

This is why we must understand separation of powers correctly. The argument that these city-states made other fellow Grecians/Romans into meek and secondary people is true, but it is also true that often this was not the primary case until threats within the city-states occurred, and infiltrated offices under a relaxed (idle) populace skewed the public narrative. Even truer is the fact that among themselves as members of a city-state they were equals in their freedom to do as they wished. Prior to cultural threats to their personal liberty these people lived side-by-side with other cultures and religions in many ways. Only in supporting their state by becoming nationalists over the foundations of liberty and the patriotism they were based on were their cultures crushed. Therefore, while it was a republic, the Romans turned themselves into a security firm, and by protecting membered regions whose citizens were granted full citizenship (except for involvement in the governance of Rome Prime, the City of Rome). Rome was able to usher in hundreds of years of peace under the Roman Republic—the true Pax Romana, not the one spoken of after the Triumvirate ruined the Republic.

Peace doesn't mean no fighting, no war. It means relative calm, no tyranny. And since tyranny means, "government oppression by force," the Romans didn't have a government over themselves, because they were freemen. They had a government over government, as did the U.S.

But once they did gain a government of the People, they slipped into being the Roman Empire, as did the U.S.

163

THE INFORMED REPUBLIC

Part Three:
THE AMERICAN
REPUBLIC

PREAMBLE

MUCH OF THE position of this work is proven in the American Republican (or Anti-Federalist) public and legal works. So, this will be the longest section in the book. The American Republic is heavily focused and based on Greek and Roman confederations, with "federal" checks and balances as an internal function (management of the auxiliary). Relations to British Common Law are generally overinflated or false altogether. There is also a long-held belief this nation is Christian. This is highly incorrect and stated equally false in the Treaty of Tripoli. That religion simply has shared views on key aspects of personal liberties over human governments, but like most of its competing religions, it violates many other liberties to use government to force non-members of its faith to follow its edicts despite the faith's own restrictions from government and the U.S. Bill of Rights' Separation of Church and State, to be used for such purposes. A violation atheists equally commit.

The American Republic's "general government" has no actual power over living individuals who are not elected, hired, or licensed agents of the governing body titled The United States of America. Its system is separated from all religious and social legal intermingling. The debates on the Constitution reveal many positions of the individual being separate from the political body both nationally and statewide. They are clear on its direction over the states in key regards and in restricting foreign influence over all levels of government. Much of the Founders' establishment of our system and our public dissolution from England used the Law of Nations (which I recommend you read for yourself as I do not go into it much) as the reference in which most of my positions on migrants and citizenship are validated, but the Founders' further study into the Republics of antiquity beyond that work are key to their intentions and the spirit of the law in connection to the deeper research by Enlightenment thinkers such as John Locke.

The one thing that keeps holding up the advancement of liberty are the early-Enlightenment writers' appeals to government, and modern man's need to appeal to artificial authority due to a total misunderstanding of Natural Law, thanks to some of this subterfuge, a far worse offense in the European works than that of the American Enlightenists of the '76 era—Yes, that's right, America is a (the) Nation of the Enlightenment. The tendency and necessity for writers to make subversive works appeal to the upper crust in that era resulted in lots of sentiments of pro-government and pro-judicial stances being accepted by the modern politicos as supporting government and judicial opinion, despite overt statements by the writer(s) to the right of the individual to create and forcefully end a government's reign. The entire occurrence of America's rebellion speaks to the reality that the Enlightenment was a march to the eventual removal of government, not only the justifiable limitation of it, and the redemption of the self-governed individual (power to address and manage matters in public forum personally or privately).

Even in keeping the view of the rebellion simply to "limiting government" (though I contend they wanted an evolution into its total repeal), the classical liberal (libertarian) position attributed to Locke and ilk has advanced into republicanism and the position that a "government" is intended to only interact with other governments and only to assure a people's way of life, not to alter the people to conform to an external or internal governing body. Put another way, *constitutions* are restrictions and declarations/contracts on governments and their assets, not real people, except again, *for those employed by it* (officers, agent, representatives, titled, etc.) or serfs under a "positive government." Resistance by powermongers to this concept is why we see the growth of licensing and permissions from government and arguments for "positive" government (a political body that permits, or lords over the people).

Leadership knows this is true and uses loopholes—or, more accurately, misinterpretation—for themselves while making us think they're just securing the general welfare, as was done with the Stamp

Act or more recently the Patriot Act, for instance. More importantly, Americans were declared free in 1776 under a pre-existing liberty that can never be given up, even willfully. The government in the U.S. Republic does not act without explicit consent of the People as we read about in Rome with Polybius, and not on the whims of the representatives (democracy), and must assure the minority or dissenting's right to refuse participation and to be protected in that position, not prosecuted. Generally, this is where internationalism, statists, nationalists, or globalists take advantage of ignorance and manipulate public perception with arguments of advancements of and forming of new societies under government's direction, as well as labeling dissenters as un-mutual to the cause. If you'll notice those positions are almost always for global or national governance via a central authority through "representational democratic government" (trustees, often the influential from a district), but not necessarily real representative government under free persons.

By these factors I'll inform you of how liberty was quickly subverted by the Federalists to get the Constitution in place. Thus, the Republican guarantee being installed to somewhat rectify this criminal action. Though in the end we have a bloated overburdened system with trust in a government that was never to be trusted, and a citizenry backward in their understanding of freedom, begging for serfdom to a state in order to keep their preferred lords and political bodies employed, instead of commanding their own lives.

ALTERING THE LAW, A SECTION OVERVIEW

In studying America's Foundation, we find a problem regular to the general populace and their shared understanding when examining the historical republics. Many trying to save the Constitution and what they think is their national heritage tend to think the legal process's channels and state sovereignty made America the Land of the Free. But does that make sense? Needing collective agreement or a magistrate's (majesty's) affirmation to act is freedom? Liberty? Isn't that still serfdom and trusting government (group-controlled mechanisms), the very source of our oppressions? Isn't that slavery?

We are conditioned to think our political operation comes from the establishment of legal codes or Biblical fixtures, but in what we've seen of republic in this work so far, this is clearly not true, as code laws, judicial interpretations, and religious doctrine were used for tyrannical means regularly in monarchies, theocracies, tyrannies, and despotism alike. Real legal codes usually come up to address something that already occurred, meaning the body politic was already in motion and authorizes a community standard which is a suggestion in case of an event happening again, or known to happen at times. It is simply an option available for finding a solution to a dispute that must be initiated for solution by a citizen or citizens, not a government agent's best judgement, like we saw in how the Consul must be directed by the people to act. The judiciary only really issues an opinion with no power of enforcement, but for by the winning party. Though it is true that there were times in the old courts (and as is illegally done today) when you gave up freedom to refute a claim and risked incarceration when you participated with the judiciaries to the outcome of that opinion. However, in purity, the citizen who won is then socially protected to enforce the ruling, not entitled have the government solely enforce the ruling.

Theocracies of all kinds attempt to place rules through governments out of their religious book upon people who do not even participate in the religion. How is there freedom in that? And what weak God thinks men should be acting on its behalf?

Liberty allows for the individual non-titled being to refuse the determination of an artificial body, even one claiming to be of a particular God, like it or not. That is real freedom and what America was really trying to accomplish and advance against a system that believed it could revoke personal freedom for decorum offenses.

ar ti fact[71] (*or artificial*)

1. a: a usually simple object (such as a tool or ornament) showing human workmanship or modification as distinguished from a natural object

Misunderstanding this can be detrimental to a republic being founded or one already in play for many reasons we've seen so far. Focus on this mis-evaluation must be addressed. First off, prior to 1776 America was still stuck dealing with governing officials, domestic and foreign, trained in British legal standards that in truth are based in Roman Imperial Law (Code Law) dressed up in the Bible. You can call this Church Law or Vatican Law or whatever else, also. It was and is *all* artificial, human-constructed to control behavior, so the power structure feels safe. This is admitted in the Bible by God defining this as Man's Law or the Laws of Men. All of those laws fall to what the Christian calls God's Law (though they too ascribe too many human behavioral codes to that), or what the Enlightenment and even Aristotle rightly called Natural Law, which if you are a Christian, is what Jesus was actually teaching, the true Living Word. "Nature's law" and "nature's God" is not just the ability to reason. It's the reality that you and nature (the living ever-changing environment) determine how comfortable your life is at the end of the day, only then aided by other freemen no matter what the artifacts of pulpit, throne, community or legislature claim. Natural, true, and existing with or without human interpretation of it.

So, when we turn to artificial legal documents highly based in judicial perception, we give men rule over the natural state of other

---

[71] https://www.merriam-webster.com/dictionary/artifact

men and damage the natural liberty existence has placed in everyone's hands evenly. Equality/equity. Legal texts and judicial opinions being based on Roman Imperial Law, as we've now learned over the course of this book, are not based on the Roman or Antiquity Republics which predate modern religions. U.S. Founders are overwhelmingly clear that they researched the liberty societies (republics) of Sparta, Athens, Unified Greece (Like the League of Corinth) and Rome, focused on assuring what we read above from Xenophon per 'Hiero," the "private citizen," is as free as possible.

Additionally, the Founders and Anti-Federalist Framers are very clear in their works that the majority of European countries calling themselves republics at that time were not republics and were often corrupt to the core. So legal documentation and exchange with these bodies and appeals to long-installed powers cannot be seen as the driving intent to the political purpose of America. Only as the means by which it may respond to a corrupt world in the moment.

If they were trying to end the old ways, why would they use the popular Imperial style when appealing for independence as some may claim? Well, they used it to codify in public courts of record (Forum) their legal dissidence against the Crown and its misuse of the legal codes and statutes. In other words, the documents filed and served were just to present a claim in a form the Kingships and churches had been conditioned to as a record of violations. They were using the enemy's system against itself which still uses a lot of the old styles, hidden from the general public's understanding. However, no sane Founder, studied in what the real problem was, believed there would be "legal remedy" *by that means*. For example, their legal pleas to the House of Commons and the Crown that were often ignored, which lead to the domestic chant of "No taxation without representation." Keep in mind a person involved in the Founding being a university-schooled lawyer seeking such "peaceable" legal remedy was not necessarily competent in liberty or natural law even if they were a prominent figure.

Thomas Jefferson[72]

When the Declaration of Independence was released it used the existing powers accepted from of public record proclamation to completely end the rule of Roman Imperial Law over freemen first, and then the political States of the New World. However, it did not appeal to the Old World or even domestic State authority. It appealed to Nature and whatever the God of Nature is. Christians play up in their minds the generalization it must be the Christian God or British Common Law, but Thomas Jefferson's works imply otherwise (look into *Revisal of the Laws: Drafts of Legislation*).

---

[72] https://www.whitehouse.gov/about-the-white-house/presidents/thomas-jefferson/

Even the editor's note at Archive.gov on the *Revisal of the Laws* says:

> This resulted partly from its purpose, which was
> not that of forming a collection of laws then in
> force but of reforming the entire structure of law
> so as to strip it of all vestiges of its earlier
> monarchical aspects and to bring it into
> conformity with republican principles.[73]

Yet, along the way bear this in mind:

> Laws are made for men of ordinary
> understanding and should, therefore, be
> construed by the ordinary rules of common
> sense.[74]

I want to give a timeline on the colonies into the Republic, but I need to clarify Common Law for you first.

Madison wrote in depth on the subject of Common Law as generally understood being incompatible with our new system (There is a lot here, I know, and I do not agree with it all, but Madison covers a major aspect of common law.):

> The committee refer to the doctrine lately
> advanced, as a sanction to the Sedition Act, 'that
> the common or unwritten law,' a law of vast
> extent and complexity, and embracing almost
> every possible subject of legislation, both civil and

---

[73] https://founders.archives.gov/documents/Jefferson/01-02-02-0132-0001

[74] Thomas Jefferson letter to Judge William Johnson 1823, https://founders.archives.gov/documents/Jefferson/98-01-02-3562

criminal, makes a part of the law of these States, in their united and national capacity.

The novelty, and, in the judgment of the committee, the extravagance of this pretension, would have consigned it to the silence in which they have passed by other arguments which an extraordinary zeal for the Act has drawn into the discussion; but the auspices under which this innovation presents itself have constrained the committee to bestow on it an attention which other considerations might have forbidden.

In executing the task, it may be of use to look back to the colonial state of this country, prior to the Revolution to trace the effect of the Revolution which converted the colonies into independent States, to inquire into the import of the Articles of Confederation, the first instrument by which the Union of the States was regularly established, and, finally, to consult the Constitution of 1787, which is the oracle that must decide the important question.

In the state prior to the Revolution, it is certain that the common law, under different limitations, made a part of the colonial codes. But whether it be understood that the original colonists brought the law with them, or made it their law by adoption, it is equally certain that it was the separate law of each colony within its respective limits, and was unknown to them as a law pervading and operating through the whole as one society.

It could not possibly be otherwise. The common law was not the same in any two of the Colonies, in some the modifications were materially and extensively different. There was no common legislature by which a common will could be expressed in the form of a law, nor any common magistracy by which such a law could be carried into practice. The will of each colony, alone and separately, had its organs for these purposes.

This stage of our political history furnishes no foothold for the patrons of this new doctrine.

Did, then, the principle or operation of the great event which made the Colonies independent States imply or introduce the common law as a law of the Union?

The fundamental principle of the Revolution was, that the Colonies were co-ordinate members with each other and with Great Britain, of an empire united by a common executive sovereign, but not united by any common legislative sovereign. The legislative power was maintained to be as complete in each American Parliament, as in the British Parliament. And the royal prerogative was in force in each Colony by virtue of its acknowledging the King for its executive magistrate, as it was in Great Britain by virtue of a like acknowledgment there. A denial of these principles by Great Britain, and the assertion of them by America, produced the Revolution.

There was a time, indeed, when an exception to the legislative separation of the several component and co-equal parts of the empire obtained a degree of acquiescence. The British Parliament was allowed to regulate the trade with foreign nations, and between the different parts of the empire. This was, however, mere practice without right, and contrary to the true theory of the Constitution. The convenience of some regulations, in both cases, was apparent; and as there was no legislature with power over the whole, nor any constitutional pre-eminence among the legislatures of the several parts, it was natural for the legislature of that particular part which was the eldest and the largest to assume this function, and for the others to acquiesce in it. This tacit arrangement was the less criticized, as the regulations established by the British Parliament operated in favor of that part of the empire which seemed to bear the principle share of the public burdens, and were regarded as an indemnification of its advances for the other parts. As long as this regulating power was confined to the two objects of conveniency and equity, it was not complained of nor much inquired into. But, no sooner was it perverted to the selfish views of the party assuming it, than the injured parties began to feel and to reflect, and the moment the claim to a direct and indefinite power was ingrafted on the precedent of the regulating power, the whole charm was dissolved, and every eye opened to the usurpation. The assertion by Great Britain of a power to make laws for the other members of the empire in all cases whatsoever, ended in the discovery that she had a right to make laws for them in no cases whatsoever.

Such being the ground of our Revolution, no support nor colour can be drawn from it for the doctrine that the common law is binding on these States as one society. The doctrine, on the contrary, is evidently repugnant to the fundamental principle of the Revolution.

The Articles of Confederation are the next source of information on this subject.

In the interval between the commencement of the Revolution and the final ratification of these Articles, the nature and extent of the Union was determined by the circumstances of the crisis, rather than by any accurate delineation of the general authority. It will not be alleged that the "common law" could have had any legitimate birth as a law of the United States during that state of things. If it came as such into existence at all the Charter of Confederation must have been its parent.

Here again, however, its pretensions are absolutely destitute of foundation. This instrument does not contain a sentence or a syllable that can be tortured into a countenance of the idea that the parties to it were, with respect to the objects of the common law, to form one community. No such law is named, or implied, or alluded to, as being in force, or as brought into force by that compact. No provision is made by which such a law could be carried into operation; whilst, on the other hand, every such inference or pretext is absolutely precluded by Article II, which declares "that each State retains its sovereignty, freedom, and independence, and every power, jurisdiction, and right which is not by this Confederation expressly delegated to the United States in Congress assembled."

Thus far it appears that not a vestige of this extraordinary doctrine can be found in the origin or progress of American institutions. The evidence against it has, on the contrary, grown stronger at every step, till it has amounted to a formal and positive exclusion, by written articles of compact among the parties concerned.

Basically, the U.S. Constitution doesn't create a system with power to tell the States what their general laws are, and it is not under some religious construct of behavioral norms. However, other works of his are clear it does limit the States' legal capacities from abridging personal liberty and political liberties, which does by his standard constitute a Common Law, just not the common law that's often appealed too by religites, politicos, and lawyers. I will go forward generally under the use of the term *Common Law* as applying to the

Constitution beneath the Liberty which is what most Founders were setting our new society under. Freedom being the true Natural Law, but in conjunction with the doctrine restraining government away from it being Common.

Quick side note; "an empire united by a common executive sovereign, but not united by any common legislative sovereign," Denoting the King commands military security, arbitrated some law matters, and acted with diplomatic power (which cannot undermine domestic/national law) to solve disputes. Basically, Britain was simply a protectorate.

Through the act of Independence by the Revolution, Lockean Philosophy was then put into practice. Adherent's to the old Blackstone style were quick to use old law style to introduce the U.S. Constitution, which in truth was restrained only by the Republican Guarantee and the people's authority in arms under the Declaration. Note also Madison calls the Constitution of 1787 "the oracle," meaning that in the way religious oracles were consulted in Greece, in our society it is not the Church or priest consulted, but the written contracted restrictions on the body politic. Madison and others hoped the judiciary would do the right thing and stick to the law as drafted, but it was mostly a hive of Blackstonians reinterpreting it to their political ideal of the time. The Hale loving, Blackstone adherents called "Federalists" lied through media, law education, and legal procedures to the people to convince them the practice of American Law was still legislative redefinition and judicial interpretation. Eventually, this practice of deception was being taught in the universities, and it is not true.

All legal documents and judicial opinions are suspect of attempting to steal away natural rights, often, falsely done under the claim that the society abdicates them to a function of government for equity under Codified Law (legality). In truth, rulings are public opinions related to lesser arbitrary rules to protect a claimant to respond to a wrong, and though on public record they are not equal to personal claims, private filings, the societal charters of power, and of course reality (nature), despite the popular claim to the contrary. Beings, observed events, and in-person statements are facts in republic law. Also, the Anti-Federalist position was the Common Law document says what it means and means what it says. A return to law as it was when written in stone or wood. Which is also why it is applied to titled agents and not the general person(s).

Pointing to any codified legal work prior to the Declaration of Independence in 1776 is almost useless as it was abolished. Some of the most freedom-expanding movements came after '76. Pointing to anything codifying Government over personal behavior or non-abdicated State rights to command behavior via the Confederation/ U.S. Constitution/State Constitution's /Biblical Common Law is in violation of, or secondary to the Law of Nature. The American Republic's intention was personal liberty first, State liberty second.

As is noted by Sam Adams in his *The Rights of the Colonists* submitted in 1772, we have a prime example of using the old bad law (an appeal to some artificial authority or a religion's God) to announce the rebuking of such lesser criminal statutes and wrongly relinquished or stolen personal powers. In which he said:

> In short, it is the greatest absurdity to suppose it in the power of one, or any number of men, at the entering into society, to renounce their essential natural rights, or the means of preserving those rights; when the grand end of civil government, from the very nature of its institution, is for the support, protection, and defence of those very rights; the principal of which, as is before observed, are Life, Liberty, and Property. If men, through fear, fraud, or mistake, should in terms renounce or give up any essential natural right, the eternal law of reason and the grand end of society would absolutely vacate such renunciation. The right to freedom being the gift of God Almighty, it is not in the power of man to alienate this gift and voluntarily become a slave.

Because they are still connected to Britain, Samuel Adams appeals to the people's position as *subjects* a lot in the full document. At least it makes a good point. He's even said it simply:[75]

> The natural liberty of man is to be free from any
> superior power on Earth, and not to be under the
> will or legislative authority of man, but only to
> have the law of nature for his rule.

This claim liberty can't even be voluntarily abdicated is resoundingly echoed by multiple Founders from the 1740's throughout the Revolution and beyond until the dissolution of the "Federated" Republic into the Federal Democratic Corporate Communism we have had since 1865. Do you notice how Adam's claim isn't, "If States through fear, fraud, or mistake, should in terms renounce or give up any essential natural right," because political liberty or civil liberty, or whatever other false dichotomy to imply community or a religious god gives you permission to be free in some way, wasn't the real primary goal. We have to see through the minutia of appeal to authority that implies men could even give up freedom, so we are sure to notice every time a liberty thinker throughout history (especially in the American Founding) was clear that we really can't give it up or have it taken. It is always in our purview to call forth, redeem and self-enforce. Republic.

So, let us move forward, well-saturated in the true tenants of the American Republic's enlightened position that the will of the majority must not overrule the will of the dissenting, the human law and religious doctrine cannot overrule the natural law, that the titled must remain in their defined roles, that which was created cannot rule the creator, and consider what that must then mean to and how it built a brand-new republic. A place where the trumpeting call is the declaration to govern one's self, to not be taxed, fined, or charged without representation accountable to the individual, to consent or

---

[75] http://www.samuel-adams-heritage.com/quotes/freedom-liberty.html

refuse, and a place where there is no requirement to be involved with a body politic.

THE COLONIAL REPUBLIC

SETTLERS, MIGRANTS, AND INHABITANTS

On wooden ships they arrived in the late 1500's. The first Pilgrims of importance to the construct of the American Republic came to the US to be free from the Crown and most importantly religious rule through government. Meaning they were pioneers leaving oppression to try something new, and not say invaders (not here to conquer), colonists (not here for the motherlands expansion, but for in the minds of their former crazed lords), immigrants (they did not come to a foreign nation as the natives had no claim over the land per their belief system), or even refugees as their nation was not necessarily "war torn," though the term refugee may apply to the Puritans, but that is but one later arriving group. I am speaking of all people from Europe who came here for the purpose of freedom, not just the English.

I prefer the word *pioneer*:[76]

pioneer

pahy-uh-neer

noun

a person who is among those who first enter or settle a region, thus opening it for occupation and development by others.

Note: The Native did not settle, generally speaking and were not prepping the region for regular occupation or any development. They

---

[76] https://www.dictionary.com/browse/pioneer

wandered often and learned settling for stable living generally from the Westerner.

For the moment let's expand on "pilgrim" as it is regularly used to define these worshipers of freedom. The term *pilgrim* means:[77]

pil grim

ˈpilgrəm/

noun

1: one who journeys in foreign lands: wayfarer

2: one who travels to a shrine or holy place as a devotee

3 capitalized : one of the English colonists settling at Plymouth in 1620

The core of the definition simplified and regularly used is "someone who travels to a holy place." Well, was America the Holy Land for the Christian? No. Their holy land is in the Middle East, the Land of Judah. This land untouched by the old empires was a holy land for any man seeking freedom. Sure, a people wanting religious freedom would be very happy here, but most people of the Old-World religions just can't keep from forcing their form of faith on others. Here the intention was personal freedom from group authority, religious and political.

---

[77] https://www.merriam-webster.com/dictionary/pilgrim

Portrait of John Locke by Sir Godfrey Kneller[78]

---

[78]
https://commons.wikimedia.org/w/index.php?search=Portrait+of+John+Locke+by+Sir+Godfrey+Kneller&title=Special:MediaSearch&go=Go&type=image

PART THREE: THE AMERICAN REPUBLIC

The conspiracy crafted by the Enlightenment thinkers like Algernon Sidney, John Locke, Walter Raleigh and Francis Bacon to get people to the New World was to assert a society of liberty away from the serfdoms of the Old World. The pilgrim was not truly a migrant/pioneer or a colonist. The colonist was politically linked to England. The Pilgrim was off to establish their culture in a new land. In the case of the liberty-minded pilgrim (a worshiper of Libertas\freedom) the true, free pioneer, this was a new culture separate from even the religious refugees fleeing to the New World. A land where individuals could live as they wished bound only by natural response, or limited law encompassing the true Golden Rule "Do no harm," not the authoritarian rule of "Prevent any possible harm."

A point to this is made in a comparison on Sidney and Locke in a printing of Sidney's *Discourses Concerning Government*, edited by Thomas G. West. In the Foreword West writes in discerning the difference between Locke's more libertarian acceptance of needing government versus Sidney's "classical republicanism" (notice that distinction):

> John Locke wrote Two Treatises of Government at the same time Sidney was working on the Discourses. Since Locke's book is much better known today, it is worth comparing to Sidney's.
>
> While some scholars have assigned Locke to an emerging bourgeois or liberal tradition of natural rights, especially property rights, Sidney is said to belong to a supposed tradition of 'classical republicanism' stemming from Machiavelli and ultimately the ancients. But other scholars have noted that Sidney does not fit this paradigm very well. Sidney is as much a natural rights and contract man as Locke. Both advocate government by elected representatives. Both maintain that natural liberty is governed by the natural law. Both argue for limited government and the people's right to revolution. Both are spirited

185

proponents of liberty. Sidney and Locke are 'republicans' as well as 'liberals.

Notwithstanding these similarities, there are differences, and they are important. Sidney proves to be closer to the Greek and Roman classics than Locke is. It is characteristic that Sidney quotes frequently from the ancients while Locke hardly ever does. But the ancients were not "classical republicans" in a Machiavellian sense. Their political thought always began or ended with the individual human being, not in the sense of an isolated unit, but as a being oriented by human nature to a life in accord with reason.

Portrait of Algernon Sidney[79]

---

[79]
https://commons.wikimedia.org/w/index.php?search=Algernon+Sidney
&title=Special:MediaSearch&go=Go&type=image

A quick note that Locke was seen as growing middle class, "an emerging bourgeois." Recall Solon came from the middle class. A repeat of the closing:

> Their political thought always began or ended
> with the individual human being, not in the sense
> of an isolated unit, but as a being oriented by
> human nature to a life in accord with reason.

Is this not what has been presented to you through what you have been reading here about republic? Though, the slight difference is that a single human living in nature in accordance with reason can be a human being who is an isolated unit. That by reason and nature should be respected.

Mind you, I'm not saying these men didn't have their own conditioned thinking to a religious or authoritarian rigidness of the time. Which West seems to pay some apologetics for in his Foreword, but I also believe they understood the folly in the use of religion in the body politics and "governance." Also, West may be misunderstanding Machiavelli. This confusion can come from the work *The Prince*, where Machiavelli notes the weaknesses of republic, but regularly warns the Principalities that if they wish to control those people it will be a hard battle and that the republican dislikes being controlled (governed) as they are very jealous of their liberties. He is defining things in a modern term for his era, but Machiavelli's understanding is very much of ancient republic in nature.

The lack of a central power made the New World the Holy Land for freemen, and thus your early Virginian settlers were coming here to grow personal wealth, to be free from the dominance of the Old Crowns and to worship liberty. They were truly and more accurately *Pilgrims of Libertas*.

Sir Walter Raleigh by an unknown English artist;
oil on panel, 1588[80]

80
https://commons.wikimedia.org/w/index.php?search=Sir+Walter+Raleigh&title=Special:MediaSearch&go=Go&type=image

Walter Raleigh's first colony was established about 1585 and was a wholly private venture and likely a hopeful test run that failed. His next was the infamous Roanoke Colony which disappeared, possibly due to a hurricane and merging with natives. However, the importance of these Colonies is in acknowledging that they were free (private) people unlike what we see with the later townships. This leads me to believe men like Bacon used the corporateers of Britain to finance the New World for a more likely success then the first excursions with an intention of the "companies" (not the pioneers themselves) failing, which would then force the King to end the Corporate contracts returning the people to natural state and making a transition back to Natural Law from British Common Law easier.

As evidence to this need of religites of the Old World constantly needing to force their faith on others I mentioned earlier, consider this: You have it drilled into your mind that the Pilgrims landed on Plymouth Rock seeking religious freedom. True enough of the Puritans. You are then focused on the Plymouth colony pretty thoroughly. Yet, the first successful colony preceded Plymouth by 15 years and was the primary center of trade, independence, and wealth. But, you aren't made too familiar with the landing in Chesapeake Bay as much. The colony of Jamestown is taught at first in history class, but not focused on. It was not founded by religious zealots like Plymouth, but because *all* of Europe was Christian, the pioneers are automatically lumped in as Christian by both English officials charged with aiding the pioneers, and English government (Crown) officials at home trying to claim authority in-and-over the new land for their national church or the Vatican they answer to, let alone the religious followers all trying to claim their God's dominion over free land.

This relation pervades despite the fact most people wanted liberty from the Crown's edicts and the National Churches, including the Vatican. We must remember the Crown cloaked everything it did under the claim of expanding in the name of its God, whether Catholic, or Protestant or whatever. That doesn't mean it was really the average pioneer's goal. The New World was established by entrepreneurs and independents looking to be freed from England's social controls. It was a dangerous endeavor, fraught with violent natives in places and new strange beasts, but the outcome well worth it.

The "legal" claim upon the colonies is by the companies that sold space to bring the settlers here, and the King who *allowed* them a charter, in which were made the religious links to one form of Christianity or another, for operation in areas they up and claimed cause of an explorer visiting the region... because that totally makes something already inhabited yours.

The charters gave the people under the companies almost total autonomy in their governance on local matters. King James I revoked the Charters and turned them into Royal Colonies due to the Virginia (London) Company going under. Though this had them under governors they had councils run by elected officials of the people and established their own civic and criminal laws. Virginia was placed in this status making it a self-governing colony in 1624, before Massachusetts. During this time the General Assembly defanged the Governor and took over control, placing representatives in command of the body politic. The People took over from the executive, but it wasn't a democratic coup as the reps were landowners (or freeholders) answerable to landowners. Thus, the freeman owned and ran the government due to a social upheaval, thanks to the Virginia Company failing to secure the people and who was attempting to place the Colonies into perpetual war with the natives (a violation of the charters), including the King freeing them in their internal affairs which the companies oversaw. Thus, they became a de facto republic. Unfortunately, being people breaking out of mental abuse, they often relapsed back into serfdom... a little too often.

In coming to the New World, the pioneer is accompanied by the migrant who either paid in full or more likely got a loan from the London Company. Here we can make a distinction that will help you better understand the difference between our true Founders and designer pilgrim pioneers and the migrant and immigrant tools of the Crown.

migrant

noun

mi ·grant

1. a : a person who moves regularly in order to find work especially in harvesting crops

So, a migrant is an employee likely from a foreign land come to work, often, seasonally.

immigrant

noun

im·mi·grant

a : a person who comes to a country to take up permanent residence

…

immigrant or emigrant?

Both of these words come from the Latin migrare ("to move from one place to another"), and both have definitions in English that hew closely to their etymological roots, but there is a definite difference between how you would use each one. Emigrant is used in reference to the country that has been left ("an emigrant from Canada"), while immigrant is used in reference the country that one is destined for ("an immigrant to Spain").

Ah! We have an abuse of language here. "Immigrant" tries to imply a person becoming a permanent resident. Now if you recall the purpose of Grecian Cities, and Rome limiting foreigners from involvement in the political body, we now have a better understanding of what that was and why. A resident isn't a native nor naturalized "person." They are workers staying in the area long-term. More importantly, using the term *immigrant* correctly, it really means a worker from somewhere else who decided to live somewhere permanently. In doing so they need to show loyalty to the local body politic to be involved with actual passing of measures, rules, laws... whatever. And thus, we learn why the Colonies were not originally colonies, but settlements of liberty men, hijacked by British employees whose benefactor, the King of England claimed their settlements in legal works hiding the actual purpose and reality of the founded communities. Through migrants the settlers are undermined by an overwhelming loyalist work force and the public records they were establishing. The upside is being that far away from the Crown creates an independent lifestyle, which the Crown tried to undermine with its titled officials. This was known to many Founders by the term *usages,* but so separated in general understanding that I believe this is why they never set the record straight and used the term *colonist* far too often.

This worker or employee, or most accurately indentured position was true for the Pilgrims under the Plymouth Company as well. Meaning most of the Puritan "Pilgrims" came as corporate slaves until their loans were paid back. If you didn't "owe," your land was yours, and I contend most the freemen likely grabbed land outside the Companies' area of control and the King's domain once established, though this was a dangerous move leaving one in the wilds.

That was the case, until James I emancipated the colonists, then returned the people to and brought the Colonies back under British Common Law from private corporate laws and regulations. You can bet the financers weren't too happy. In 1629 King Charles basically granted Massachusetts autonomy and in 1630 the people there specifically created the Colony of Massachusetts. How is this different than Virginia? First, they weren't really independent. Yet, the domestic people were already doing their own thing, and as authority feeling disempowered does, the Kings would make an action or structure the People were using "official" by some decree to "lord" his authority over them, or make it look like his idea. This creates confusion for the historical record and a leg for the monarchial and theocratic apologist to stand on when they try to make it look as though the Old World was always connected in the New World's political spectrum. Former Vice-President of the Confederacy Alexander Stephens wrote in his post-Civil War history work *A Compendium of the History of the United States*:

In 1629 the proprietors of this purchase of public domain, who were residents of England, obtained from Charles I., King of England, who had succeeded his father James I., a charter, granting them powers of government over colonists who might settle within its limits. The title of the corporation created by the royal grant was "The Governor and Company of Massachusetts Bay in New England." About three hundred persons soon after embarked for the new colony of Massachusetts.

In 1630, for the purpose of stimulating emigration to the new colony, the proprietors agreed "to form a council of those who should emigrate, and who might hold their sessions thereafter in the new settlement" or colony. Under this arrangement John Winthrop was chosen the first governor of the colony of Massachusetts, so planted —

We need to really understand this migration better, though. These were more Englishmen coming to be English and not necessarily pioneers leaving the old world like those from the 1580's on. Note how he discusses the proprietors being residents? It is claimed that Francis Bacon wrote two of the Company Charters for the Authorization to spread to the New World. In the Charters are some relatively liberating statements, as to the powers of those who have paid their debts to travel here, and the interest applied. There was high chance of the Companies that brought folk here to turn them into perpetual slaves, but there was the equal chance and reality that many of the leaders that traveled would die, as many did. The transition to Royal Colonies from Companies was actually a good thing and it set the settlers in place to become unrepresented in England, thus, autonomous in their living.

Secondly, we also need to really keep in mind there were people who paid in full to come on their journey here, and immediately moved out of the boundaries the Companies claimed as their operating area, legally making those people free inhabitants and separate from the "Colony," a term that implies under the migrant's originating nation's privy. Again, not actually the pioneers' goal. There is tendency to apply legal codes of trade to those inhabitants but in truth they are independent. This is why the later Articles of Confederation specifically defined *protections* to free inhabitants:

> The better to secure and perpetuate mutual friendship and intercourse among the people of the different States in this Union, the free inhabitants of each of these States, paupers, vagabonds, and fugitives from justice excepted, shall be entitled to all privileges and immunities of free citizens in the several States; and the people of each State shall free ingress and regress to and from any other State, and shall enjoy therein all the privileges of trade and commerce, subject to the same duties, impositions, and restrictions as the inhabitants thereof respectively, provided that such restrictions shall not extend so far as to prevent the removal of property imported into any State, to any other State, of which the owner is an inhabitant; provided also that no imposition, duties or restriction shall be laid by any State, on the property of the United States, or either of them.

This is a hundred years-ish after a lot of the first settlers yet sentiments are still there. Such as, its point to having to be subject to "duties, impositions, and restrictions as the inhabitants thereof." This is a return to the domestic protection from peoples living outside the city-states of old and vice versa from those who might take advantage of success or their complete lack thereof by creating jealousy. It is just making sure everyone who is imposed by any membered political body is equally imposed. Though it excludes paupers, vagabonds, and fugitives a State can still provide these protections to those people. The Confederation simply doesn't. However, that is also to discourage impositions and duties, period.

There were still those who desired to tax the people and profit. Such clauses reduced the likelihood of this happening by causing equal strife by such actions. If you aim to impose on those trading, you need to be imposed upon in your trade as well. Yet, none of that has to do with personal property. At all. The rights, privileges (which are domestic rules) and immunities (which are usually liberties already but are also "rights" for specific persons involved in some community recognized action) of the free citizen, and free inhabitant are the same. No preference can be played. Even still the words *free citizen* automatically gives legal protection from any of these "permitted" activities, and thus a free inhabitant is equally in liberty and equal in political interactions. Essentially, it is a trigger if liberty is infringed upon, against any political body attempting to do so. The free are also being recognized as protected in any and all legal (political) "rights" when traveling. So that means you can vote where someone else is voting, for example. Sadly, these distinctions were lost at the time, even on Founders like James Madison.

As a modern example to that, since a person can have an ounce of marijuana in their possession in Colorado, Texas cannot ban them from bringing it into their State. They do, but it's a violation of the Constitutional compact they're in now, and also of our natural rights. People are just ignorant of the true law. Texas can politicly (legally) stop me from selling it, if they've banned their own people from selling it, unless there is a U.S. Constitutional protection (which technically there is as you have property rights that entail the right to dispose of property as you wish). You have the personal authority to the property regardless. For in truth, restrictional clauses and regulations are under lesser laws.

Under the Colorado Constitution, Colorado's Supreme Law, I can have as much marijuana as I want and internally sell all the marijuana I want per Article III. Section 3.

So, let's say you drive to Texas with that ounce of marijuana on you as a Coloradan. Even if Texas has laws (which are lesser rules) against its possession, use, and transportation, Colorado, which you are of does not. How does Texas think it can violate this cultural identity and artificial/natural protection of yours? It's not supposed to, or it has started a war with *all* of Colorado. This dispute can be solved in the Supreme Court, taken there by either the wronged citizen (who are to be free to respond to the Texas law agents violating his rights with force at moment of usurpation) or by their home state per the U.S. Constitution, for in America's case both states have agreed to not war on each other … until they change their minds. This fact is codified by the Privileges and Immunities clause in the U.S. Constitution:

> "The Citizens of each State shall be entitled to all Privileges and Immunities of Citizens in the several States." — U.S. Const. Article. IV. Section. 2.

To get a good historical definition for *free inhabitant* online, well… you won't. You only get the text from the Articles of Confederation. They don't want you knowing what that is, because you can't take command of anyone freely inhabiting outside the claimed authority of a region, which is only ever perceptual power. So, here is the general dictionary definition of inhabitant:

> inhabitant:
>
> : one that occupies a particular place regularly, routinely, or for a period of time

Microsoft's Bing gives us:

> inhabitant:
>
> 1. a person or animal that lives in or occupies a place.
>
> 2. US a person who fulfills the requirements for legal residency.

… HA! Legal! HAHAHA!

Noah Webster 1828 says:

> inhabitant:
>
> noun, A dweller; one who dwells or resides permanently in a place, or who has a fixed residence, as distinguished from an occasional lodger or visitor; as the inhabitant of a house or cottage; the inhabitants of a town, city, county or state. So brute animals are inhabitants of the regions to which their natures are adapted; and we speak of spiritual beings, as inhabitants of heaven.
>
> 1. One who has a legal settlement in a town, city or parish. The conditions or qualifications which constitute a person an inhabitant of a town or parish, so as **to subject the town or parish to support him**, if a pauper, are defined by the statutes of different governments or states.

So, add "free" to those and we get one that is not restrained at all in or by where they occupy. But the general definition still doesn't imply serfdom or allegiance. It basically means to dwell. They are outside legal jurisdiction as they are not membered at all as free inhabitants. This is Bing's second definition to imply an inhabitant after "legal residency," which means local regulatory acceptance as living in a political area.

This is predominantly how Emerich de Vattel defines inhabitants in the *Law of Nations § 213:*

> The inhabitants, as distinguished from citizens, are foreigners, who are permitted to settle and stay in the country. Bound to the society by their residence, they are subject to the laws of the state, while they reside in it; and they are obliged to

defend it, because it grants them protection,
though they do not participate in all the rights of
citizens.

The Constitution notes "inhabitants" can run for office so living in the U.S. is enough to initially qualify for some offices. This was to minimize outskirt uses of tyranny as we saw with Athens. So, you are protected in all your natural rights at all times, or they'd cut out inhabitants being free. Of course, politically they aren't totally at liberty, because the Constitution requires additional certain requirements be met to run for an office, beyond and including being an inhabitant.

Example:

"No Person shall be a Representative who shall
not have attained to the Age of twenty five Years,
and been seven Years a Citizen of the United
States, and who shall not, when elected, be an
Inhabitant of that State in which he shall be
chosen."

— U.S. Constitution

This was often done in many of the original settlements.

GOAL OF THE PIONEERING REPUBLICANS

British expansionism was not on the pioneer's agenda. It was on the government of England's agenda. The pioneer's agenda was freedom. Libertas. Leaving the throne and broils of Europe. This was the beginnings of our Republic which existed nearly 150 years before it was even officially recognized as one during the rebellion. Something that was noted by multiple Founders in the 1780's during the debates on the Constitution.

In specifically Jamestown, the goal was a crop of trade and a free society. The tendrils of democracy that took root along those coastal trade states over time is the same sickness that overtook Athens's "republic" and even England's Monarchy—uncontrolled merchants with loyalty only to profit and recognition (titles), the East Indian Company to name one. It would do us best to bear in mind that America was "settled" by companies authorized by the King to do business, and had they not bankrupted and dried up, the King would not have necessarily made us Royal Colonies and the companies would have attempted to keep some people enslaved to paying constant interest on the travel debts, perpetual debtors. However, I have always thought that a cover to get us here as the focus on liberty being the settlements' main purpose is huge in the historical works.

Remember during Colonial times the Crown had to permit you to do business. So, all businesses of England were technically government-owned, even when privately-funded, as is the case in any country where the government requires licensing. Yes, including the modern U.S. We are still dealing with the problem of merchant malfeasance and cronyism today. Luckily, the "colonies" had force in numbers that Athens and most old republics didn't have or were too indoctrinated to authority to act against. Numbers found in a truly powerful land-ownership culture. Something Rome once pervade much in, and why Solon required landowners not to be able to sell. Your home was your castle under its own rules and laws (within reason) as was the land you held, commonly known as *Castle Law*. Especially, once the Companies died and for those deemed dead by proclamations like England's Cestui Que Vie Act of 1666. A "law" which states if you are overseas from England for seven years or more you are freed from your land and wealth debts and considered lost at sea. De facto freedom.

The definition of the Castle Doctrine as it is legally known is as follows:[81]

> The Castle Doctrine is a self-defense theory which gives a homeowner the right to protect his home with the use of deadly force. The Castle Doctrine originally emerged as a common law theory.

It's another law of nature they have skewed with codifying over time for central government to violate personal liberty, but the name itself is clear on the purpose. The definition avoids noting the fact that you can set law upon your property completely different from the public realm beyond... cause it's your land. It also goes together with the Stand Your Ground Doctrine to face threats anywhere when you were not being one. Additionally, we're told by the modern codes of these laws that you are required to flee if you can. The requirement comes from an overreaching political body, which may fly in a serfdom, but not in liberty as a freeman is never required to *flee*. This position is per the Rome and Greek societies who had similar ideals.

These laws are basic natural rights completely imbued into the purpose and spirit of American Law, needed in their autonomy in the wilds of the New World. They are not needed to be stated as they were commonly understood to be personal powers. When codified it is the officers and agents that must flee. The charter authorizing Virginia notes a lot of factors allowing the Colonies to self-govern without Britain's involvement, with again, the recognition that anyone not logged with England after seven years deemed "dead" releases that person if alive from the laws of England altogether. This mentality of the right to address a threat on a freeman is what will

---

[81] https://criminal-law.freeadvice.com/criminal-law/violent_crimes/castle-doctrine.htm

play into the rebellion that overthrows the King of England from the American shores.

The point of our political republic was not that the landowner was some unstoppable force with no restraint over his commanding of the "state," but that the landowners who often were their own community and laws unto their individual self could not have their liberty stolen by city-states run by plebeians (immigrants), or British and foreign workers/businessmen/politicians. Their land, their community, their conditions, their agreed remedies were applicable to their unique situations by their voluntary participation.

The downside is that the landowner would keep the immigrant and indentured (and slave) work forces ignorant of both the natural and political republic, property rights, and individual authority/self-responsibility in being over the general government. This is evidence to the danger the continued corporate mentality and ownership would have presented. The political body the indentured and leased man was ignorant of, only had a duty to assure trade and funds to the trade protectorate, which was England. In other words, we took on England as a security firm and if not careful, British immigrants would vote it into power, which they kind of did multiple times. The problem in the domestic landowner's action was in keeping the fact of natural law secret, which could lead to dissent against the landowner when they would treat a freeman in contract to them like their servants, and which the freeman could then use his knowledge to misinform the under-educated servants. Not to mention the dangers of an informed slave class to predatory masters. This in turn spread to the political process when indentured men, immigrants, and freed slaves were able to participate in the process, as what happened with Rome and the involvement of the plebeians.

Had the landowner never hid the truth that a worker can leave their governance any time, battles with the Empires would have been easier and not led to a collapse of the Confederation into a corporate democracy barely checked by a "Federated" Republic over the succeeding years after the revolution. Knowledge is power and the individual always knowing their right to part ways with others is dangerous to leaderships and power mongers, but necessary for a republic to maintain its condition of freemen.

PART THREE: THE AMERICAN REPUBLIC

Though England always sent its infiltrators to our shores the distance between the New and Old World was vast, but not insurmountable. Central power claims weren't going to work when a costly long journey is the only way you can get troops to back you up against a rebellion. So, local "government" took the appropriate position even when the settlements were created. People would be gathered for limited communal matters. Voting pools had to come from the locals. Pre-determined leaders selected before sailing only mattered if the bastards survived. Even then time would take its toll, and the governors would only be able to provide a symbolic role in mediating public forums, and limited courts. Many preferred being in England and went back as often as they could leaving the settlements on their own. This is enough to keep enslaved minds attached to the Old World, but it sows seeds of liberty, basically, how we ended up with England as our protectorate even though most families that came here did so in separation from the Crown.

VOTING IN THE SETTLEMENTS AND BEYOND

Google gives a good background on early voting in America and like many mainstream sources it does a bang-up job of backing this book's position that they manipulate reality to suit the position of centralized power and what made this New World a republic. In the ever-continuing effort to push democracy as the never-ending goal of the elite, Google states on voting in the Colonies:

> Becoming a freeholder was not difficult for a man in colonial America since land was plentiful and cheap. Thus, up to 75 percent of the adult males in most colonies qualified as voters. But this voting group fell far short of a majority of the people then living in the English colonies.
>
> After eliminating everyone under the age of 21, all slaves and women, most Jews and Catholics, most free black men, Indians, plus those men too poor to be freeholders, the colonial electorate consisted of perhaps only 10 percent to 20 percent of the total population.[82]

Ah! But they ignore what was the domestic population of those settlements. The Indian didn't get a vote because they have their own society and culture. I'll get to some other points in their claim in a moment, but a quick side note on Catholics. Catholics were banned from politics in most of the "colonies" for the reasons mentioned here again by Sam Adams:

---

[82] https://artsandculture.google.com/exhibit/EQIyltleTp-cLg; Review: —https://www.encyclopediavirginia.org/ Elections_in_Colonial_Virginia#start_entry

> The only sects which he thinks ought to be, and which by all wise laws are excluded from such toleration, are those who teach doctrines subversive of the civil government under which they live. The Roman Catholics or Papists are excluded by reason of such doctrines as these, that princes excommunicated may be deposed, and those that they call heretics may be destroyed without mercy; besides their recognizing the Pope in so absolute a manner, in subversion of government, by introducing, as far as possible into the states under whose protection they enjoy life, liberty, and property, that solecism in politics, imperium in imperio, leading directly to the worst anarchy and confusion, civil discord, war, and bloodshed.

They (Catholics, et. al.) have a tendency to use their religious laws on anyone they want, not just their disciples, as do Muslims, which is noted by Jefferson and others who had to deal with the Barbary Pirates. Jefferson was clear after reading the Quran that Islam is completely incompatible with our system, for as he was told by the Barbary "Our God is our government." So, they are a theocracy and thus cannot keep their God out of the body politic. As such, those types of religions shouldn't be allowed in a civil law system not of their making, particularly a centralized one. Shocker Google doesn't know that! Guess disdain is only for the Reformation sects.

The preceding quote misses a few things. Notice how it said only 10 to 20 percent of the population could vote. Despite their own poor ability to do math in admitting 75 percent of men held land. In what type of election couldn't the "majority" vote in? Union, state, local election? Generally, they are implying at the Union level, but grammatically they just imply voting altogether. Not to mention this wasn't America (yet) so the States were separate self-governing bodies with differing rules in each one. Being in a population doesn't necessarily give you the right to engage in a native culture's activities, which we've seen demonstrated throughout this work. We have Google making an attempt at encouraging mob rule over domestic tranquility and cultural security, tactics you need to be aware of when researching. If the overall population dislikes the native body's tendencies and actions, they need to return to whence they came, move elsewhere, or establish something of their own externally. The beauty of a liberty republic is if you want to establish something different within, you just need to assure it applies to only your participants. Applying your new action (way) to the body as a whole is an act of war on the predecessors in liberty.

Then there is the reason for why it was the man of the household who could vote, and that sex and racial (cultural) exclusion was, again, a local matter. Women and men "of color" were voting in some of the States and local municipalities and like Rome and Greece there were usually exceptions—for example, a widow would not be silenced. However, the Head of Household was the primary person responsible for the welfare of those on his land, which was generally a man. You know, the guys who would go with their sons to fight the wars, and had the actual land to lose, not to mention the primary goods/resource suppliers. Yeah... screw those guys!

We have been indoctrinated that the American Aristoi was the same as the European, but how could they be? Where was the fast reacting Army to come to their aid? It wasn't the worker class migrants that "couldn't vote" who would have to take up arms (short of stationed British troops), at least not until criminal conscription during the Civil War. It was the landowning, multiple employing persons, their families and the domestics and immigrants they employed—they didn't all have slaves, and where they did they couldn't necessarily trust the slave to use arms to defend them, though you can bet the workers on those private lands willingly got active too, else the enemy was likely to kill them as well.

Still, those landholders needed to keep any foreigner pro-centralist serfs from determining the general laws. Again, notice how the people who could vote have the highest stakes in the possible loss of the nation/society? The foreigner can go back home, or start something new, but since many of them were suckling off what existed they need(ed) to be limited in altering the general political course.

Oh, and Google's shared claim that "the colonial electorate consisted of perhaps only 10 percent to 20 percent of the total population" is argued against by EncyclopediaVirginia.org:

> On average, about 50 percent of adult white male Virginians qualified by outright ownership and another 20 percent entered the electorate as life tenants...

Meaning 70 percent of Virginians were eligible to vote. This of course depended on the laws at the time too. At one point we could argue *all* of Virginia was eligible to vote.

The voting populace in the early U.S. tended to be the gentry:[83]

> Of landed but not noble lineage, the gentry established themselves in Virginia as tobacco planters...
>
> The term "gentry" was imported from Britain, where it referred to similar groups of well-to-do men in England and Ireland, normally not members of the titled nobility, who owned extensive country estates and lived off the rental income of their tenants.

So, in other words, *gentry* are the middle-class real estate holders which at a time didn't have to be specifically white. For as Google notes there were "free black men." Again, it's all a matter of where the historian wants to focus your attention to play your emotions. Then we should ask, how long had their families worked that land personally? How long had they built their prestige?

---

[83]

https://www.encyclopediavirginia.org/Gentry_in_Colonial_Virginia

Ignore those questions, so you can focus only on the inequality their progeny had, who added forms of democracy where it fit them, were scrupulous and only that way because they had it good as oligarchical fat cats of a "republic," even though their political station was more from a tyrannical monarch's attached construct to our political body, as opposed to the actual communal activities. Definitely ignore when those landholders were British and not actually of the colonies... I'm being facetious.

When looking into what was needed to run for office it's interesting most searches will be bombarded by what one needed to have to have a right to vote, mainly because the only real thing that kept you out of office in the colonies for legislator (representative) positions was religion. Why? Because some religions can have a tendency of legally hijacking a society as noted above, and other religious sects wanted to control the political narrative like the aforementioned sect. Otherwise, if you were a trusted member of a community you could run or be nominated for office often regardless of economic class, though relation to Christianity would tend to be required, and again this depended on what eras are being looked at. Also, prior to 1776 we have a lot of religious-exclusion laws people try to reference, after which point that became criminal on the national stage as an affront to liberty and representation, and often those restrictive rules were installed on the early pioneers after the communities had been active for a time, and by overreaching British directives.

Of course, there were a lot of differing local rules. Lucky for the populist they can point to a bunch of the ones that had some race, sex, or land requirement, and ignore the dozens that had no such restraints or the far many more unincorporated self-sufficient persons unconcerned with how other individuals were living. The later was the primary example of a true American Republic noted by James Madison in his *Republican Distribution of Citizens* printed in the *National Gazette*:

> The class of citizen who provide at once their own
> food and their own raiment, may be viewed as the
> most truly independent and happy.

Playing off emotions to gain a democracy is a lot more important than noting why it was the long-domiciled natives, main fighters of war, and primary trade/craftsmen were the only ones who would be directing political policy and diplomacy. Oh, the Demos and their shows! I might add being a tradesman or craftsmen didn't make you a *merchant*. You *provided to* merchants and had an ethical standard to control their behavior when it threatened the culture, including using force.

As our protector, we paid England well and in return they kept sending infiltrating businesses (merchants) and undermining immigrants who would cry for more Crown involvement, especially regarding the "barbarous" natives that most the landowners and freemen had little problems with, and in fact often admired the culture of, despite the modern politically-driven, socially-minded historical claims. For this action of using migrant warfare, think of the use of U.S. troops sent to sway the "public vote" on Hawaii joining the Union. Servicemen of a foreign land lived there for work, then voted for Hawaii to join the Union. The vote was not left to solely the native Hawaiians. How can anyone other than the natives have a say on that, and yet, U.S. citizens willingly living on the island were allowed to vote out a nation's sovereignty to make it a member in the Union. That's a criminal action and act of war on freedom that should have angered every American, as similar tactics could, and would eventually be used in every State of the Union to grow federal government's power. On the upside, had we not, you can bet Japan would have conquered the island at some point.

To hold legislative office, you did not have to be a landowner to run or hold Colonial, or many pre-revolution State offices. It was a local power to determine what made an eligible candidate and voter, most those bodies required the *voter* to have land, not necessarily the potential agent/officer. Again, this is only for political representation which the people were the authority over, and the rep, not a trustee but a servant to. The body politic in a republic is not to command social or behavioral activities, which democracies and trustee-based systems tend to think is in their power. Now, England didn't care about that and passed lots of overreaching powers by its residing agents' decrees, but I firmly believe separating political governors from the homeland and getting people back into the wild was all part of the goal for men like Francis Bacon, Walter Raleigh, and John

Locke. It most definitely was Jefferson's goal when he made the Louisiana Purchase. This returns people to understanding they are free beyond the political bonds, which was the case in many settlements and the intention of many pioneers that became the so-called gentry.

If we look over EncyclopediaVirginia.org we find that the requirement of owning land didn't occur until 1670 and could easily have been the brainchild of Englishmen, not Americans:[84]

> In 1670 the assembly limited the right to vote for burgesses to adult men who owned land.

This restriction becomes worse as the aristoi ignorant of homeland British oppression and friendly in relations with local monarchial regents grows. For example:[85]

> While economic status in the form of land holdings became the central criteria for determining the franchise, other laws added restrictions based upon age, sex, race, and religion. The law excluded those under age twenty-one in 1699; that same year women also lost the vote…

Wait—we're told women could never vote by oh-so-wise Google and liberal educates! Do you know when it was this was occurring? No, not just in 1699, but when the King of England decided to take notice of what was going on in the colonies due to the Bacon Rebellion. Then, suddenly intrusive laws started propping up, and even before that, the King's henchmen and loyalists were running

---

[84]
https://www.encyclopediavirginia.org/House_of_Burgesses#start_entry
[85] https://www.encyclopediavirginia.org/
Elections_in_Colonial_Virginia#start_entry

rampant. Happy English Lords of Luxury were already causing problems with similar laws, all along American history. Though in some cases British authority seemed to be trying to keep the peace with native tribes, often it was a key instigator in local skirmishes with the tribes. For example: The Bacon Rebellion which did result in over-barring laws on the colonists being overturned for a time, was caused by a British-born and educated corporateer who hadn't been here long. Yet, he is bundled up with *all* of American history as the act of the regular migrant to the New World. Right or wrong in his actions, British incompetency caused a lot of problems with our North American family.

The other Crowns were trying to use the natives to steal the land, not coexist. After the foreign empires of England, France, and Spain had stoked wars between the natives and the new American race (defined so by Founders due to the fact we were migrants of an entirely separate ideology from Old Europe) the internal study by Americans began, and they started to understand their system, so they could manage their own affairs, an act often lumped in with the term *self-government*. This was a reaction due to the perception created throughout the process that wrapped the New Native (the American settler) in with the foreign English Colonist that were invading, voting, and implementing the necessary regulations for government on behalf of England. The "Colonies" were making their own decisions as independent nations, but it was also an opportunity to advance the cause of liberty. Yet, the "grasping of liberty" had to be legally applicable to America's "global peers" to escape the Old-Worlds' legal claims of power and avoid all the Crown fighting for the new world to come together against the new nations here. In this study, it was clear the "colonists" had governed their own actions when living far from the main seat of power and while often abandoned by their governors when the governors would leave to live it up in England or deal with Crown skirmishes for extended periods.

The advancement to liberty philosophy in the U.S. was heavily out of Massachusetts and Virginia. Virginia was the primary leader in revolting against England with the dissolution of the House of Burgess and had by that point passed freedom of religion acts and moved towards citizen rights based on Enlightenment concepts of Natural Law, early, sometimes unaware actions that solidified the republic before they even got into the study of it. In the realization of our system men like Patrick Henry, John Hancock, and Sam Adams were touting the fact of our republic's existence (as mentioned above) well before the Articles of Confederation and the improperly installed U.S. Constitution. It is lost on many that America is by intentional planning of men like John Locke and Francis Bacon, the Nation of the Enlightenment. The Enlightenment spanned from 1650 to 1800 and most Founders were Men of the Enlightenment—the above-mentioned men, and including Benjamin Franklin, Thomas Jefferson, Benjamin Rush, Thomas Paine, and many others. In fact, the number of men who could be listed as aligned with the Enlightenment ideals in America likely far exceeds any list of European thinkers of the whole era. Much of the American "gentry" and town locals were fairly literate, far more-so than their European counterparts.

A couple of important notes here. First, it is popularly assumed that the perception of the sovereign governance of the Colonies comes from England subverting their charters during taxation after the French and Indian War, while this might only be the claim of the colonists who reestablished their loyalty to England after King James II was overthrown and William showed favor to our self-governance. Stationed governors and officers still mean England *governed* them, at least in England's mind. Additionally, there are fun quotes I ran into from William Blackstone that note my points to the Lockean principles:[86]

> They (the legislature) held that this misconduct of King James amounted to an endeavour to subvert the constitution; and not to an actual subversion, or total dissolution, of the government, according to the principles of Mr. Locke: which would have reduced the society almost to a state of nature; would have levelled all distinctions of honour, rank, offices, and property; would have annihilated the sovereign power, and in

---

[86] Sir William Blackstone, Commentaries on the Laws of England, https://oll.libertyfund.org/titles/
blackstone-commentaries-on-the-laws-of-england-in-four-books-vol-1

consequence have repealed all positive laws; and
would have left the people at liberty to have
erected a new system of state upon a new
foundation of polity. They therefore very
prudently voted it to amount to no more than an
abdication of the government, and a consequent
vacancy of the throne;

Blackstone, who is arguing this during the Founder's era,
perfectly sums up Locke, the beauty of our form of society, and the
length which the titled masters will go to in assuring their position of
power so the commoners stay beneath them, as we saw them do when
hijacking the prior mentioned republics of Greece and Rome. He's
also incorrect about the distinctions of property. The property of lords
and title agents is property of the government and is relinquished to
the public when their positions are dissolved. It does relieve all
individual's property, like the gentry prior defined.

Oh, one more brief quote from the so-imperative to British
common law, Blackstone. I have been very direct about the powers
bestowed on the individual in a republic to thwart undermining of
freedom by public and private officials/servants through personal
force, though I think the information on the Roman Manumission and
Twelve Tables addresses this fact nicely. Blackstone in his appeal to
monarchial authority and grandeur of titles and honors, defines very
precisely the description I have been and will continue to give you on
republican power:

On the other hand, over-zealous republicans,
feeling the absurdity of unlimited passive
obedience, have fancifully (or sometimes
factiously) gone over to the other extreme; and
because resistance is justifiable to the person of the
prince when the being of the state is endangered,
and the public voice proclaims such resistance
necessary, they have therefore allowed to every
individual the right of determining this

expedience, and of employing private force to
resist even private oppression.

Let me translate that for you: "The republican faction finding total
obedience absurd, and because resistance is justifiable when the King
(prince) is endangering the state (political body), has made the liberty
of using force against any usurper of freedom a personal power
against even private violators." Thus, supporting this work's primary
position of what republic is. But I digress. As evident here in a very
simple line:

> "A pirate, an outlaw, or a common enemy to all
> mankind, may be put to death at any time. It is
> justified by the laws of nature and nations."
>
> — Patrick Henry[87]

But I digress. Later, Charles II annulled (nullified) most the
colonial charters. This is important because the ego of the monarchist
leads to their taking over ownership of the lands from the
corporation, but the reality of true contract law is that act of Charles
II completely liberated the people from control of England, which the
big colonies responded to by instituting stronger assemblies for
independent actions. They screwed up by re-aligning with the King
of England when the monarchy is replaced by a king favorable to
them. Though, this popular claim, and the response later of their
independence of operation due to "no taxation without
representation" seems to tell us the governors were more like
Alexander's commanders or the Roman Republic's Praetors left to
protect membered communities defensively and less to direct they're

---

[87] Speech Before Congress June 7th 1788,
https://teachingamericanhistory.org/document/speech-delivered-at-the-virginia-convention-debate-of-the-ratification-of-the-constitution-june-7-1788/

behavior. Thus, my summation they employed England as a *protectorate*.

Colonel Isaac Barré of the British House of Commons, a supporter of the Colonies and the claimed inventor of the term "Sons of Liberty" once exclaimed:

> They planted by your care? No! Your oppressions planted them in America. They fled from your tyranny to a then uncultivated and unhospitable country ¾ where they exposed themselves to almost all the hardships to which human nature is liable, and among others to the cruelties of a savage foe, the most subtle and I take upon me to say the most formidable of any people upon the face of God's Earth. And yet, actuated by the principles of true English liberty, they met all these hardships with pleasure, compared with those they suffered in their own country, from the hands of those who should have been their friends.
>
> They nourished up by your indulgence? They grew by your neglect of them: as soon as you began to care about them, that care was exercised in sending persons to rule over them, in one department and another, who were perhaps the deputies of deputies to some member of this House ¾ sent to spy out their liberty, to misrepresent their actions and to prey upon them; men whose behavior on many occasions has caused the blood of those Sons of Liberty to recoil within them; men promoted to the highest seats of justice, some, who to my knowledge were glad by going to a foreign country to escape being brought to the bar of a court of justice in their own.
>
> They protected by your arms? They have nobly taken up arms in your defense, have exerted a

valour amidst their constant and laborious industry for the defense of a country, whose frontier, while drenched in blood, its interior parts have yielded all its little savings to your emolument. And believe me, remember I this day told you so, that same spirit of freedom which actuated that people at first, will accompany them still. But prudence forbids me to explain myself further. God knows I do not at this time speak from motives of party heat, what I deliver are the genuine sentiments of my heart, however superior to me in general knowledge and experience the reputable body of this House may be, yet I claim to know more of America than most of you, having seen and been conversant in that country. The people I believe are as truly loyal as any subjects the King has, but a people jealous of their liberties and who will vindicate them, if ever they should be violated, but the subject is too delicate and I will say no more.

This is a strong recognition that despite America's alliance with England the success and the resistance against the rest of the Old-World authorities was of their own doing and it is what Founders like Patrick Henry are really defining when they spoke of the *American Republican*. I wish to also inform you, I knew nothing of this speech prior to drafting most of the positions in this section on America. It relates the reality of our nation that this book poses versus the claims of English, loyalist, and scholarly mythologies via legal doctrines of the Founding era. This single speech vindicates much of what is noted about many being outside the areas of general political power, "¾ where they exposed themselves to almost all the hardships to which human nature is liable, and among others to the cruelties of a savage foe," for instance. Even better defense of this work is his admission English officials were sent to imply power they didn't have and to make the people appear troublesome.

Second, several Colonies were originally of other nations, and, or were self-governed and unassociated/unincorporated with the old

216

Crowns. The constant use of "companies" seems so corporate, and the claiming of land under the old crowns quite odd, and generally the position of the Old World while not necessarily that of the settlers making their way in the New World. Though there are many scribes and thinkers of the time that appeal to the commune with England it seems clearer the travelers from the Old World were here for independence from it, not for expansion of its power, but for those direct officers of those nations (government agents) conscripted to those brave travelers.

Thirdly, many States took the position that the King's usage of power and attempt to undermine their civil protections caused an automatic dissolution of the English government, at least locally, authorizing them the power to form new governing structures, per Lockean philosophy, which as we already read, terrified people like Blackstone.

ADDENDUM, THE SUCCESSFUL COUSIN

This is a brief overview as there were Enlightenment events of republican nature occurring in Europe in tandem, especially among the old Crowns, but I am not going to go into great detail. The lessons in this work noting the tendencies of true republic should help you see the relations this section draws.

Let us not think a monarchy with republican ideals are completely inseparable. We are noting that republic is only applicable to *public matters*, and the actions of the many (politics) are both limited in scope and always beneath personal freedom. So, a community selecting a single head over the public matters does not mean the full freedom of the individuals are automatically subjugated. Of the Enlightenment two nations were prominent, one being the American States ("united" as an attempt at a real multi-national republic), and the other being the preceding Kingdom of Prussia under Frederick the Great, who with few exceptions was for unfettered markets among his own people, free speech, freedom of religion, and regularly mocked foreign monarchs' ridiculous decrees upon their own productions and trades. He was so good at mocking them, the well-known sarcastic wit of Benjamin Franklin was even fooled a time or two, unsure if Old Fritz was joking or not. This may arguably be the Enlightenment's first great success — that being the reign of Frederick the Great — though even his great grandfather Frederick William had instituted many similar concepts about 100 years prior to creating the Kingdom of Prussia.

Self-considered an "enlightened absolutist," Frederick the Great (Frederick II) believed he was a servant of the people under their political body calling himself, "the first servant of the state." Embodied by Frederick's shift of his title as King *in* Prussia to King *of* Prussia, making him ruler unanswerable to external power and empowered by the nation, or "of" the People. Whereas a king "in" was a dignitary regent for the Holy Roman Empire beneath papal power. Sounds like his interest in ancient works helped him understand the Greek Kings and Roman Consuls. He understood his position as the ruling servant in the body politic and assurer of the private citizen's authority to live life as they choose, with a duty to preserve their trades and wealth as the lord over the state agents who assure the citizen's way of life. He, as many other crowns linked to him, knew his position was permitted by those he "ruled," not by some imbuement from God.

One of his concerns were the dubious merchants that worked the border near Germany. Germany, mostly hobbled Roman duchies, was the hotbed of the Counter-Enlightenment at that time and beyond. Quickly the Counter-Enlightenment can be wrapped up in Wikipedia's entry on it:

> Although the term 'the Counter-Enlightenment' was first used in English (in passing) by William Barrett in a 1949 article ("Art, Aristocracy and Reason") in Partisan Review, it was Isaiah Berlin who established its place in the history of ideas. He used the term to refer to a movement that arose primarily in late 18th- and early 19th-century Germany against the rationalism, universalism and empiricism commonly associated with the Enlightenment.

Forming modern socialism, and where the Roman Empire authorized the empowerment of banking in a bid to alter itself from a religious form into a more anonymous financial empire operating under the mask of a family named Rothschild — in my view, a scheme to try and stop the Enlightenment that was freeing the New World and poisoning the Old by undermining it with, "rationalism, universalism, and empiricism." At this time the collapse of the Roman adherent kingships begins, partly due to kings finally rebelling against the old papist rule, partly due to King Henry the 8th's insurrection against the Vatican two hundred years prior, and largely due to the Renaissance growing into the Enlightenment with these educated royal individuals who understood the republic histories of Antiquity that Rome — through the church education system — was shoving down their throats their whole lives.

I direct you here for this brief acknowledgement because Old Fritz's reign spanned from 1740 to his death in 1786. It directly correlates with the U.S. Revolution. Frederick and Thomas Jefferson even had a brief meeting during the construction of our republic, as well as Franklin and Arthur Lee, an interesting confluence of events, a meeting of minds soaked in liberty, though Fritz wouldn't take a direct stance with America as to avoid war with England. Also, I find all actions in the succeeding years that try to legally tie Prussia and Germany together are in this writer's opinion a long coup, hellbent on destroying Prussia's independent image, and setting Germany as some long-connected relation despite Frederick the Great's disdain for the German people's culture, and likely due to Germanic Roman's contempt to the fact Prussia had regularly routed them. This also creates a false relation to the Counter-Enlightenment's "duty to a nation," which was an ideal of the Kaisers' that would have disgusted Old Fritz. It got Rome back in power, though, by eventually overthrowing the Kaisers via the legislatures.

The relation to Prussia is important. It is important to understand Fredrick was disgusted by the Germans who were financially backing most European conflicts since the Rothschild authorizations as the new arm of the Roman Empire called *banking* started in—yes, 1776. Not a coincidence the Vatican's empire had both lost all control over the New World and the Old Crowns who were joining the cause of liberty, the Scottish and English Enlightenment had spawned into France and most of Europe. Leaders like Charlies III of Spain, Catherine and Peter the Great, and possibly even Napoleon were highly influenced by the Enlightened leadership of Frederick the Great. It is latter ascendants to the Prussian throne that are related to things like Prussian education, united Germany, and duty-to-country-type socialism spawned out of the Frankfurtian-style social elites. In in my view, Frederick wasn't ever interested in uniting "Germany," but removing Roman control, and reestablishing the Old Roman Republic ideal that a leader is a representative working for their people, not lording over them.

The Jacobins of the coinciding French Revolution, which takes place about three years after Frederick's death, is dressed up as a republican revolt in love with liberty. This is a clear lie based on their actions. A sect of the Jacobins (Robespierre's political party) declared war on Austria and Prussia using the success of the French

Revolution to gain support. Robespierre and ilk were more like the Thirty Tyrants, and started wiping out everyone they deemed an enemy. By-and-large their false republic movement was more a democratic oligarchy, and a far cry from the more respectfully moving *enlightened absolutists* around them. You can see how those Enlightenment-based leaders were a threat to Roman authoritarian and socialist democratic panders of the counter-enlightenment.

In fact, we see Wikipedia note:

> Robespierre turned his attention away from the
> assembly of provincial lawyers and wealthy
> bourgeois in favor of the lower classes of France,
> particularly Jews, Blacks, and actors.

Now, any mistreatment of these people legitimately of the region (natives or due time) is unacceptable, but this coupled with actions Robespierre defended in the Reign of Terror (the span of time they were executing anti-revolutionists) finds a tactic on par with Peisistratus and Critias, so let's not fool ourselves into thinking this man with a law background, including being a judge, didn't know who that was or the tactics they used. It also implies Robespierre regularly abandoned the middle class, something the bulk of political parties happily overlook in most European revolts, the people we've historically seen who tend to be the best protectors of a republic, though there were plenty of usurpers in the French Revolution for us to think Robespierre alone was to blame, and maybe he was in the end just a scape goat.

I myself, believe the Jacobins were actually part of plot to route old Crowns on behalf of the fresh financial system Rome authorized. Robespierre, for example, dies without debt. Most U.S. Founders couldn't accomplish this type of wealth retention. How should we think a man in a broke ass country going through massive revolt managed to do so? This hypothesis of conspiracy against the pro-liberty Crowns is backed by the action the enlightened absolutists (or despots) were taking in freeing the people from regulatory and debtor hell. It has even been claimed that latter populist Karl Marx was funded by the Rothschilds. Could they have been using the same tactic they used in France in the Revolutionary days?

Political rebellion through parliaments was proven by America to be actionable and successful, as we'll see, so such rebellion was conceived in France and throughout Europe, but this time perpetrated by agents of the elite, not done by real free private landholders, as in America. Both Austria and Prussia would be targeted in the later world wars with Prussia eventually being buried, because their leaders and kingdom had regularly crushed Germany where the new Roman banking empire was located. After which, Austria was the home of fluid economics (free market for lack of a better term) that the communist worker hated but elitists loved. The American Founders were for free trade, not free markets, given free markets make it so a foreign business like the East Indian Company can come in and influence laws and control trade ports through contracts.

When you research the timeline for yourself, you'll find Frederick influenced many of the crowned leaders, nearly all their nations targeted during the world wars, especially, Catherine the Great's Russia. She was Prussian-born, her husband Peter III was a supporter of Frederick the Great, and she herself a major proponent of Enlightenment theory. Historians even like to note how much the Russian Revolution at the beginning of the 20th century was like the French Revolution, and how many European and Old World revolutions were like France's, not like America's, the founders behind those insurrections being a big reason for that. It's also interesting how hard and long the Counter-Enlightenment had to work to collapse those nations, even well after some of their leaders had turned away from the Enlightenment.

To me, the targeting and destruction of the separate people of Prussia and their history maliciously absorbed and falsified as related to Germany cements the reality of Frederick's intentions and the success his reign established for his preferred form of English and French Enlightenment. Though, it's not like his decedents did a great job of extending his ideals, and thanks to his anti-enlightenment nephew and his offspring, the Germans were able to become a connected political power and hijack the Prussian history as their own, though it is apparent the only thing that ever related the two people was the authoritarian rule of the Holy Roman Empire.

Republic spoke through the ages to intellectual elites of the 18th century, despondent with the status quo where a trust in the middle class was rearing its head to slay the centralists of the Empires as it did when Brutus killed the kings, and that had to stopped. Yet, the biggest threat of this revival was still a world away.

In France there was a fast reduction of the liberty rebellion into a tyrannical state system that took a good 50 years longer to apply in America. For as in America men disguised themselves as for liberty (such as Hamilton, Webster, and Burr) while in reality they were either egos trying to gain power for themselves or agents of the merchants shoring-up domestic regulatory power. The Federalists managed to put a lot of that centralist construct into place in America's fresh republic, though, which lead to the Civil War.

DECLARATIONS OF FREEDOM

Knowing the people who came here already considered themselves separate from the political body of England and the Old World in general is paramount to the American Republic. As we grew our political will, the most influential Founders made it excessively clear they were designing this system upon Enlightenment ideals and that the New World was a sacred land, John Locke being an essential philosopher in this process and ideals of our culture. Repeatedly, it is stated in Enlightenment works that unlike the Old World, where it was believed government gave the People rights, ours was a liberty society where *freemen* gave their "government" rights (permissions) to assure personal liberty, and the individual gives up no power to do what any government can do, whatsoever, in the process. Any claims otherwise are part of the deception by the deceived or the deceiving.

To review, we really do need to understand the Colonists weren't British. The pilgrims and liberty men who came here left England and were divorced from that construct. They were no longer of England. In time, they considered those prior people cousins. Yet, the former tag-a-long legal system was chronically implying domestic subjugation, which is how and where a lot of the history that implied we were happy to have a sympathetic king (King William, for instance) come into power, and why we were happy to rejoin with the Crown comes from. No legal doctrine or English loyalist makes that statement and position a historical reality over the intentional way the freemen came here. In other words, such doctrine and personal opinion do not supersede the general popular actions of the settlers, or foundational intentions as they are usually claimed by Crown sympathizers/agents. A sympathizer in such issues should be disregarded. Most natives who were Americans, authorized to direct political activity or were free in their own cognizance, were private landowners who found the Crown separate from their domestic being. That is the real legal majority opinion of the era.

To this, the merchants of England had a role in subverting our trade using their pull with the Bank of England as a regulator growing out of a "free" market. It was a return to some of the crushing merchant laws that helped dissolve both Greece and Rome. Today we use maritime merchant terms all throughout our laws. People in motor vehicles are called CARGO, you hold your LANE, the middle of the road is called the MEDIAN or ISLAND. You also, need a WRIT called a driver's license to operate your own property while engaging in commerce, making you a privateer and not a private citizen. So... police are just harbor patrol who claim to already own your boat and control your right to travel. Savvy?

This pressure of merchant control over trade through resettled migrant workers, the use of stamped paper (basically government embossed documents) and production permitted by the Crown erupted into what we know as the Boston Tea Party. Articles of Association were drafted in 1774. This follows the style of the Virginia Association which was responding to the Townshend Acts which, using Wikipedia's breakdown said:[88]

"The purposes of the Townshend Acts were:

• to raise revenue in the colonies to pay the salaries of governors and judges so that they would remain loyal to Great Britain,

• to create a more effective means of enforcing compliance with trade regulations,

• to punish the province of New York for failing to comply with the 1765 Quartering Act, and

• to establish the precedent that the British Parliament had the right to tax the colonies."

Note the need to pay off officials so they stayed loyal? Notice how they need to set a precedent to collect taxes, because they weren't allowed to prior? I need to point out that the Associations are similar legal documents that are relating the colonies as subject to the Crown. I cannot stress enough that this is a mindset in the body politic caused by the long usurpation by the King's officers and migrants. Thus, the

---

[88] https://en.wikipedia.org/wiki/Townshend_Acts

need to keep them paid off so they did not help the Colonies redeem their more generally understood true independent position as settlements for liberty. The Wikipedia page even begins the topic on the Acts by saying they "were a series of British Acts of Parliament passed during 1767 and 1768 and relating to the British in North America." This is a distinction that means the Act does not apply to the native tribes, but it would also not apply to people not associated with Britain as subjects, like say *landowning freemen*, which includes all the people who fled persecution, oppression, and those sent into exile here. If they were exiled from England how can England have rule over them?

The Articles of Association were in response to the British Parliament's attempts to shut down the Boston Harbor after the Tea Party, known as the *Coercive Acts*. Yeah, totally not tyrannical. They responded to the acts with decorum, but weakness. As admitted subjects how could they expect the Crown and its loyal lords to care about the opinions and wants of lessers?

Three years later the Second Continental Congress drafted the Declaration of Independence. There are students nowadays being taught that this document is null and void claiming it met its purpose and informed the Crown and other governments of our separation from England. This is a gross misrepresentation. The Declaration of Independence is a Charter of Freedom. This is even how the document is labeled by the U.S. Government at archives.gov:

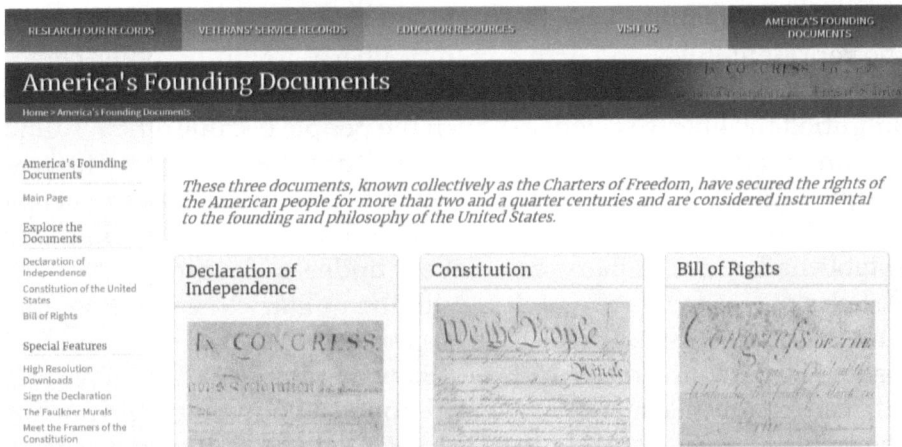

"*These three documents, known collectively as the **Charters of Freedom**, have secured the rights of the American people for more than two and a quarter centuries and are considered instrumental to the founding and philosophy of the United States.*"[89]

In other words, it is a recognition of personal liberty of every individual (people are persons, persons are always individuals, individuals are always free) under the Power of the Supreme Creator, Nature, or Roman-ly speaking *per Libertas*, who adorns the top of the U.S. Capitol dome as Freedom. In fact, Libertas has been a persona for the New World from almost the beginning as Columbia. This further aids my position that this goddess and antiquity are the basis of America's society. The Declaration of Independence was a Legal Charter in a format the Old-World had no choice but to recognize, per their own rules. It stands over all governments as a monument to the People's power over their government and right to abolish it at any time, a lesson Americans have long forgot and that schools are doing their best to distort the truth of.

The Declaration of Independence was created after many attempts to solve the rift with the Crown peacefully through representatives sent to reassert the "Colonies'" awareness that England had no direct power in local affairs and trade, often resulting in those representatives being imprisoned or executed. In the King's

---

[89] *Archives.gov screen captured October of 2018*

intention to steal our freedom and claim power over our homeland the representatives and active men of liberty found no other choice but to sever their connection with their cousins. The Declaration solidified the liberty society in which the people became officially and self-anointed under the authority of Natural Law as free. The free people could from there authorize any association they desired at any time. The initial representatives who rebelled against England established a preliminary association under a doctrine called The Articles of Confederation to deal with the military threat of England. The States membered with it were political bodies. The individual people living in the nations of the "State" operations could have and still can establish a new unassociated political body at any time, while the political agents and political bodies tended to be restricted from doing such things. Only those willing members participating with a representative to the Continental Congress with the Articles of Confederation under the State political body were required to abide by its proceedings and agreements, not necessarily every person in a community which had a representative there. That's not freedom or liberty if that's the case. All of this transpired under the Charter called the Declaration of Independence.

Writing the Declaration of Independence, 1776
by Jean Leon Gerome Ferris, 1932[90]

---

[90] https://americanheritage.org/the-creator-god-the-basis-of-authority-law-and-rights-for-mankind-in-the-united-states/

I will include the full Charter at the back of the book, but here is the primary invocation to its purpose and cause:

> The unanimous Declaration of the thirteen united States of America, When in the Course of human events, it becomes necessary for one people to dissolve the political bands which have connected them with another, and to assume among the powers of the earth, the separate and equal station to which the Laws of Nature and of Nature's God entitle them, a decent respect to the opinions of mankind requires that they should declare the causes which impel them to the separation.
>
> We hold these truths to be self-evident, that all men are created equal, that they are endowed by their Creator with certain unalienable Rights, that among these are Life, Liberty and the pursuit of Happiness.--That to secure these rights, Governments are instituted among Men, deriving their just powers from the consent of the governed, --That whenever any Form of Government becomes destructive of these ends, it is the Right of the People to alter or to abolish it, and to institute new Government, laying its foundation on such principles and organizing its powers in such form, as to them shall seem most likely to effect their Safety and Happiness. Prudence, indeed, will dictate that Governments long established should not be changed for light and transient causes; and accordingly all experience hath shewn, that mankind are more disposed to suffer, while evils are sufferable, than to right themselves by abolishing the forms to which they are accustomed. But when a long train of abuses and usurpations, pursuing invariably the same Object evinces a design to reduce them under absolute Despotism, it is their right, it is

their duty, to throw off such Government, and to provide new Guards for their future security.

The Founders did a lot of study on the ancient republics, and likewise I have examined those republics which led to the conclusion so commonly and intentionally misinterpreted by "experts" and "scholars," most notably our own. Under this notion "to secure these rights, governments are instituted among Men" it is clear government does not direct our behaviors. The usage of the word "safety" is not a matter of other freemen's actions not being able to endanger you. Life is dangerous. Fellows and foreigners alike cannot push you (or us) into submission via political bodies; government generally speaking, all collective agreements more broadly speaking. This is the greatest threat to all freemen and where we need safety for our happiness.

Then, "it is the Right of the People to alter or to abolish it, and to institute new Government, laying its foundation on such principles and organizing its powers in such form, as to them shall seem most likely to effect their Safety and Happiness," meaning the People (free individuals) can then institute new government, but they don't have to, especially if it seems that government would adversely impact their safety and happiness.

Of the greatest importance in this work are our "unalienable rights, that among these are Life, Liberty and the pursuit of Happiness." If our life is *un-a-lien-able* how can a cop kill you for non-compliance? He can't. You have to be an active danger (firing a gun, stabbing at people, being clear you are trying to harm), and non-compliance to a command for a lesser code violation does not authorize the use of force by the Law of Nature, the Spirit of the Law, or the restraints upon an agent. It is through lesser codes and regulations government officers have mystically imbued law enforcement (once only called peacekeepers) to kill you for not listening to them. Which in turn authorizes you to kill them right back and respond preemptively as they have standing orders to kill you for non-compliance. That is a criminal action, banditry, piracy, mercenary, and gang warfare by "government" in a republic. You can't be free if you have to obey your servant, which is also why many police agencies are dropping the saying, "To protect and serve" from their pledges and sayings.

Liberty is noted clearly too. Simply, you are naturally protected in your liberty. The error in this natural authority by men comes from the ignorance of where liberty comes from and covered earlier in this book, but I will mention this a little more in-depth when I get into the powers the Constitution permits government later in this section of the book.

Finally, *Happiness*. If you'll notice these three concepts: Life, Liberty and Happiness are large ideas. They cover a wide range of activities and embodiments. Life is the simplest of the concepts. People shouldn't just kill and imprison each other. Liberty is actually simple too. Happiness is the most abstract "right" defined, but also makes the expansion of where we are protected from encroachment by our servants vast. Benjamin Franklin wrote an essay on pain in the 1720's. He noted that it is the right and goal of all living things to alleviate themselves from pain. As such, the Declaration of Independence (which Franklin worked with Thomas Jefferson, John Adams, Roger Sherman, and Robert R. Livingston on) is assuring the world knows the commoner understands the government's duty is to alleviate strife, not create it. Thus, our Natural Right (liberty) to be, or at least seek being happy.

The Articles of Confederation were established on the intentions and principles set forth in the Declaration, meaning the later Constitution was also built upon the same concept as it claimed to be authorized by the Continental Congress which was empowered by the Articles, and by the very same minds behind the rebellion from England who made a public claim as to why they did what they did. This means as with the Constitution they are bound to the assurance of our life, liberty, and power to seek and obtain happiness. The Confederation is, however, formed by the States under the States. The Article's preamble does not levy it under the power of the People (all free persons) and so they could be perceived as being allowed to violate personal liberties internally. That is, if it weren't for the reality they were structured right after the claim of the liberation of all men from and into power *over* all government per the Declaration, and were they not all involved in the drafting of the Declaration, or political bodies of The People. Yet, they are just that.

As is noted above the Articles are quite clear on the fact the States have free citizens, and free inhabitants. The former a clear distinction from the natives who were not members of the Union. The Constitution later makes sure this fact is clear in its limitation of powers "and excluding Indians not taxed" helping us understand the position of the Articles was the same and only applicable to citizens and inhabitants of the membered States. One membered with a "tribe" clearly already belongs to another political body and is thus "excluded."

This is not necessarily how many Framers (different in some cases from Founders, but not in all instances) of the Constitution understood these clauses in the Articles or the Constitution, partly out of ignorance, and partly out of intention to skew a view that implied the Articles were insufficient in want of political power. This generally came from disingenuous positions that state or imply the Articles failed to accomplish something. Worse, some of our trusted Founders make excuses in later works trying to cover and redirect the improper use of the Articles as to protect the legacy of their work on the Constitution's improper construct, where although they bettered our brotherhood in liberty of United States, the deficits were in their failure to properly tie the limitations, and lack of power the Articles and Constitution have to the realities of liberty. Again, because we are dealing with people that often didn't fully grasp the use of the term *liberty* or the power of the individual they, with good intentions, were fighting on behalf of, but terrified to the reality of total freedom. What I am defining for you is the actual power to the clause per the concept of liberty not always what was done, but there are plenty of works which note these limitations are as I define.

THE ARTICLES

The Articles of Confederation followed up the serfdom-based Articles of Association, an initial attempt at colonial unity while still pledging loyalty to the crown. The newly declared independent States renewed their vows to each other in a loose association based on the Old Greek Confederations, Old Roman Republic, and Iroquois traditions of co-operative being without required adherence.

Let's start with the first three Sections of the Articles.

I. The Stile of this Confederacy shall be

"The United States of America."

II. Each state retains its sovereignty, freedom, and independence, and every power, jurisdiction, and right, which is not by this Confederation expressly delegated to the United States, in Congress assembled.

III. The said States hereby severally enter into a firm league of friendship with each other, for their common defense, the security of their liberties, and their mutual and general welfare, binding themselves to assist each other, against all force offered to, or attacks made upon them, or any of them, on account of religion, sovereignty, trade, or any other pretense whatever.

This was a confederation in form, and in a "stile" (framework) of a union. The member States stay "sovereign" where they did not authorize the union *permission* to delegate key matters. They are going to aid each other in protection of liberty and security (different than safety) to be sure of their good condition, welfare. As such, the Confederation's primary purpose was as the hand of diplomacy. No membered State was to independently involve their own or accept foreign delegates from another nation directly. They had to go through the Confederation as the moderator, as no State was to get special treatment in trade dealings over any of the others. This would minimize external corruption and imperialism by the membered States against the weaker States. Whether you like free trade or not, the reality is when you are dealing with tyranny their goal is their expansion over your region through markets, and they will use your neighbors to do so. This is easy for them when your neighbor is already a serfdom with either no understanding or a dislike for liberty and freedom of the individuals.

The jurisdiction applies to the States, again political bodies, not the actual individuals in the States. The States in Section 4 (earlier noted in this book) are required by the jurisdiction they gave to the

United States to assure individuals political protections and that regulation in trades are equally respected across the board, for reasons I've defined and continue to define all throughout this work.

The Articles retained a lot of freedom to the members, still, such as entering into treaties with each other so long as the Congress of the Confederation was informed, and the treaty exposes in total in its dealings and limitations. It noted the power of States to determine lesser officers for military actions from colonels and lower ranks (most Congressmen were colonels during the war) and as with any good republic it assured its member's local communities would be well-armed and readily-trained. Most importantly, the position I've regularly noted on republics and note with a prior section from the Articles above is clarified in Article IX:

> IX. The United States in Congress assembled, shall have the sole and exclusive right and power of determining on peace and war, entering into treaties and alliances, provided that no treaty of commerce shall be made whereby the legislative power of the respective States shall be restrained from imposing such imposts and duties on foreigners, as their own people are subjected to, or from prohibiting the exportation or importation of any species of goods or commodities whatsoever...

Though the Congress determines war it must be understood it does not mean the States are bound to wait for a response when under attack. Thus, the available armories to the local regions. No treaty of commerce can stop a State from taxing foreigners in the same way it taxes its own people. As was noted by Section IV of the Articles of Confederation impositions had to apply equally across the board. Most significantly, nothing could be prohibited from *trade*, period! This intention was not altered when the Constitution implied regulatory powers, which are powers to make trade regular (assured). Markets cannot be stopped from trading. Enemy Merchants and business can be.

Representatives were extended protections they usually have as private citizens, and as in the U.S. Constitution they could not be stop from presenting a vote by arrest and detainment, but for security and national sovereignty "treason, felony, or breach of the peace" were the exceptions. Furthermore, they were not to work any other capacity than delegate nor be paid by the Confederation:

> Section V: No State shall be represented in
> Congress by less than two, nor more than seven
> members; and no person shall be capable of being
> a delegate for more than three years in any term of
> six years; nor shall any person, being a delegate,
> be capable of holding any office under the United
> States, for which he, or another for his benefit,
> receives any salary, fees or emolument of any
> kind.

For if you serve the people you do so as a duty and it was up to your state to fund you. Non-delegates could be paid. So, if you were a diplomate sent overseas you could receive funds for your work. Otherwise, you were doing a duty to your people. The U.S. Constitution adds the abilities for reps to get paid—a beginning of politics becoming a *profession* in the settlements and not a *service*. This created a need in the mind of reps to be working to earn their pay despite the reality that these structures intend for reps to be away and in private life far more than they are to be in congress and active in public matters, which again, are few and far-between.

There isn't much to really go into beyond these points that weren't already covered as the goals and purposes of confederations and republics, or that won't be noted in the Constitution's intentions, short of the assurance of funding for and availability of weaponry, training, and ammo for the militias in the membered State's communities the Articles require. The Constitution maintains these same requirements upon the Union. The point of such clauses are not central power of the "United States" over the State militias though, except for when called forth in the protection of the members and whole of the Union, which is a temporary event and goal. It is for the general assurance that any and every State, and every connected community is able to defend itself at a moment's notice upon its own will, *even against the Confederation and Constituted General (Federal) Government.*

The proper and barely-used argument as to why the Articles should be replaced was that they served their purpose. A Confederation is a political agreement to accomplish a task—fight bandits, Persia, England, or whatever. Once accomplished the agreement is fulfilled. The power structure does not stay in place and continue its authority, as I noted with Alexander and the Corinthian League. The problem with the Constitution is they did not form it outside the Confederation after disbanding it.

CONSTITUTED TREASON

In the thralls of removing England many representatives believed the Articles of Confederation to be weak. There was no way to enforce dues (taxes) were paid to the Confederation. However, unlike today where this is designed to keep us in perpetual debt under funds going out to public works projects and "public" services, back then it was just to recover costs for protection duties of the Union, funds for soldiers who had to take action, or most often to shore up the forts and local armories in townships *during the war,* and to pay off what we owed to allies who provided financial aid for the *war, only.* So, why would some States keep paying after the war was over? Well, the debts incurred not being paid to foreign lands could cause another war, to be fair. That doesn't change the fact the Confederation served its purpose.

The Constitution is a result of a power struggle among the representatives. The Federalists were pushing for central control over the whole Union like the United Kingdom has, with Estate Lords, while the Anti-Federalists were trying to assure state rights for autonomous governance *under* freemen. The Articles of Confederation covered this need, but the Federalists were unhappy with the Congress as they could not forcefully excise taxes from the States and the connected municipalities, which was intended (as

Franklin stated before Congress during the debates framing the new Constitution) since taxes were originally at-will when paid to England, and it was hoped we'd do the same where most states would aid each other in any deficits causing hardship on their peoples:

> Let the weakest State say what proportion of money or force it is able and willing to furnish for the general purposes of the Union.
>
> Let all the others oblige themselves to furnish each an equal proportion.
>
> The whole of these joint supplies to be absolutely in the disposition of Congress.
>
> The Congress in this case to be composed of an equal number of delegates from each State;
>
> And their decisions to be by the majority of individual members voting.
>
> If these joint and equal supplies should, on particular occasions, not be sufficient, let Congress make requisitions on the richer and more powerful States for further aids, to be voluntarily afforded; so leaving each State the right of considering the necessity and utility of the aid desired, and of giving more or less as it should be found proper.
>
> This mode is not new; it was formerly practised with success by the British government with respect to Ireland and the colonies. We sometimes gave even more than they expected or thought just to accept; and in the last war, carried on while we were united, they gave us back in five years a million sterling. We should probably have continued such voluntary contributions whenever the occasions appeared to require them for the

> common good of the empire. It was not till they
> chose to force us, and to deprive us of the merit
> and pleasure of voluntary contributions, that we
> refused and resisted. Those contributions,
> however, were to be disposed of at the pleasure of
> a government in which we had no representative.
> I am therefore persuaded that they will not be
> refused to one in which the representation shall be
> equal.[91]

In the end Congress still wouldn't be able to force taxes, but had the tools put into the Constitution to imply they were allowed to take taxes when it suited them. However, we see Franklin state that a State will receive *aid* according to what it pays. If it doesn't pay it receives no aid. Making the tax an at-will payment for service, not a tax. This was the case in every real republic ever.

Furthermore, the Federalists wanted more central control over interpersonal activity, but in pushing for the "federal constitution" they cloaked themselves as pro-liberty men simply trying to strengthen the Union. Anti-federalists understood what such a power grab leads to and were doing everything they could to guide the Convention to a weaker position. They couldn't stop it, because the Federalists were comprised of the businessmen and local influencers (as noted above). The Federalists eventually unveiled themselves as the wolves they were and pushed to construct a new "federal" constitution.

This is interesting as there was no federal constitutions in the first place. Thus, the term *confederation,* meaning *to be against* (con-) federation. Federations can command their counter-parts, and being ours was modeled after the Roman, Greek, and Iroquois confederations, this is a suspect position, and a claim that begins to reveal the treason of putting forward a *Federation* in a *Confederation*. Too bad many Founders reiterated this misnomer, though in some major cases it was the writer talking to someone in terms they understood and not necessarily a defense in the use of the term. The term *federal* is used to define a check-and-balance system from the old

---

[91] https://franklinpapers.org/framedVolumes.jsp?vol=45&page=51

Roman Empire, to keep branches of government policing (policy-ing) each other. However, as with the use of voting this is a tool and when the term *federal* is used for *the* government in common speak, in founding times it is written or printed in lowercase, noting it is a descriptor but not a title. Thus, the object is not actually *Federal*.

Wikipedia at least describes this relation, but they also expose the modern conspiracy misusing the terms:

> The terms 'federalism' and 'confederalism' both have a root in the Latin word foedus, meaning "treaty, pact or covenant." Their common meaning until the late eighteenth century was a simple league or inter-governmental relationship among sovereign states based upon a treaty. They were therefore initially synonyms. It was in this sense that James Madison in Federalist 39 had referred to the new United States as 'neither a national nor a federal Constitution, but a composition of both' (i.e. neither a single large unitary state nor a league/confederation among several small states, but a hybrid of the two). In the course of the nineteenth century the meaning of federalism would come to shift, strengthening to refer uniquely to the novel compound political form, while the meaning of confederalism would remain at a league of states. Thus, this article relates to the modern usage of the word 'federalism'.

> Modern federalism is a system based upon democratic rules and institutions in which the power to govern is shared between national and provincial/state governments. The term federalist describes several political beliefs around the world depending on context.

First, "confederalism" doesn't exist at all and they were never really synonyms, not if you know how to read anyways. *Federalism* exists because it is the worship of the central government as a nation with intermingling political bodies (states) jointly ruling the populace. We see plainly their "modern" usage slaps democracy right on there and can tell there must be a difference from the republic concept the Constitution ended up with by their reference to Madison's usage, or more accurately his rebuking of the term "federal." We also see the definition, "have a root in the Latin word *foedus*, meaning "treaty, pact or covenant."

As above noted "con" in this usage means *in opposition to federation*. They mangle this usage too, "neither a single large unitary state nor a league/confederation among several small states, but a hybrid of the two." This is slightly incorrect in a very damaging way, but correct enough so you the reader can now understand **there is no nation of the "United States of America."** Confederation is neither a large unitary state (central authority), nor an everlasting league over the unified members at all. As I've noted a few times. It is a temporary joint body to address a danger or accomplish a task, meaning the "league of small states" is the primary point of fact to the Articles of Confederation. A federation is not that, which is why he said our system is *not that*, and why the Constitution guarantees us a *republic*.

Federal implies total central control over political decision-making and *public policy* (people management) of a region. The Republic (political republic) is more continuous than a league or confederation and more voluntary, but it is as, if not more limited, in its power over joined members. In our case, the States gave up diplomacy powers, key trade powers, they use the Republic to assure armories and armies of the regions for defense and use it as central body for keeping States from violating the personal liberty of the People of the Republic.

It is a government that manages governments, not people. This is the Republic's primary goal under the Declaration of Independence.

So, we did not become a nation-state, and we did not become a league or confederation (under the Constitution) by Madison's claim. A nation-state is something Sparta attempted when running their Grecian League, and it caused a lot of problems. However, that was exactly the Federalists' intension, by the reality of the title they gave

241

their political party and what was revealed by Alexander Hamilton's ilk in their actions. Hamilton's *Continentalist* exposes this intent as he believed most representatives native to the States were incompetent to international operations. He wrote:[92]

> It would be the extreme of vanity in us not to be sensible, that we began this revolution with very vague and confined notions of the practical business of government. To the greater part of us it was a novelty: Of those, who under the former constitution had had opportunities of acquiring experience, a large proportion adhered to the opposite side, and the remainder can only be supposed to have possessed ideas adapted to the narrow coloneal sphere, in which they had been accustomed to move, not of that enlarged kind suited to the government of an INDEPENDENT NATION.

"… the remainder can only be supposed to have possessed ideas adapted to the narrow coloneal sphere." This was a jab at Jefferson and other Anti-Federalists.

"Not of that enlarged kind suited to the government of an INDEPENDENT NATION." Here he's talking about the nation in inter-national affairs and command of the union as though it has a central power structure.

The U.S., again, is not a *nation*. If it is, the State cannot command the general government. The general government would *have to* command the States so they don't cause an international incident, which means Old World politics… the very thing we were altering because of its corruption and undermining of personal liberty. This piece is his outing as the fascist he really was and exposes how false many of his statements in the Federalist papers were. Remember, this

---

[92] https://founders.archives.gov/documents/Hamilton/01-02-02-1179

is the man who told Thomas Jefferson, "Caesar was the greatest man who ever lived."

The form of our system is stated in the U.S. Constitution with no uncertainty:

> The United States shall guarantee to every State in
> this Union a Republican Form of Government.

Seeing that it's a *republic* may seem that puts it in line with the concept of confederation, and liberty. The Constitution's illegality is in the process that formed it being outside of the Articles' authorizations and the Spirit and Purpose of the Law. The Confederation and the Constitutional Republic use a "federal" layout over *offices*, not over the people who empowered the political body. *Government* implies these managed persons then manage us—a lie. Thus, why the objective term is *federal* and not *Federal* in old writings. By this their power was limited and not technically Federal until the American Federalist Party began illegally using the Supreme Court to re-interpret the U.S. Constitution to command of the public and using the military in form of police in a tyrannical style to enforce their "rulings," as done over the proceeding century/centuries, especially through the Civil War, which was always their goal, and why they pushed for the Philadelphia Convention of 1787 to undermine the Articles.

Scholars defined the creation of the Constitution as meeting the Articles' requirements because the Annapolis Convention sent word to the Continental Congress that they met and decided to alter the Articles with a new Constitution. In other words, they met the requirement to inform Congress of a meeting to determine the Articles insufficient. The problem is the clause noted by these apologists reads as:

> ... unless such alteration be agreed to in a
> Congress of the United States, and be afterwards
> confirmed by the legislatures of every State.

The Articles already defined what the Congress of the United States *is* (Continental Congress) and the requirement it agree to a new structure or alteration *before* the State legislatures met—the exact *reverse* of what was actually done. Otherwise, it is a conspiracy against the Confederation.

One of the great factors that weighed on the Republic's Founders in not forcing an armed revolt to this criminal action against the Federalist Party was the fact that there were so many immigrants and natives in the cities conditioned to needing a central protective force over the years through English or some Crown's oppression. Even though, as Patrick Henry and other Republicans noted, the "republican" gladly and thanklessly picked up their arms and defended their nation. They used no uncertain terms in pointing out how the republican fought for our liberties in the Seven Years' War and the revolt. Men, with and without land who respected each other's brotherhood of republicanism, without which there was no winning any war. Those Founders would have fought a civil war against the Federalist then, but the city dwellers were so accustomed to serfdom they would have had the cities running back to the old Empires in some fashion or another. Additionally, their businesses and media were nearly all controlled by monocrat federalist merchants, men accustomed to commanding people in their employ in a very monarchial-like hierarchy that they considered *uneducated commoners*, commoners mentally and financially indebted to their employers, the employer knowing they were keeping the worker dumb. Despotism 101.

Thomas Jefferson in his *Notes on Professor Ebeling's Letter* satets that:[93]

> Two parties then do exist within the US. They embrace respectively the following descriptions of persons.
>
> The Anti-republicans (Federalists) consist of

---

[93] https://founders.archives.gov/documents/Jefferson/01-28-02-0391

1. The old refugees and tories.

2. British merchants residing among us, and composing the main body of our merchants

3. American merchants trading on British capital. Another great portion.

4. Speculators and Holders in the banks and public funds.

5. Officers of the federal government with some exceptions.

6. Office-hunters, willing to give up principles for places. A numerous and noisy tribe.

7. Nervous persons, whose languid fibres have more analogy with a passive than active state of things.

The Republican part of our Union comprehends

1. The entire body of landholders throughout the United States

2. The body of labourers, not being landholders, whether in husbandry or the arts"

Though I'd say the laborers were likely the American-born workers and farmhands, not the migrants the anti-republicans shipped in, working in the cities. Note closely 2. and 3., in relation to what I've been writing to you:

British merchants... composing the main body of our merchants

And

American merchants trading on British capital.

Additionally, Jefferson adds of the Federalists:

> They all live in cities, together, and can act in a
> body readily and at all times; they give chief
> employment to the newspapers, and therefore
> have most of them under their command.

There are many that also try to argue the Constitution did not
violate the Articles of Confederation because, the rule for the
Convention was *plenipotentiary*, meaning:

> Plenipotentiary:
>
> plenəpə'tenSHərē, plenəpə'tenSHē erē/
>
> noun
>
> noun: plenipotentiary; plural noun:
> plenipotentiaries
>
> 1. a person, especially a diplomat, invested with
> the full power of independent action on behalf of
> their government, typically in a foreign country.

Yet, again we have a definition that does in the apologist's
perception—"on behalf of their government" not necessarily on
behalf of "the people." For if under "the people" they would surely
be limited by those people as a "representative." In the case of the
Confederation, the State governments were already under agreement.
Their members were not able to do anything outside the power the

Articles granted. So, they were only "plenipotentiary" where those powers allowed or did not restrict. Any and every action taken to act outside of the Spirit of the Confederated Agreement means an end to that contracted organization (Locke 101), and thus all activities happening under the permissions or rules of said group becoming invalid among all permitted by that body, to which the representatives acting didn't exactly go get externally authorized to proceed in their doings as community reps by the Congress. They acted as Confederation members. This would be a different matter if they were simply acting upon their own personal intent or internal interest in matters only applying to themselves, or as reps in a new, separate organization after exiting the Confederation.

So, to hide their deception the public claim by the Conventioneers was to alter the Articles of Confederation not replace it. Yet, they moved forward in a dissolution of the Articles all done under the claim of "We don't have enough power," part of the Federalists' ability to "act in a body readily and at all times." That alone should have resulted in their execution by fellow members, but there was a crisis in the weakness of the Congress to excuse the power grab, and good men restrained themselves. None the less, the convention overextended its authority and this is echoed by Franklin, Jefferson, Madison, and multiple delegates. It's a main reason Patrick Henry left the convention, altogether.

The *Dissent of the Minority of the Convention of Pennsylvania* stated:

> It was at this time that the want of an efficient federal government was first complained of, and that the powers vested in Congress were found to be inadequate to the procuring of the benefits that should result from the union. The impost was granted by most of the states, but many refused the supplementary funds; the annual requisitions were set at naught by some of the states, while others complied with them by legislative acts, but were tardy in their payments, and Congress found themselves incapable of complying with their engagements, and supporting the federal

247

government. It was found that our national character was sinking in the opinion of foreign nations. The Congress could make treaties of commerce, but could not enforce the observance of them. We were suffering from the restrictions of foreign nations, who had shackled our commerce, while we were unable to retaliate; and all now agreed that it would be advantageous to the union to enlarge the powers of Congress; that they should be enabled in the amplest manner to regulate commerce, and to lay and collect duties on the imports throughout the United States. With this view a convention was first proposed by Virginia, and finally recommended by Congress for the different states to appoint deputies to meet in convention, "for the purposes of revising and amending the present articles of confederation, so as to make them adequate to the exigencies of the union." This recommendation the legislatures of twelve states complied with so hastily as not to consult their constituents on the subject; and though the different legislatures had no authority from their constituents for the purpose, they probably apprehended the necessity would justify the measure; and none of them extended their ideas at that time further than "revising and amending the present articles of confederation." Pennsylvania by the act appointing deputies expressly confined their powers to this object; and though it is probable that some of the members of the assembly of this state had at that time in contemplation to annihilate the present confederation, as well as the constitution of Pennsylvania, yet the plan was not sufficiently matured to communicate it to the public.

This is the third paragraph in the public address titled, *The Address and Reasons of Dissent of the Minority of the Convention of the State of Pennsylvania to their Constituents*. Most of the things I've noted as problems for these people are reiterated so you can see this first-hand account for yourself. There is much important classification in the whole document that plays to the claims of the U.S. being a nation and things of that matter. Misgivings of such and improper positions can only be corrected in review long after occurrences, but this line is of the upmost importance:

> This recommendation the legislatures of twelve states complied with so hastily as not to consult their constituents on the subject; and though the different legislatures had no authority from their constituents for the purpose, they probably apprehended the necessity would justify the measure.

Please, forgive my copying this here again, but it must sink in as the later point that necessity may justify that action can drown out the main point that the twelve legislatures did "not to consult their constituents on the subject" and "the different legislatures had no authority from their constituents for the purpose," and finally, "none of them extended their ideas at that time further than "revising and amending the present articles of confederation." Making the action criminal. Regardless of the acceptance of the activity that even the dissenters gave.

Using term *revisions* in state legislatures, Federalists were implying a necessity to strengthen the "federal constitution," and yet, there was no federal constitution to begin with. Neither the Articles nor the U.S. Constitution define themselves as *Federal*. As we read, Madison refutes any Federal power to the doctrine over the Union. Public arguments and independent titling mean nothing. The document itself must identify itself as a thing to be that thing. This is contract basics. The U.S. Constitution failed in key regards to obey Common Law standards provided by the Articles of Confederation, and the Civic Standards of the agency that designed it. It was not lawfully instituted, and it authorizes no such entity called the Federal Government, nor does it have federal power over the public.

Much of this standard can be found in Jefferson's *Notes on the State of Virginia, Query XIII*[94]. To get a proper understanding, we'll need to translate some of his points. The piece is lengthy and like with many other notations I've shared I recommend you go to the works and links cited where possible. A quick summation of what you are about to read: Thomas Jefferson is discussing the Virginia Constitution. He defines that the Constitution as of 1775 is under different style of governance from that of a republic. It is temporary and very stripped -down in scope, that at the time the "ordinary legislature" could alter the Constitution itself. This was seen as the ordinance over the government branches — again, noting the Constitutional applications still only applied to the *government agents*. His descriptions of the time also inform us the Republic requires maxims that are unalterable:

> So that the electors of April 1776, no more than the legislators of July 1775, not thinking of independance and a permanent republic, could not mean to vest in these delegates powers of establishing them, or any authorities other than those of the ordinary legislature. So far as a temporary organization of government was necessary to render our opposition energetic, so far their organization was valid. **But they received in their creation no powers but what were given to every legislature before and since**. They could not therefore pass an act transcendant to the powers of other legislatures. If the present assembly pass any act, and declare it shall be irrevocable by subsequent assemblies, the declaration is merely void, and the act repealable, as other acts are. So far, and no farther authorized, they organized the government by the ordinance entitled a Constitution or Form of government. It pretends to no higher authority than the other ordinances of the same session; it does not say, that it shall be perpetual; that it shall

---

[94] http://xroads.virginia.edu/~hyper/jefferson/ch13.html

be unalterable by other legislatures; that it shall be
transcendant above the powers of those, who they
knew would have equal power with themselves.

Basically, the convention was only to assure resistance to
England, and couldn't do much else. I again must stress he is
speaking mostly of the Virginia Constitution during rebellion, and
writing this around 1787. So, when he notes the Virginia Constitution
can be altered as ordnances, it applies to that Constitution prior to
Republican Government (Political Republic):

> Meeting as a House of Delegates in General
> Assembly with the new Senate in the autumn of
> that year, passed acts of assembly in contradiction
> to their ordinance of government; and every
> assembly from that time to this has done the same.
> I am safe therefore in the position, that the
> constitution itself is alterable by the ordinary
> legislature.

An operation like that is of despotic monarchy, and tyranny.
However, he is noting this is among the Assembly itself not against
any higher power. What is the higher power? The *freeman*, always.
Even still, once a Republic, the *law* is locked down by the stated
purpose, and can only be changed where allowed in the designated
powers. That is why Jefferson notes it was not yet, "a permanent
republic." Thus, why I define it as *against institution*. If it were fully
institutional the ordinary legislature would be bound to everything
the general government legislates. Ordinary in law means:[95]

> Ordinary meaning rule is a principle of statutory
> interpretation that when a word is not defined in a
> statute or other legal instrument, the court

---

[95] https://definitions.uslegal.com/o/ordinary-meaning-rule/

normally construes it in accordance with its
ordinary or natural meaning.

Or, as I've argued throughout, the legislature would be legislating
by the Common Language or Common Law, but not beyond the
defined powers.

This gets heady, and I will do my to best explain afterwards… Get
ready for some more serious reading:

> 2. They (the House of Delegates in General
> Assembly (Virginia)) urge, that if the convention
> had meant that this instrument should be
> alterable, as their other ordinances were, they
> would have called it an ordinance: but they have
> called it a constitution, which ex vi termini means
> `an act above the power of the ordinary
> legislature.' I answer that constitutio, constitutum,
> statutum, lex, are convertible terms. `Constitutio
> dicitur jus quod a principe conditur.'
> `Constitutum, quod ab imperatoribus rescriptum
> statutumve est.' `Statutum, idem quod lex.'
> Calvini Lexicon juridicum. Constitution and
> statute were originally terms of the (* To bid, to
> set, was the antient legislative word of the
> English. Ll. Hlotharii & Eadrici. Ll. Inae. Ll.
> Eadwerdi. Ll. Aathelstani.) civil law, and from
> thence introduced by Ecclesiastics into the English
> law. Thus in the statute 25 Hen. 8. c. 19. (symbol
> omitted). 1. `Constitutions and ordinances' are
> used as synonimous. The term constitution has
> many other significations in physics and in
> politics; but in Jurisprudence, whenever it is
> applied to any act of the legislature, it invariably
> means a statute, law, or ordinance, which is the
> present case. No inference then of a different
> meaning can be drawn from the adoption of this
> title: on the contrary, we might conclude, that, by

their affixing to it a term synonimous with ordinance, or statute, they meant it to be an ordinance or statute. But of what consequence is their meaning, where their power is denied? If they meant to do more than they had power to do, did this give them power? It is not the name, but the authority which renders an act obligatory. Lord Coke says, `an article of the statute 11 R. 2. c. 5. that no person should attempt to revoke any ordinance then made, is repealed, for that such restraint is against the jurisdiction and power of the parliament.' 4. inst. 42. and again, `though divers parliaments have attempted to restrain subsequent parliaments, yet could they never effect it; for the latter parliament hath ever power to abrogate, suspend, qualify, explain, or make void the former in the whole or in any part thereof, notwithstanding any words of restraint, prohibition, or penalty, in the former: for it is a maxim in the laws of the parliament, quod leges posteriores priores contrarias abrogant.' 4. inst. 43. -- To get rid of the magic supposed to be in the word constitution, let us translate it into its definition as given by those who think it above the power of the law; and let us suppose the convention instead of saying, `We, the ordinary legislature, establish a constitution,' had said, `We, the ordinary legislature, establish an act above the power of the ordinary legislature.' Does not this expose the absurdity of the attempt?

I tried Google translation for Jefferson's different definitions as I have no deep training in direct Latin, but my reading comprehension for its application in English is strong. This is how it would read if we went with those translations and didn't think through them:

- *Constitutio dicitur jus quod a principe conditur* is said to be "of the right which it is hidden from the prince of"

- `Constitutum, quod ab imperatoribus rescriptum statutumve est`, the commanders of the copy *statutumve* – '`Statutum, idem quod lex`, the same as the law of the.'

As I've noted there seem to be some intentional translation issues with Google. Using these translations as a base we can get the idea though. In my view they are more accurately translated as:

- 'The direction/director of the principle conduct.',
- 'the commanding doctrine of the statutes.'
- 'Statutes of the Law.'

Understanding the meaning of what is being said is a little more important than an exact translation, but I believe this to be very accurate. As such, Jefferson is saying that all these meanings are that the Constitution sets out the mission of the Law the legislature is to follow. Meaning a constitution is superior over that established under it.

> It is not the name, but the authority which renders an act obligatory.

You cannot be compelled to obey a law they have no power to pass else they are warring on you. This applies to any political body.

> But of what consequence is their meaning, where their power is denied?

And to the crux of the point we get. The alterations can only apply to the context of power given:

notwithstanding any words of restraint,
prohibition, or penalty, in the former.

Notice there is also a maxim, "quod leges posteriores priores contrarias abrogant," or "whereby the laws after the first are contrary they are abrogated." For the record, I am not pulling these definitions out of my ass. I'm breaking them down into parts when translation programs I'm accessing make no sense per dictionary root terms. That, and Latin and English are highly connected so it doesn't take much thought to figure out what they are saying. For example, *posteriors* means (essentially) later, but we can understand this as *posterity,* meaning our children/descendants, or those who come later.

By the way, a search for *quod* tells us via Wikipedia that:

Per quod is a Latin phrase (meaning whereby).

Yet Google Translation defines quod as "and." Seems like an important distinction, in my opinion.

Further, Jefferson writes:

3. But, say they, the people have acquiesced, and
this has given it an authority superior to the laws.
It is true, that the people did not rebel against it:
and was that a time for the people to rise in
rebellion? Should a prudent acquiescence, at a
critical time, be construed into a confirmation of
every illegal thing done during that period?
Besides, why should they rebel? At an annual
election, they had chosen delegates for the year, to
exercise the ordinary powers of legislation, and to
manage the great contest in which they were
engaged. These delegates thought the contest
would be best managed by an organized

government. They therefore, among others, passed an ordinance of government. They did not presume to call it perpetual and unalterable. They well knew they had no power to make it so; that our choice of them had been for no such purpose, and at a time when we could have no such purpose in contemplation. Had an unalterable form of government been meditated, perhaps we should have chosen a different set of people. There was no cause then for the people to rise in rebellion. But to what dangerous lengths will this argument lead? Did the acquiescence of the colonies under the various acts of power exercised by Great-Britain in our infant state, confirm these acts, and so far invest them with the authority of the people as to render them unalterable, and our present resistance wrong? On every unauthoritative exercise of power by the legislature, must the people rise in rebellion, or their silence be construed into a surrender of that power to them? If so, how many rebellions should we have had already? One certainly for every session of assembly. The other states in the Union have been of opinion, that to render a form of government unalterable by ordinary acts of assembly, the people must delegate persons with special powers. They have accordingly chosen special conventions to form and fix their governments.

The importance in this section in my view is in his query of the lack of rebellion. It is made clear we were busy at war with a superpower. Squabbling with the local aristoi may not have been in our best interest. The delegates deciding how they would run things surely kept Virginians focused on that fact and found it quite the excuse for their behavior. Today this position is abused even more-so and misapplied to make us think we aren't to rebel but win through the different branches, a farce invited by political scientists and politicians terrified of what the people would do if they realized their fields are in cahoots to obstruct knowledge from the people. The fact is, once we are back to the usurpation by our government, rebellion returns as a proper response. So, they keep us focused on foreign wars and claim these same violations are necessary due to global political (and nowadays literal) climate. The Query ends with this commentary:

> Our situation is indeed perilous, and I hope my countrymen will be sensible of it, and will apply, at a proper season, the proper remedy; which is a convention to fix the constitution, to amend its defects, to bind up the several branches of government by certain laws, which when they transgress their acts shall become nullities; to render unnecessary an appeal to the people, or in other words a rebellion, on every infraction of their rights, on the peril that their acquiescence shall be construed into an intention to surrender those rights.

Again, this statement is abused by the political player to imply we play the game and go through the same motions for every violation that occurs until we have an election, legislative fix, judicial opinion and it goes around and around from there. When the Democrats hold the house and pass a law violating the Bill of Rights, Republicans claim we should avoid armed rebellion until they've had a chance to file a lawsuit and see it play out, or until the next election. Then while Republican Party guys are in, we are to wait until they've had a chance to institute some repealing, but more often replacement legislation. When that doesn't happen, they say, "We'll remove him next election." When they lose that election, we are supposed to wait until the following election from that, or try to beat the usurpers in the next most local body by trying a local nullification, say in a county or city body.

Yet, who runs the bodies and defines their regulations? The same ones abusing the State and general bodies. The merry-go-round never ends for most of them. It's fine to attempt this but you aren't supposed to take generations to accomplish it like the Founders had too. They still only went through two, maybe three generations in their patience. That's the point of this *republic*, to know We are the People in charge, and they are to behave or be removed by bloody force. Eventually, one can get some of these mindless party players to admit they think we are *never* to engage in armed combat. Yet, the Father of American Independence says otherwise. If the branches and process fail to nullify the transgressions against us it is a call for rebellion. And *rebellion* was understood by all Founders to be a violent overthrow of the established "government."

"Guard with jealous attention the public liberty. Suspect every one who approaches that jewel. Unfortunately, nothing will preserve it but downright force. Whenever you give up that force, you are inevitably ruined." - Patrick Henry

CONSTITUTIONAL PURPOSE & POWERS

With all that noted I will layout the branches of the Constitutional "Government" and examine it as I have briefly with the other republics. There is more depth here as it is the document claimed to be actively in command over the United States at this time, and there is a lot more documentation available on what occurred than with the republics from nearly 2,500 years ago. There is still a lot of freedom alluded to and enforced in this document, but its intention was always subterfuge of the public will and erosion of personal liberty by monocrats who loved the British serfdom, wanted it here, and wanted their shot at king and lordships — our Federalists.

As I've tried to note in this book, there is severe ignorance that *liberty* is not the same as *freedom,* an ignorance that can't seem to grasp those concepts are part and parcel. Crazed minds regularly defile liberty with the claim that it is a collective permission by the community — a baseless concept by people incapable of discerning the difference between liberty and rights. It takes a highly uninformed or diluted mind to not accept the piles of historical works that speak of liberty and freedom hand-in-hand. This, from the Preamble to the U.S. Constitution:

> We the People of the United States, in Order to form a more perfect Union, establish Justice, insure domestic Tranquility, provide for the common defence, promote the general Welfare, and secure the Blessings of Liberty to ourselves and our Posterity, do ordain and establish this Constitution for the United States of America.

First and foremost! This is a Constitution *for* the United States of America. It did not come *from* the United States of America. It founded the political structure from a greater source. The artificial concept that is the governing body *for* these States that are *of* America which is *of* the People. So in a fun, confusing factor, The People *of* the United States are in truth *of* the People *of* America. You need to pay attention to this wording, for a Constitution of the United States that came *from* the United States and is thereby part and parcel, alterable by condition, but a Constitution *for* the United States was made by something else for its benefit — in this case, "We the People." What benefits? Well, they're listed there. You've just read them, but the most important benefit is, "And secure the Blessings of Liberty." What the hell does a person who thinks liberty is a social permission think that means?

The Declaration of Independence is clear regarding *inalienable rights* under the "laws of nature and nature's God." Those are liberties. Governments are to secure our liberties, meaning the liberties are there before we form community bodies. As such, who do they think blesses us with liberty? Our fellow men? That takes some effort in denying basic observances of nature and ignorance in nearly all fundamental works by the American Enlightenists. Some will say Nature, or God, but then when it doesn't suit their agenda the opinion of men suddenly supersedes that factor. The Blessings of Liberty are defined in multiple works, noted within this book, as a fact of existence and being. By calling them *blessings* the writers, drafters, and signers accept its preexistence to the document being laid out:

> "Under the law of nature, all men are born free, everyone comes into the world with a right to his own person, which includes the liberty of moving and using it at his own will. This is what is called personal liberty, and is given him by the author of nature, being necessary for his own sustenance."
>
> —Thomas Jefferson

And:

> "Law is often but the tyrant's will, and always so when it violates the right of an individual."
>
> —Thomas Jefferson

Could a person believing *men* permit *men's* freedom be more insincere to such a claimed belief in liberty than that? When a man says he believes in freedom then denigrates liberty to a social permission that man is only capable of discussing the freedom of communities, generally of nations or states, and is incapable of understanding personal liberty, such a man is a tool to collapse large centralist regimes but cannot be trusted after that event to stop a new one, as he is looking to only install a better tyranny of his own choosing. He has no mind for the true tumults of freedom.

Thomas Jefferson is also quoted as saying:

> I would rather be exposed to the inconveniences attending too much liberty than those attending too small a degree of it.

So, what does the disingenuous liberty mind think he is saying? He'd rather have too many permissions from his fellow men than not enough? Or is he stating he'd rather have unrestricted activity in freedom for all than rule by peers limiting possibilities? Permissions mean there is restriction on the act regardless of whether you can or cannot do it, so it must be the later query. His works and many other Founders make it clear liberty and personal freedom are one in the same, and the security of the "Blessings of Liberty" automatically force all Branches and related government beneath a man's personal freedom to assure it, not impede it, as is clearly defined in the Declaration of Independence.

A secondary game to this is played where about your personal freedom is impeded by lesser law. It is claimed this is done so someone else's personal freedom is protected. In this game they'll use the word liberty, so reworded:

> *Such laws are so someone else's liberty isn't damaged or impeded.*

For instance, they issue you a speeding ticket because you *could* hurt someone and violate their liberty to be unharmed. Well, that means you didn't impede someone's liberty so how can they punish you? They can't. But *stopping you while traveling does impede your liberty*. In fact a government official endangering people but not accomplishing the task of protecting liberty is a different matter altogether. *They* (the traffic cop, for example) *can* be ticketed and punished *as servants* as the codes are set by artificial bodies and thus can only affect the artificial titles. They know this, despite the fact they chose to become servants, and so they turn the rule around and hold you responsible to the lesser laws only applicable to them. You have no requirement to secure the Blessings of Liberty but for yourself first and for others through the power of your own virtue, and in securing your liberty from titled agents' abuses. Those oathed and ordained under a contract do have duty to secure its meaning, meaning they are not at liberty to violate …liberty. Nor are they at liberty to keep you from violating liberty. You can't *harm*, as you'll see below. Thus, the point to my rant is the entire Declaration is subject to securing *our* personal liberty, first.

Let us also not forget the reality of our right to happiness. The powers of the U.S. Constitution must meet the intention of the declaration/charter (or agreement) that founded the society. Chiefly, the Declaration of Independence. Again, it states:

> all men are created equal, that they are endowed
> by their Creator with certain unalienable Rights,
> that among these are Life, Liberty and the pursuit
> of Happiness.

Wouldn't any imposition on you make you unhappy? That renders the imposition nullified, unless the person is willing to accept it in the moment. Not primitively by secondary or tertiary decree.

Being a Coloradan, our Bill of Rights in our Constitution states:

"All persons have certain natural, essential and inalienable rights, among which may be reckoned the right of enjoying and defending their lives and liberties; of acquiring, possessing and protecting property; and of seeking and obtaining their safety and happiness."

— CO Const. Art. II Sect. 3

If I have the right to seek and obtain my happiness no lesser law may impede this unless I have harmed, not *may harm*. A few States make sure this type of clause made it into their constitutions. Some failed, and yet the Declaration extends this protection to all of them as this is one of the "innumerous" rights men like James Madison noted a Bill of Rights may not mention but are still included in our inalienable rights (protections/natural authority) by the Blessings of Liberty and Natural Law.

These factors bind the U.S. Constitution, regardless of what it says or is implied to say. Even more important, The Constitution was said by Jefferson to be best only when applied to Foreign nations, period.[96]

The true theory of our constitution is surely the wisest & best, that the states are independent as to everything within themselves, & united as to everything respecting foreign nations. Let the general government be once reduced to foreign concerns only, and let our affairs be disentangled from those of all other nations, except as to commerce which the merchants will manage the better, the more they are left free to manage for themselves, and our general government may be reduced to a very simple organization, & a very unexpensive one: a few plain duties to be performed by a few servants. but I repeat that this simple & economical mode of government can

---

[96] https://founders.archives.gov/documents/Jefferson/01-32-02-0061

never be secured if the New England states
continue to support the contrary system.

It is in other works of Jefferson where we find his distrust for
Federalists of the North, and this quote is noting the case if the
intrusive ideals being sought had been abandoned. They weren't, and
thus why I note the Constitution takes commerce and activities of
merchants over to protect the Union. Merchants engaged in foreign
trade would still apply to Jefferson's description, and in truth the
Republic form and use of terms in the Constitution still reduce the
government power to only assuring trade, and maintaining forts and
armories. Also, the States are independent to everything within
themselves, but not the power to violate personal liberty. For men like
Jefferson this went without saying because… **there was a *war* over it.**

The powers to "establish Justice, insure domestic Tranquility,
provide for the common defence, promote the general Welfare" are
all very simple, really. To establish justice means to provide courts for
solving disputes when asked, and tribunals for trying *agents* for
crimes — not for trying *citizens* but for the limitations of treason,
piracy, counterfeiting. All other claimed crimes are "inferred," which
literally means they're bullshit and not in the general government's
power to prosecute. Though, if one looks over the Crimes Act of 1790
you will see it applies to government agents mostly on the grounds
of the three crimes listed in the Constitution. The Constitution must
define the clause to be enforced by a power to punish for a crime to
be committed at that level.

For instance, to violate the Constitution in any way as a State,
State official, or Constitutional Official is *treason*, and an Act of War.
Violating it and the Bill of Rights brings aid and comfort to our
enemies and is *real* insurrection. Good luck getting a government
official to admit this or even understand how these powers are
enforced upon each other. *Domestic tranquility* is the power to stop
insurrections, quell rebellions (ones against liberty), and stifle
infiltrations; the *common defense* is the power to assure forts and
armories, and the promotion of the general Welfare (not General
Welfare) means the general government can support and inform the
best actions to aid the States being in a good condition, but it has no

power to enforce the general Welfare, because the word used is "promote." All done to secure the Blessings of Liberty.

The Branches

Legislature

(Congress: Representatives and Senators):

America's House of Representatives (House of Commons) and Senate make up Congress. That means they're *all Congressmen*: Instead of separate agendas with some overlapping areas of power they are required to check each other's legislative house in order for any legislative paperwork to be deemed "legal" after a review by the executive. Should he deem their legislation "vetoed" (refused) they can resubmit the work to each other and pass it by a democratic (mob) vote restrained by consensus – a rule requiring a 60 percent majority to pass. However, this is only in the spectrum of what power we gave them and not in power that they claim or interpret they have. Court opinions on such matters are just that, opinions. The court can claim a legislation unconstitutional but has no real ability to enforce. The President is the one who is to enforce court rulings. If he doesn't the criminal legislation will likely be enforced by Congress, and most "federal" law enforcing agencies. Know that I'm defining all of this by the document as written and not by Amendments made after the original 10 Amendments in the Bill of Rights.

The Branches and officers are given no power over the people. Their authority is over the management of the General Body and it's agents, which is given few powers – many revolving around diplomacy, trade assurance, monetary stability (mostly to subdue financer influences), and inter-state defense. These are the areas defined in Congress's Powers which apply to member governments, foreign governments, their officers and agents (including anyone or thing licensed or permitted by them). In all places the free people are in power over the Constitution's officers, but politically involved directly in few operations. Specifically, in one place after the Preamble. U.S. Const. Art I. Sect. 2:

HOUSE OF REPRESENTATIVES

The House of Representatives shall be composed
of Members chosen every second Year by the
People of the several States, and the Electors
(Voter) in each State shall have the Qualifications
requisite for Electors (Voter) of the most
numerous Branch of the State Legislature.

This is the only place other than the Preamble in which the People are
mentioned. This is because we are to control the General Government
(Republic) by directing the House of Representatives. We can address
any agent personally, but we as a group only have power through the
House of Representatives in directing the Republic by the
Constitution's confines. This is the only position in which there is a
popular vote to select General Government agents because the
Government works for the States of the People. The House selects the
Speaker of the House from among their body and manages their own
officers. That is an internal power. They have the sole power over
impeachment, with their seats added to by a counting of the
population of a state, and to which the election of a representative is
limited to whatever requirement is domestically required to vote for
a State House of Representatives officer or similar populist chamber.
However, I argue by use of the words "People of the Several States"
they wanted limited infringement on any person in a State having a
say in their Representative.

SENATE

(U.S. Const. Art. I Sect. 3)

The Senate of the United States shall be composed
of two Senators from each State, chosen by the
Legislature thereof, for six Years; and each Senator
shall have one Vote.

Senate is supposed to be selected by the State legislatures, because again, the General Government is a State-invented body by their power *under* the People. Like the House, they pick their own internal officers. Senate is the only house of Congress that has a say in treaties, departmental leadership positions, and upholding impeachment charges. It is supposed to be overseen by the Vice President who is really only ever supposed to be the runner-up—though it seems advantageous to have a running mate defined from a separate pool, you want the loser to be there to equalize the winner in policy. However, they are supposed to always be on the same page of understanding the limitations on the General Government and in keeping it operating to Statute.

Both these bodies (Houses) make up the Congress where the public and the State entities have an equal presence to direct a large trader protectorate called "The United States of America." The Houses set the rules and manage their own officers.

There is no power in Congress to command us as they are not privileged over us. They are *permitted*. The proof to my claim is in Article I Section 9 of the U.S. Constitution:

> No Title of Nobility shall be granted by the United States: And no Person holding any Office of Profit or Trust under them, shall, without the Consent of the Congress, accept of any present, Emolument, Office, or Title, of any kind whatever, from any King, Prince, or foreign State.

"No Title of Nobility shall be granted by the United States."

Nobility is defined as:[97]

---

nobility

1. (Government, Politics & Diplomacy) a socially
or politically privileged class whose titles are
conferred by descent or by royal decree.

Some of Noah Webster's definitions are:

2. Antiquity of family; descent from noble
ancestors; distinction by blood, usually joined
with riches.

3. The qualities which constitute distinction of
rank in civil society, according to the customs or
laws of the country; that eminence or dignity
which a man derives from birth or title conferred,
and which places him in an order above common
men. In Great Britain, nobility is extended to five
ranks, those of duke, marquis, earl, viscount and
baron.

4. The persons collectively who enjoy rank above
commoners; the peerage; as the English nobility;
French, German, Russian nobility"

— Websters Dictionary 1828

Titled people tended to be those authorized to own land and have
a major say in political operations. Who can own land in America?
Anyone. As no Title of Nobility can be granted by the United States,
the President, Vice President, Congressmen, Senators and alike those
men also are not "a socially or politically privileged class," which was
once the way political officials were defined in old republics,
monarchies, theocracies, and despotisms alike. Public officials have
no power *over* us individuals in this republic. We the People are over
them and equal to each other. Again, were this not the case there
would be a specific clause stating the General Government's power

over the people in specified regard. Things such as legal cases involving individuals have to be brought before the constituted courts and can only be on the matter the court is defined to have power to oversee. In most cases the government can't just take you to court, either.

The Branches have power only in the confines of what they are directed to. This work put time into talking about the auxiliaries of old republics, so let's examine America's auxiliaries and limitations of power. These auxiliaries being the 13 delegated powers and operations the Constitution defines for Congress. I wager we'll notice as with the other auxiliaries of past republics it has little to do with personal activities. It is even likely far more repressed than they were, as they still surround the object called *cities,* not sprawling nations.

First it is important for you to know Section 2 of Article I:

> Representatives and direct Taxes shall be apportioned among the several States which may be included within this Union, according to their respective Numbers, which shall be determined by adding to the whole Number of free Persons, including those bound to Service for a Term of Years, and excluding Indians not taxed, three fifths of all other Persons.

Their powers in Article I Section 8 of the U.S. Constitution are as follows:

> The Congress shall have Power To lay and collect Taxes, Duties, Imposts and Excises.

On anything and everything? No. Only…

> to pay the Debts and provide for the common
> Defence and general Welfare of the United States;
> but all Duties, Imposts and Excises shall be
> uniform throughout the United States;

These charges must be uniform throughout the United States and *only apply to the states*, not the individual. The free persons' numbers are only calculated for the States' dues assessments.

We are not to be personally charged by the general government.

Any amendment that does so is void as the Union applies to political bodies... which are fictions. One State can't be charged more (per capita) than another, an equity under the law. What is the "general Welfare"? The assurance of personal liberty first and foremost, always. This is per the Preamble. The Preamble is clear they can only *promote* (advertise or fund) the general Welfare. The General Government has no power to *direct* the general Welfare. So, they are not to take money to assure you have food on your table because someone else does. Equally, it doesn't mean a person who hordes the production of food (especially a business) from the masses through persuasion, influence, affluence, and perseverance is protected from retribution, but that reaction must be initiated by a free person or people, first, either by a claim in court or direct resistance. Government cannot just act in our best interest against a non-governing, non-agent, "unofficial" party.

The loophole? Committing yourself to servicing the public a good, product, service, and especially a necessity you are aiming to take over creation of, for the betterment of mankind. Thus, you choose serfdom to the People. Getting licensed to do so makes you a government agent and officially subject to the People. This is addressed shortly. Also, if the Union perceives that a *group* acts as an intentional threat against its cause (securing personal and community liberty), it can deem them bandits or pirates and act.

> To borrow Money on the credit of the United
> States...

271

This does *not* authorize the creation or power to regulate us with an external or internal private bank. It is for leveraging the good name of the Union to borrow funds when needed in cases of diplomatic or infrastructure emergencies. This is a treasury power for stable financing in trade of materials of production. Not control of those materials or means. At least, not in a republic. In a federalism they believe they can do what they want to.

> To regulate Commerce with foreign Nations, and among the several States, and with the Indian Tribes...

Notice how it defines foreign nations *first!* The primary goal is minimizing foreign infiltration of commerce, then keeping States and merchants from lording over each other. This is to manage governments and tribes involved in trade with the United States, not them personally in their affairs, but in their behaviors when here in our affairs. This does not actually give them power to determine the goods and products that are in the market, but assures they are equally available across the Union. To be precise, goods are not to be impeded or used to extort power. In this case businesses, merchants, governments are servants and are not private entities as they have chosen to provide to the public at-large giving the People the natural power to observe and limit them.

As this book has noted, merchants are a major threat to a native populace if not monitored. However, this does not empower the government over them at the national or even state level to command the goods or products themselves. Only how things are logged and charged for port costs. This has nothing to do with individual non-government connected bodies. It has to do with trade agreements when allowing non-liberty societies to access our people through an influence, manufacture or good and our own merchants who are interacting with said societies from membered States when following those State's trade rules (regulations).

I have repeatedly stated the goal of a republic is to assure trade. This position is vindicated by James Madison to this specific section in the Constitution. He told Joseph Cabell in a letter:[98]

> 1. The meaning of the Phrase "to regulate trade" must be sought in the general use of it, in other words in the objects to which the power was generally understood to be applicable, when the Phrase was inserted in the Const.

> 2. The power has been understood and used by all commercial & manufacturing Nations as embracing the object of encouraging manufactures. It is believed that not a single exception can be named."

Encouraging, not commanding, not restricting.

> To establish an uniform Rule of Naturalization, and uniform Laws on the subject of Bankruptcies throughout the United States...

It can define how someone not born of America becomes an American with native political rights (natural rights/liberties are absolute). It does not empower them to decide immigration policy.

It sets how a freeman with debt in need of forgiveness can be aided, not punished. Though this is to help out a financier or lender by repaying some level of the sum due, when the bankruptcy process works in total favor of the debtee (the one owed) it is adding the servant over the sovereign. The opposite of its purpose. Something to think about.

---

[98] https://www.loc.gov/resource/mjm.22_0553_0561/?sp=3&st=text

> To coin Money, regulate the Value thereof, and of foreign Coin, and fix the Standard of Weights and Measures...

Not *print* currency (which was being done in those days). *Coin money!* Tied to physicality, assuring its value. They can then address the relation of a foreign coin to the domestic coin, which is often done by input from private financial professionals and researching the total products and goods in trade[99].

> To provide for the Punishment of counterfeiting the Securities and current Coin of the United States...

Thus, punish currency printers stealing wealth and extorting people. Like... the Federal Reserve. Remember the banker came into power about this time. Jefferson and other Founders were well aware of the schemes happening in Europe. Hamilton was trying to implement it here to be a world power player. So early on many were trying to thwart currency schemes.

Also, this doesn't actually state there can be no other monies in use. It just says the Congress can regulate the value of other coins, which is a comparative evaluation, and should be based on hard numbers, not subjective value, which is where digital money punches itself in the throat, but I digress.

> To establish Post Offices and post Roads...

This is to assure communication throughout the Union. This does not empower government to be the *only* postal provider. The public, by financing the roads, has every right of using them as we pay for

---

[99] As a side note: Bitcoin is, a coin... meaning the government can constitutionally regulate it.

their creation and upkeep in multiple ways. Thus, why communication lines are claimed to fall under infrastructure which the government is claimed to maintain. This in no way implies they control it, and in reality, the Constitution makes no mention of infrastructure (do a search for the word), as that is a State's or people's prerogative, respectively. Yet, there is another imperative purpose intentionally not mentioned, but historically evident in the reason for postal roads. Roads were invented so armies could move smoothly throughout a nation in cases of emergency (invasion and such) which also worked in favor of traders. Who is the legitimate military in the U.S.? *You and me.* We are then by these roads able to get to the aid of fellow freemen quickly, including accessing the capitols in case we need to rebel. Where do they get off charging us fees to access them as this is already their duty to maintain in the foundation funding purposes?

> To promote the Progress of Science and useful
> Arts, by securing for limited Times to Authors and
> Inventors the exclusive Right to their respective
> Writings and Discoveries...

This is a matter of money, which they oversee. It is not to *fund* the arts. It is to assure artists and inventors of their right to recognition for their creation, and a financial assurance to funds earned by manufactures and producers in corporations using their innovations. To assure someone who did not create something isn't becoming a financial powerhouse and endangering the public welfare, nor that a manufacturer is using a man's invention without recognizing his innovation and paying him for his contribution to society. The Founders were not for free markets and they understood the importance of a man creating something to be recognized as the creator. It encourages creation. Basically, under this clause correctly enforced, Edison would be outed as the fraud he was. This is also not intended to be a perpetual protection beyond the creator themselves. For instance, Disney has lobbied for decades to extend their trademark laws to protect their holding of Mickey Mouse, because once he enters the legal public domain anyone can put Mickey on a product and sell it without paying the corporation. But Walt Disney is dead, and their action is an abuse of the system, not technically protected or authorized by the power granted to the General Government.

> To constitute Tribunals inferior to the supreme Court...

Both houses can hold hearings to try for crimes, but the Supreme Court can overrule their judgements.

> To define and punish Piracies and Felonies committed on the high Seas, and Offences against the Law of Nations...

They can determine maritime law and when mutual respect built over the course of historical relations between nations has been violated by government agents. This has nothing to do with you on a boat, or you an American in a foreign nation, but when an unaffiliated person, group, or officer from abroad or one of our officers abroad commits an act of disrepute and corruption. This has to do with government officers or licensed entities. Pirates were often operating under "letter of marque" and were de facto agents, privateers. Jefferson noted how when a private citizen (different than a privateer) was in a foreign port and their property was searched without a warrant, it was an Act of War and the full force of the Navy should be ready to be brought down on that nation. An act equal to searching a foreign King simply because another nation suspected him of deception.

> To declare War, grant Letters of Marque and Reprisal, and make Rules concerning Captures on Land and Water...

Set standards for warfare and to authorize official participants and actions.

> To raise and support Armies, but no
> Appropriation of Money to that Use shall be for a
> longer Term than two Years...

They can encourage militia growth. The armies, however, cannot be appropriated funds longer than two (2) years. Not the same as forts and munitions being funded to assure domestic defense. So, how is our Army still so active and funded? Those who support the military claim it is because the world is different, that requires the military stay readied nationally. Along with pointing to constant convenient conflicts needing our vigilance that per the Monroe Doctrine have nothing to do with our *actual* national interests. This is a lie as I'll note in the next power. The people are the only legal standing army. I will expand an important point to this in discussing the Second Amendment later on.

> To provide and maintain a Navy...

The Navy is not technically a military arm, but a guard unit. Responsive/defensive only. Militaries, or armies (best defined as "regulars") can be preemptive. Done correctly, the Air Force should have been created by Convention of the States (Article V of the U.S. Constitution) once it broke off and can be then funded as regularly as the Navy as an air guard unit. Instead, it is an illegitimate military power. As evidence, this original term for army via Etymonline.com:[100]

---

[100] https://www.etymonline.com/word/army

Word Origin and History for army

n.

late 14c., "armed expedition," from Old French
armée (14c.) "armed troop, armed expedition,"
from Medieval Latin armata "armed force," from
Latin armata, fem. of armatus "armed, equipped,
in arms," past participle of armare "to arm,"
literally "act of arming," related to arma "tools,
arms" (see arm (n.2)). Originally used of
expeditions on sea or land; the specific meaning
"land force" first recorded 1786. Transferred
meaning "host, multitude" is c.1500.

The Old English words were here (still preserved
in derivatives like harrier), from PIE *kor-
"people, crowd;" and fierd, with an original sense
of "expedition," from faran "travel." In spite of
etymology, in the Anglo-Saxon Chronicle, here
generally meant "invading Vikings" and fierd was
used for the local militias raised to fight them."

"Fierd was used for the local militias raised to fight them."
Meaning built upon the arrival of the threat. Thus, the last-mentioned
section's reason for being written as "To raise and support Armies."

To make Rules for the Government and
Regulation of the land and naval Forces…

Again we see the term "regulation." This is a matter of assurance
as with commerce, and money stability. They are to assure land and
naval forces and supply recommended protocols. The terms "rules"
is what covers how people conceive the term "regulation" in these
clauses. Does "To make the Rules for the Government and Rule of the
land and naval Forces" make sense as a statement applied to you?
Then that's clearly not what this clause is saying. It applies to the

General Government and the forces it raises. However, using these clauses to regulate the public by required adherence to guidelines was how the Federalists want these sections interpreted and what they used the Supreme Court to accomplish. Wrongly, and intentionally. With malice and deception. The Rule being for the government can only apply to the government and its agents which it cannot conscript you to as that power is not defined in the constitution.

> To provide for calling forth the Militia to execute
> the Laws of the Union, suppress Insurrections and
> repel Invasions...

This empowers the Body Politic to call upon each State's armed citizens to help defend the Republic, Spirit of the Law, and Constitutional provisions but restricts the power they have when acting. Additionally, the prior section to this is allowing for the type of rules that if the militia is working under the Body Politic and it violates the rules applied, militia members can be brought to Tribunal. However, Congress can only call them up. The States do not have to answer. Else, how are they free?

> To provide for organizing, arming, and
> disciplining, the Militia, and for governing such
> Part of them as may be employed in the Service of
> the United States, reserving to the States
> respectively, the Appointment of the Officers, and
> the Authority of training the Militia according to
> the discipline prescribed by Congress...

They can define the best training and operational methods while the militia is called up, but the actual power of appointing officers and training soldiers is supposed to be left to the States, as is the implementation of training. General Government direction over the militia cannot be made a regular activity. An illegal action done ever since the U.S. Government criminally created the National Guard and stole the State militias.

> To exercise exclusive Legislation in all Cases
> whatsoever, over such District (not exceeding ten
> Miles square) as may, by Cession of particular
> States, and the Acceptance of Congress, become
> the Seat of the Government of the United States,
> and to exercise like Authority over all Places
> purchased by the Consent of the Legislature of the
> State in which the Same shall be, for the Erection
> of Forts, Magazines, Arsenals, dock-Yards, and
> other needful Buildings; — And...

They can create and legislate the cases (this doesn't mean behaviors, but legal matters which are few) in the small area designated as the *seat of government* of the United States, not *seat of government* over the whole nation. They can buy things in that *area only* per the permission of the State(s) in where the capitol is, to build protective enclaves. These are the same things they are required to assure are regularly maintained throughout the Union which We the People are at liberty to access and use at *all* times. This section is abused to imply the Government can own land. Untrue. As has already been clarified about a republic, anything the public funds go to is owned by the people as a whole. In this case we all own the "forts, magazines, arsenals, dock-yards, and other needful buildings" in D.C., the state it is located in, as well as D.C. itself. The forts in other states are for their people first and foremost, but still jointly maintained by the People of the United States of America.

> To make all Laws which shall be necessary and
> proper for carrying into Execution the foregoing
> Powers, and all other Powers vested by this
> Constitution in the Government of the United
> States, or in any Department or Officer thereof.

They can make laws (rules under the Spirit and Purpose of the Society) regarding powers given to the government under this contract, and that is it. Not one thing mentioned above applies to you and your dealings, not even money usage. Nor, does it imply Congress can define terms in the Constitution itself. Those terms used in the Constitution are defined by common use definitions of the time.

This government is wholly-criminal and out of control. It is by its own terms above, a pirate organization.

The Constitution was written so an 8th grader in an agrarian (farmer) culture could understand it. The idea it's so complex you need a law degree to understand it is a primary example of subterfuge and piracy at the governing and legal level. A position and claim that is totally criminal and treasonous. If not true, the Constitution would be a book's worth of laws and regulations. It is not.

Beyond the list of can-do's there is a specific list of can't-do's. For instance, Congress's power over immigration is something most political parties use as an issue. Well it came to an end in 1808 and no Amendment gave the government power to decide migration after 1808. That's right. The U.S. Government has no authority over immigration but for invasions. It is a State matter or matter of the people. Only under extreme and limited circumstances can they suspend *habeas corpus*. In fact, the following Section notes multiple places Congress is restricted and Section 10 restricts member States:

> Section. 9. The Migration or Importation of such Persons as any of the States now existing shall think proper to admit, shall not be prohibited by the Congress prior to the Year one thousand eight hundred and eight, but a Tax or duty may be imposed on such Importation, not exceeding ten dollars for each Person.

Congress met in 1808 and focused on ending the slave trade under Jefferson. In the process they failed to authorize a change to the powers in Sect. 9 and gave up authority over State immigration matters. Does the line "shall not be prohibited... prior to" imply after

1808 the government can prohibit it? No. In order for the government to have power to do something it has to be specifically expressed. As you'll read in the 10th Amendment.

The Privilege of the Writ of Habeas Corpus shall not be suspended, unless when in Cases of Rebellion or Invasion the public Safety may require it.

No Bill of Attainder or ex post facto Law shall be passed.

No Capitation, or other direct, Tax shall be laid, unless in Proportion to the Census or enumeration herein before directed to be taken.

No Tax or Duty shall be laid on Articles exported from any State.

No Preference shall be given by any Regulation of Commerce or Revenue to the Ports of one State over those of another: nor shall Vessels bound to, or from, one State, be obliged to enter, clear, or pay Duties in another.

No Money shall be drawn from the Treasury, but in Consequence of Appropriations made by Law; and a regular Statement and Account of the Receipts and Expenditures of all public Money shall be published from time to time.

I think most these are self-explanatory, however, the level to which they violate this last clause alone should have caused a revolution decades ago. They do not inform us of *all public money* use out of the claim of "national security." Yet we — the armed people — are the primary power of national security and *are to be told where the money goes*. Bootlickers and servicemen all seem to not mind this violation of the law as long as it fits their needs.

> No Title of Nobility shall be granted by the United
> States: And no Person holding any Office of Profit
> or Trust under them, shall, without the Consent of
> the Congress, accept of any present, Emolument,
> Office, or Title, of any kind whatever, from any
> King, Prince, or foreign State.

By the way, here is a breakdown of the only crime the government can actually punish for as noted in the Kentucky Resolution drafted by Thomas Jefferson:

> 2. Resolved, That the Constitution of the United
> States, having delegated to Congress a power to
> punish treason, counterfeiting the securities and
> current coin of the United States, piracies, and
> felonies committed on the high seas, and offences
> against the law of nations, and no other crimes
> whatsoever.

Meaning most felonies and capital crimes you could commit are not in the power of the U.S. Government to trial or carry out punishment of.

The next section is a statement on the limitations on the States membered in the Union. This section basically, kills the claim the Constitution has no power to limit the States. Which the Articles of Confederation also did, to assure personal freedom and that no State ruled over the others, which the creation of Washington D.C. into having a vote in Senate is the attempt at making a State power ruling the other States:

> Section. 10. No State shall enter into any Treaty,
> Alliance, or Confederation; grant Letters of
> Marque and Reprisal; coin Money; emit Bills of
> Credit; make any Thing but gold and silver Coin a
> Tender in Payment of Debts; pass any Bill of

Attainder, ex post facto Law, or Law impairing
the Obligation of Contracts, or grant any Title of
Nobility.

We see powers that might make a preferred class or risk the
security of the Union by a member State joining with bodies that may
infiltrate the Union through member States is stripped. When
Maryland attempted to enter the Confederacy during the Southern
Secession it violated this clause and created the real legal authority
for the Union to war on the South, something regularly ignored by
Southern Apologists and general historians.

No State shall, without the Consent of the
Congress, lay any Imposts or Duties on Imports or
Exports, except what may be absolutely necessary
for executing it's inspection Laws: and the net
Produce of all Duties and Imposts, laid by any
State on Imports or Exports, shall be for the Use of
the Treasury of the United States; and all such
Laws shall be subject to the Revision and Controul
of the Congress.

Any tax upon a traded good from abroad or between domestic
States is only a power of the United States unless needed to fund
inspection costs, only permitted by Congress. This is the inspection of
foreign goods for safety, not for say in whether a good can be traded
or not, and then profits go to the Union. Though Congress can revise
these laws, it is under only the reasons given. Another power
Congress regularly overreaches with.

No State shall, without the Consent of Congress,
lay any Duty of Tonnage, keep Troops, or Ships of
War in time of Peace, enter into any Agreement or
Compact with another State, or with a foreign
Power, or engage in War, unless actually invaded,

or in such imminent Danger as will not admit of delay.

States cannot on their own charge access to ports based on vessel capacity. No state can have standing armies of their own making, unless in direct and immediate danger. They have always readied militias (armed citizens) and available armories for these needs

Before I get to the Presidency there is an important matter. Section 7 of Article I states:

> Every Bill which shall have passed the House of Representatives and the Senate, shall, before it becomes a Law, be presented to the President of the United States; If he approve he shall sign it, but if not he shall return it, with his Objections to that House in which it shall have originated, who shall enter the Objections at large on their Journal, and proceed to reconsider it. If after such Reconsideration two thirds of that House shall agree to pass the Bill, it shall be sent, together with the Objections, to the other House, by which it shall likewise be reconsidered, and if approved by two thirds of that House, it shall become a Law. But in all such Cases the Votes of both Houses shall be determined by yeas and Nays, and the Names of the Persons voting for and against the Bill shall be entered on the Journal of each House respectively. If any Bill shall not be returned by the President within ten Days (Sundays excepted) after it shall have been presented to him, the Same shall be a Law, in like Manner as if he had signed it, unless the Congress by their Adjournment prevent its Return, in which Case it shall not be a Law.

In 1865 Andrew Johnson vetoed the 14th Amendment. Congress having had a 2/3rd's agreement on passing it the first time deemed it as passed. They did not follow this procedure:

> If after such Reconsideration two thirds of that House shall agree to pass the Bill, it shall be sent, together with the Objections, to the other House, by which it shall likewise be reconsidered, and if approved by two thirds of that House, it shall become a Law.

Which does not say:

> If prior to that Reconsideration it was already passed by two thirds vote that House can send it on as though passed by vote.

The Amendment is criminal and not legal. Killing the Constitution and making the government as of that date void per Locke. There technically is no legal sitting Government for the United States at this time. All agents are operating *de facto*, meaning:

De Facto

[Latin, In fact.] In fact, in deed, actually. [101]

This phrase is used to characterize an officer, a government, a past action, or a state of affairs that must be accepted for all practical purposes, but is unlawful or illegitimate. Thus, an office, position, or status existing under a claim or color of right, such as

---

[101] https://legal-dictionary.thefreedictionary.com/de+facto

a *de facto* corporation. In this sense it is the contrary of *de jure*, which means rightful, legitimate, just, or constitutional. Thus, an officer, king, or government de facto is one that is in actual possession of the office or supreme power, but by usurpation, or without lawful title; while an officer, king, or governor de jure is one who has just claim and rightful title to the office or power, but has never had *plenary*[102] possession of it, or is not in actual possession. A wife de facto is one whose marriage is voidable by decree, as distinguished from a wife de jure, or lawful wife. But the term is also frequently used independently of any distinction from de jure; thus, a blockade de facto is a blockade that is actually maintained, as distinguished from a mere paper blockade.

In other words, it's presumed power that *must* be accepted over all for "practical purposes" to excuse criminal actions by an overwhelming force because it is just the current state of things (what's in charge). Is that freedom? Liberty?

You are in a war with this government and they just keep pushing you around.

---

[102] *plenary*, plē'nə-rē, plĕn'ə-, adjective, Complete in all respects; unlimited or full. — American Heritage Dictionary of the English Language, 5th Edition.

EXECUTIVE

(President)

(Section. 1. is discussed next, under *Judiciary* and in the *Bill of Rights* section.)

Section. 2.

The President shall be Commander in Chief of the Army and Navy of the United States, and of the Militia of the several States, when called into the actual Service of the United States; he may require the Opinion, in writing, of the principal Officer in each of the executive Departments, upon any Subject relating to the Duties of their respective Offices, and he shall have Power to grant Reprieves and Pardons for Offences against the United States, except in Cases of Impeachment.

As already said, he commands the military when active for the Union. Thus, the military is not always there nationally, or under the President's power. Why? Because sometimes the President is an enemy and needs to be slayed... like Caesar. And sometimes the military is the enemy standing over as a power of the authoritarian like with Peisistratus.

He shall have Power, by and with the Advice and Consent of the Senate, to make Treaties, provided two thirds of the Senators present concur; and he shall nominate, and by and with the Advice and Consent of the Senate, shall appoint Ambassadors, other public Ministers and Consuls, Judges of the Supreme Court, and all other Officers of the United States, whose Appointments are not herein otherwise provided for, and which shall be established by Law: but the Congress may by Law vest the Appointment of such inferior Officers, as they think proper, in the President alone, in the Courts of Law, or in the Heads of Departments.

The President shall have Power to fill up all Vacancies that may happen during the Recess of the Senate, by granting Commissions which shall expire at the End of their next Session.

He can recommend employees and hire temps.

Section. 3.

He shall from time to time give to the Congress Information of the State of the Union, and recommend to their Consideration such Measures as he shall judge necessary and expedient; he may, on extraordinary Occasions, convene both Houses, or either of them, and in Case of Disagreement between them, with Respect to the Time of Adjournment, he may adjourn them to such Time as he shall think proper; he shall receive Ambassadors and other public Ministers; he shall take Care that the Laws be faithfully executed, and shall Commission all the Officers of the United States.

The President oversees all officers of the government. In this work I tend to interchange the Representatives with officers as technically they are *all* officers. The Commander-in-Chief is the sole authority over the military once the Congress as called for war and to spite the War Powers Act (*acts* are not *laws*) he does not have the power to initiate war unless Congress is incapacitate or they are failing in their duty to defend us. This factor comes to power as he is an American and we all have a duty to defend the country from corruption. If Congress is failing to stop a direct invasion or insurrection it is common sense and thus Common Law that the Commander of the military can respond to threats. However, it is best that We the People have already engaged the enemy, and then the President would be backing up the Sovereign with what the Founders called "the regulars" — military-educated, regularly-employed military agents, such as those who tend the forts and the soldiers called forth by the Congress. The Chief is then Head of Diplomacy and meeting with heads of foreign States on behalf of the membered *States'* congress. State congressmen aren't to act as diplomats without Presidential authorization. Why? Because they cannot make deals and political promises on behalf of the U.S. or their State. The President can mitigate a deal, but not independently make treaties.

JUDICIARY

(Supreme Court)

Section. 1.

The judicial Power of the United States, shall be vested in one supreme Court, and in such inferior Courts as the Congress may from time to time ordain and establish. The Judges, both of the supreme and inferior Courts, shall hold their Offices during good Behaviour, and shall, at stated Times, receive for their Services, a Compensation, which shall not be diminished during their Continuance in Office.

(So, if the judges display poor or bad behavior they can be fired.)

Section. 2.

The judicial Power shall extend to all Cases, in Law and Equity, arising under this Constitution, the Laws of the United States, and Treaties made, or which shall be made, under their Authority; — to all Cases affecting Ambassadors, other public Ministers and Consuls; — to all Cases of admiralty and maritime Jurisdiction; — to Controversies to which the United States shall be a Party; — to Controversies between two or more States; — between a State and Citizens of another State, — between Citizens of different States, — between Citizens of the same State claiming Lands under Grants of different States, and between a State, or the Citizens thereof, and foreign States, Citizens or Subjects.

In all Cases affecting Ambassadors, other public Ministers and Consuls, and those in which a State shall be Party, the supreme Court shall have original Jurisdiction. In all the other Cases before mentioned, the supreme Court shall have appellate Jurisdiction, both as to Law and Fact, with such Exceptions, and under such Regulations as the Congress shall make.

The Trial of all Crimes, except in Cases of Impeachment, shall be by Jury; and such Trial shall be held in the State where the said Crimes shall have been committed; but when not committed within any State, the Trial shall be at such Place or Places as the Congress may by Law have directed.

Section. 3.

Treason against the United States, shall consist only in levying War against them, or in adhering to their Enemies, giving them Aid and Comfort. No Person shall be convicted of Treason unless on the Testimony of two Witnesses to the same overt Act, or on Confession in open Court.

The Congress shall have Power to declare the Punishment of Treason, but no Attainder of Treason shall work Corruption of Blood, or Forfeiture except during the Life of the Person attainted.

Section 2 shouldn't be hard to understand:

The judicial Power shall extend to all Cases, in Law and Equity, arising under this Constitution, the Laws of the United States, and Treaties made, or which shall be made, under their Authority.

That's it. They have judicial power in all cases of Law and Equity arising *under* the Constitution, first and foremost. Not cases in Law and Equity beyond its limitations found in... *The Constitution*! It then lists the differing types of cases. They must occur under the confines of the Constitution's limitations. You may note the word Citizen used much here, including a case between a State and a Citizen. I feel I have and will later continue to clarify the position of a Citizen over artificial bodies. That fact applies to Judiciary power. Here also.

Why is the last section important? First, it notes the need for the *government* to have two witnesses to the same action or by an admission in open court, meaning on public record. Again, as it cannot be stressed enough, Constitutions mainly apply to government agents, government members, or agents of other political organizations. So, the officers need two witnesses to you committing treason, or you need to admit to it in a public proceeding. Otherwise they can't do shit. Certain other courts and even individuals making a claim do not need to do this but can follow this procedure. These stipulations are not required for *you* to act against a traitor.

Next, though Congress can convene tribunals against traitors, and declare the punishment, the Supreme Court overrules them as they do any lesser court brought before them in *only* the matters they have authorization to hear. So, when a case under a Congressional Tribunal is appealed to the Supreme Court, the court stated power in the Constitution allows the Court to overrule Congress. If the issue brought before the court is defined in the listing of Congressional Power or its restrictions. Like say, a State claiming it can coin money. The Supreme Court must find on Congress's side or be rendered dead in power. Which it has been for some time due to many rulings in which it reinterpreted the Constitution and misappropriated powers.

The last line itself says Congress can declare a punishment, yet bars Congress from declaring one guilty by legislation, and to stop Congress and the Court from levying treason punishments against one's family, and things once the guilty have died. A Bill of Attainder does not (despite the claims of some) necessarily mean death and even if Congress issues the Attainder the accused can appeal to the Supreme Court. Course, Article I Section 9 already states they can't pass a Bill of Attainder. Oh, the fun doublespeak the Federalists implement for confusion of the law.

In the aspect of the U.S. Constitution, it doesn't state the Government has power over the individual person, or People. Its power is over the States where authorization to carry out tasks was given and over the States in assuring every individuals' liberty and adherence to the agreement. This is done via the Bill of Rights which every member is to respect and adhere to as protections across the board. This is evident in the 10th Amendment:

Amendment X

The powers not delegated to the United States by the Constitution, nor prohibited by it to the States, are reserved to the States respectively, or to the people.

The Bill of Rights is an addendum and as such it is an expansion of the intentions in most the last sections of most the Constitution's Articles. That is, restrictions upon the Body Politic, and in this case, most focusing on where government power is restrained when dealing with the individual who is also, the People. Further, where there is no power noted to "government," the people can give a power to their State, or retain it individually and personally act. Which would also mean, the individual cannot give up those powers whatsoever. If they could, it would violate the Declaration of Independence's proclamation "All men are created equal" and "Governments are instituted among Men, deriving their just powers from the consent of the governed." If they derive their powers from consent than the consenter must naturally retain the power to dissent and withdraw. The artificially-titled could never have the equal power to a private man or their station is superior, and they lords, meaning the individual can't give up any just power they bestowed to agents (who must always be servants). This Amendment is intended to dismantle the Federalist overreach, but can only stand if the Court does its duty correctly and does not reinterpret the meanings of the words used. Thus, they are not absolute arbiters of the Constitutions and Bill of Rights' meanings. The armed citizens *always* are.

Today, the Court skirts this responsibility by claiming words can be interpreted in old documents under the current understanding.

Any competent man understands that is an unacceptable position, but the powermongers know any attempt to establish something new risks their loss of control over the old system they defiled. They will have to work hard to build a new system and will likely be exposed. This is why the Articles of Confederation and the Constitutional Convention in Philadelphia right through to the Reconstruction after the Civil War, and Amendments done during the World Wars were the paths taken to manipulate the existing structure. Easier to misuse and abuse preexisting loyalties using trusted positions than to get people to join in on an honest attempt to subvert their own will. Especially, when they a proving so docile as to refrain from harming public officials.

BILL OF RIGHTS

The Bill of Rights was intended to assure we were aware of key personal liberties no matter what the claims of the government were in its permitted powers. It also clarified additional limitations on the government from and beneath us. Though Jefferson noted the constituted powers are about foreign governments, the Union is in charge of checking the States (which are foreign to each other) against encroaching on each other's autonomous condition and most importantly the Bill of Rights is to be a statement against any of these politic bodies encroaching on the individual's autonomous condition *at all times*. The debate leading to this was intense.

In *Federalist 38* Madison wrote:

> This one tells us that the proposed Constitution ought to be rejected, because it is not a confederation of the States, but a government over individuals. Another admits that it ought to be a government over individuals to a certain extent, but by no means to the extent proposed. A third does not object to the government over individuals, or to the extent proposed, but to the want of a bill of rights. A fourth concurs in the absolute necessity of a bill of rights, but contends that it ought to be declaratory, not of the personal rights of individuals, but of the rights reserved to the States in their political capacity. A fifth is of opinion that a bill of rights of any sort would be superfluous and misplaced, and that the plan would be unexceptionable but for the fatal power of regulating the times and places of election.

Notice the immediate concern that the government commands individuals and the discernment that a Confederation does not? Notice the excuses made by some (according to Madison) that this new Constitution is okay to govern individuals? Notice liberty of the individual is outnumbered *four to one*? This is why the Republican Guarantee and the Blessing of Liberty protection in the Preamble are so important. It places the construct under the people. In *Federalist 49* Madison states:

> If we resort for a criterion to the different principles on which different forms of government are established, we may define a republic to be, or at least may bestow that name on, a government which derives all its powers directly or indirectly from the great body of the people, and is administered by persons holding their offices during pleasure, for a limited period, or during good behavior. It is ESSENTIAL to such a government that it be derived from the great body of the society, not from an inconsiderable proportion, or a favored class of it; otherwise a handful of tyrannical nobles, exercising their oppressions by a delegation of their powers, might aspire to the rank of republicans, and claim for their government the honorable title of republic. It is SUFFICIENT for such a government that the persons administering it be appointed, either directly or indirectly, by the people; and that they hold their appointments by either of the tenures just specified; otherwise every government in the United States, as well as every other popular government that has been or can be well organized or well executed, would be degraded from the republican character.

In noting the apparatus receiving its power form "the body of the people" Madison and other republican founders are reducing the ability for government to claim its position by some other power. The Union had to have permission from the States. The State had to have been formed by some representation of the People. Unfortunately, Madison's oversimplification for the common man ignores the factor that the people individually must consent in the end, however that is also considered common knowledge due to... the Declaration of Independence. Generally, kings and churches claimed the power to govern from God's imbuement of them or arbitrary public perception. This echo's back to Frederick the Great's position as the "First Servant of the People." The people are then, again, understood by these Founders as persons, who are individuals, who are always free, but those in office are not. Thus, the concern the new construct would allow the office to more govern the individual. As happened in Polybius's day in Rome.

Also, we find Madison notes the stipulation of "Good Behavior." During this book's drafting President Donald Trump was facing impeachment. His supporters claimed it unconstitutional. As you read it is not, and if the Congress (which is either House) find the President to be behaving poorly or having poor character they can, starting in the House of Representatives, impeach him.

Do you disagree with this point? In a letter to Thomas Jefferson, Madison wrote in finding a Bill of Rights to be unimportant:[103]

> 1. because I conceive that in a certain degree,
> though not in the extent argued by Mr. Wilson,
> the rights in question are reserved by the manner
> in which the federal powers are granted. 2.
> because there is great reason to fear that a positive
> declaration of some of the most essential rights
> could not be obtained in the requisite latitude. I
> am sure that the rights of Conscience in particular,
> if submitted to public definition would be
> narrowed much more than they are likely ever to
> be by an assumed power. One of the objections in
> New England was that the Constitution by
> prohibiting religious tests opened a door for Jews
> Turks & infidels. 3. because the limited powers of
> the federal Government and the jealousy of the
> subordinate Governments, afford a security which
> has not existed in the case of the State

---

[103] https://founders.archives.gov/documents/Madison/01-11-02-0218

Governments, and exists in no other. 4 because experience proves the inefficacy of a bill of rights on those occasions when its controul is most needed. Repeated violations of these parchment barriers have been committed by overbearing majorities in every State. In Virginia I have seen the bill of rights violated in every instance where it has been opposed to a popular current. Notwithstanding the explicit provision contained in that instrument for the rights of Conscience it is well known that a religious establishment wd. have taken place in that State, if the legislative majority had found as they expected, a majority of the people in favor of the measure; and I am persuaded that if a majority of the people were now of one sect, the measure would still take place and on narrower ground than was then proposed, notwithstanding the additional obstacle which the law has since created. Wherever the real power in a Government lies, there is the danger of oppression. In our Governments the real power lies in the majority of the Community, and the invasion of private rights is chiefly to be apprehended, not from acts of Government contrary to the sense of its constituents, but from acts in which the Government is the mere instrument of the major number of the constituents.

Not only do we see the concern of religious overreach and Madison notes it's constantly happening, but it does so in the face of the fact there is a Bill of Rights in place. The law willfully ignored for the whims of *the majority,* another piece of evidence the Founders did not like democracy. Madison supplies no legitimate position as to how a Bill of Rights would be enforced or how corruption would be stopped, though in his other works he implies the best remedy is constant new charters. Basically, by creating new bodies out of the lands, society's communities can protect their liberty and nullify popular government control over them. Unlike Jefferson, Madison didn't have much in the way of guts for certain fights. Jefferson's early works are clear on our need to have *armed* rebellions like the revolution every 20 years—though in his old age his want to secure a legacy weakened his fortitude to this way, in my view. His early opinion was soaked in the realities of how a republic is secured. To that, Jefferson ended up being for a Bill of Rights. In response to Madison's point above Jefferson wrote on a Bill of Rights:[104]

1. That the rights in question are reserved by the manner in which the federal powers are granted. Answer. A constitutive act may certainly be so formed as to need no declaration of rights. The act itself has the force of a declaration as far as it goes: and if it goes to all material points nothing more is wanting. In the draught of a constitution which I had once a thought of proposing in Virginia, and printed afterwards, I endeavored to reach all the great objects of public liberty and did not mean to add a declaration of rights. Probably the object was imperfectly executed: but the deficiencies would have been supplied by others in the course of discussion. But in a constitutive act which leaves some precious articles unnoticed, and raises implications against others, a declaration of rights becomes necessary by way of supplement. This is the case of our new federal constitution. This instrument forms us into one state as to certain objects, and gives us a legislative and executive body for these objects. It should therefore guard us against their abuses of power within the field submitted to them. **2. A positive declaration of some essential rights could not be obtained in the requisite latitude.** Answer. Half a loaf is better than no bread. If we cannot secure all our rights, let us secure what we can. **3. The limited powers of the federal government and**

**jealousy of the subordinate governments afford
a security which exists in no other instance.**
Answer. The first member of this seems resolvable
into the 1st. objection before stated. The jealousy
of the subordinate governments is a precious
reliance. But observe that those governments are
only agents. They must have principles furnished
them whereon to found their opposition. The
declaration of rights will be the text whereby they
will try all the acts of the federal government. In
this view it is necessary to the federal government
also: as by the same text they may try the
opposition of the subordinate governments. **4.
Experience proves the inefficacy of a bill of
rights.** True. But tho it is not absolutely efficacious
under all circumstances, it is of great potency
always, and rarely inefficacious. A brace the more
will often keep up the building which would have
fallen with that brace the less. There is a
remarkeable difference between the characters of
the Inconveniencies which attend a Declaration of
rights, and those which attend the want of it. The
inconveniences of the Declaration are that it may
cramp government in it's useful exertions. But the
evil of this is shortlived, moderate, and reparable.
The inconveniencies of the want of a Declaration
are permanent, afflicting and irreparable: they are
in constant progression from bad to worse. The
executive in our governments is not the sole, it is
scarcely the principal object of my jealousy. The
tyranny of the legislatures is the most formidable
dread at present, and will be for long years. That
of the executive will come in its turn, but it will be
at a remote period. I know there are some among
us who would now establish a monarchy. But
they are inconsiderable in number and weight of
character. The rising race are all republicans. We
were educated in royalism: no wonder if some of
us retain that idolatry still. Our young people are
educated in republicanism. An apostacy from that

301

> to royalism is unprecedented and impossible. I am
> much pleased with the prospect that a declaration
> of rights will be added: and hope it will be done in
> that way which will not endanger the whole frame
> of the government, or any essential part of it.

Did you catch that?

"The jealousy of the subordinate governments is a precious reliance. But observe that those governments are only agents."

Meaning they are dependent on the direction of the people in their States so if those people have too much loyalty to the popular (national) government don't expect a resistance to federal overreach, and don't expect States to not coup for control of the General Government over the others. I added extended parts of the letter, so we could see Jefferson had serious concerns over the Congress's power. He was troubled greatly by lack of restraints on the Presidency, concerns which have all to come to fruition, but the legislature meddling in State and personal affairs was a much larger concern. If you note, he worries of the tyranny of the legislature. As we've gone over, *tyranny is minority rule through ruthless majority power.*

Jefferson downplays those in the legislature later responsible for the tyranny he fears as being few and not influential enough. Recall my note from him above about who the anti-republicans were, and we may see how unfortunately wrong he was on this point. Yet, he also is clear his generation is steeped in monarchial teaching (royalism), and that is those of youth more aware of republic. Juxtapose this to today's youth who are fully indoctrinated to Social Statism. As their great grandparents were long ago. But a handful today understand real "republicanism."

To back my point on why the Constitution and any government naturally binds to only it's agents anyways, and why the Constitution is criminal since the Articles of Confederation were binding on it; Patrick Henry stated before the Virginia Convention on the New Constitution for the union:

There are certain maxims by which every wise and enlightened people will regulate their conduct. There are certain political maxims which no free people ought ever to abandon—maxims of which the observance is essential to the security of happiness. It is impiously irritating the avenging hand of Heaven, when a people, who are in the full enjoyment of freedom, launch out into the wide ocean of human affairs, and desert those maxims which alone can preserve liberty. Such maxims, humble as they are, are those only which can render a nation safe or formidable. Poor little humble republican maxims have attracted the admiration, and engaged the attention, of the virtuous and wise in all nations, and have stood the shock of ages. We do not now admit the validity of maxims which we once delighted in. We have since adopted maxims of a different, but more refined nature —new maxims, which tend to the prostration of republicanism.

We have one, sir, that all men are by nature free and independent, and have certain inherent rights, of which, when they enter into society, they cannot by any compact deprive or divest their posterity. We have a set of maxims of the same spirit, which must be beloved by every friend to liberty, to virtue, to mankind: our bill of rights contains those admirable maxims.

In this case he is speaking of the Virginia Bill Of Rights, but as a guide as to the reason and need for the Bill of Rights against the new federal government being designed. He also mentions a clear point as to why I noted the Constitution was criminal in this same speech where he said:[105]

---

[105] http://teachingamericanhistory.org/library/document/speech-delivered-at-the-virginia-convention-debate-of-the-ratification-of-the-constitution-june-7-1788/

The honorable member tells us, then, that there
are burnings and discontents in the hearts of our
citizens in general, and that they are dissatisfied
with their government. I have no doubt the
honorable member believes this to be the case,
because he says so. But I have the comfortable
assurance that it is certain fact that it is not so. The
middle and lower ranks of people have not those
illuminated ideas which the well-born are so
happily possessed of; they cannot so readily
perceive latent objects. The microscopic eyes of
modern statesmen can see abundance of defects in
old systems; and their illuminated imaginations
discover the necessity of a change.

In other words, the politician imagines need for change from the
Confederation, because his desires in using the government are not
being obtained in the Confederation. So, they want a change to a more
national system, so their position is important. As such, men like
Henry demand a Bill of Rights to lock the coming leviathan down, at
least in the mind of the people it will aim to control. I highly
recommend reading this speech on June 7th, 1788 at the Virginia
Convention in its entirety, so you can see Henry's comparison and
definition of a republic.

We'll get to the Bill of Rights in a moment. First there are some
other key ways majority rule was minimized for the assurance of
liberty and so States maintained operational sovereignty.

An opt-ed by Walter E. Williams, Professor at George Mason
University gives a rather decent run down:

The Founders expressed contempt for the tyranny
of majority rule, and throughout our Constitution,
they placed impediments to that tyranny. Two
houses of Congress pose one obstacle to majority
rule. That is, 51 senators can block the wishes of
435 representatives and 49 senators.

The president can veto the wishes of 535 members of Congress. It takes two-thirds of both houses of Congress to override a presidential veto.

To change the Constitution requires not a majority but a two-thirds vote of both houses, and if an amendment is approved, it requires ratification by three-fourths of state legislatures.

Finally, the Electoral College is yet another measure that thwarts majority rule. It makes sure that the highly populated states—today, mainly 12 on the east and west coasts, cannot run roughshod over the rest of the nation. That forces a presidential candidate to take into consideration the wishes of the other 38 states.

This is important to focus on for at the time of writing this book a movement has occurred to try to abolish the Electoral College. Proponents of the action are essentially trying to get State legislatures to pass bills abolishing it, by giving a winner-takes-all mandate to the Electors, citing Supreme Court rulings that States are supposedly free to determine how their electoral is divvied up. So, this is where I will now address Section 1 of the Article II of the U.S. Constitution.

Here's the Deal. Unless you are an Elector, *you do not elect the president of the United States directly at all!* Period. No, it doesn't matter what your state has passed in the last 200 years or what the Supreme Court has interpreted in the line "Each State shall appoint, in such Manner as the Legislature thereof may direct." Public elections are just supposed to give the State Legislature an idea of who you want to be your Elector's choice from your State. And though the States can hold elections for Electors, the Electors pick the President. Let's look at two parts of the U.S. Constitution on elections:

Election for President of the United States:

Section 1.

The executive Power shall be vested in a President of the United States of America. He shall hold his Office during the Term of four Years, and, together with the Vice President, chosen for the same Term, be elected, as follows:

Each State shall appoint, in such Manner as the Legislature thereof may direct, a Number of Electors, equal to the whole Number of Senators and Representatives to which the State may be entitled in the Congress: but no Senator or Representative, or Person holding an Office of Trust or Profit under the United States, shall be appointed an Elector.

This is the 12th Amendment version:

The Electors shall meet in their respective states and vote by ballot for President and Vice-President, one of whom, at least, shall not be an inhabitant of the same state with themselves; they shall name in their ballots the person voted for as President, and in distinct ballots the person voted for as Vice-President, and they shall make distinct lists of all persons voted for as President, and of all persons voted for as Vice-President, and of the number of votes for each, which lists they shall sign and certify, and transmit sealed to the seat of the government of the United States, directed to the President of the Senate; -- the President of the Senate shall, in the presence of the Senate and House of Representatives, open all the certificates and the votes shall then be counted; -- The person

having the greatest number of votes for President,
shall be the President, if such number be a
majority of the whole number of Electors
appointed; and if no person have such majority,
then from the persons having the highest numbers
not exceeding three on the list of those voted for
as President, the House of Representatives shall
choose immediately, by ballot, the President. But
in choosing the President, the votes shall be taken
by states, the representation from each state
having one vote; a quorum for this purpose shall
consist of a member or members from two-thirds
of the states, and a majority of all the states shall
be necessary to a choice. [And if the House of
Representatives shall not choose a President
whenever the right of choice shall devolve upon
them, before the fourth day of March next
following, then the Vice-President shall act as
President, as in case of the death or other
constitutional disability of the President. --]* The
person having the greatest number of votes as
Vice-President, shall be the Vice-President, if such
number be a majority of the whole number of
Electors appointed, and if no person have a
majority, then from the two highest numbers on
the list, the Senate shall choose the Vice-President;
a quorum for the purpose shall consist of two-
thirds of the whole number of Senators, and a
majority of the whole number shall be necessary
to a choice. But no person constitutionally
ineligible to the office of President shall be eligible
to that of Vice-President of the United States.

Here the Electors are to come out of or to be sent by the State
Legislatures determined by state law, including the empowering of
the public to vote for the Electors. Electors have to be sent because
they have to elect two persons. So, they can't be given as a whole for
a State or as party-preferred winners. They have to be done by the
sending State's standards under the requirement an Elector, *picks two*

people, but one for President or Vice President must be from outside their State. Anyone who they want, regardless of what the popular opinion of the rest of the State is. Electors decide the President *as they are the Electors*. Just as Fredrick William the Great Elector was so because of his influence in the selection of the Roman Emperor. Kings in the Vatican days were the premier vote givers for the Roman Emperor from the Church's held regions. They were the representation for the region's voice. Your Elector is from your Legislature to the servants of the Constituted Government. Almost anyone can be an elector in the U.S. The biggest problem is that the parties have stolen the Electors into their primary process to elect their party guy, not the best person from your state (anyone 35 years of age and a natural born citizen) as it is supposed to be. The parties must be routed to redeem the election system.

Put another way, the electors are to act independently for the State in deciding who presides over the House and Senate… and military *when called forth*. Therefore, the President is the chief law enforcer, to first and foremost intimidate the Congressmen from conspiring against the Constitution and undermining the States.[106]

> The Senate will represent the States in their political capacity, the other House will represent the people of the States in their individual capacity. The former will be accountable to their constituents at moderate, the latter at short periods. The President also derives his appointment from the States, and is periodically accountable to them.

(The Congress may determine the Time of choosing the Electors, and the Day on which they shall give their Votes; which Day shall be the same throughout the United States.)

Pretty self-explanatory, yet some still think this means Congress can decide election protocols. No. That's already defined in the above section. So all the things you hear about nullifying elections, or

---

[106] James Madison,
https://founders.archives.gov/documents/Jefferson/01-12-02-0274

decertifying, or holding new elections are nullified already by the fact the Constitution *defines* the election process, and the power of Congress to impeach criminals holding office and remove them. You don't like that? Tough! That's the *real* law around U.S. elections.

I'm going to take this opportunity to address another aspect of the President's position and qualification to hold office:

PRESIDENTIAL ELIGIBILITY

> No Person except a natural born Citizen, or a
> Citizen of the United States, at the time of the
> Adoption of this Constitution, shall be eligible to
> the Office of President; neither shall any Person be
> eligible to that Office who shall not have attained
> to the Age of thirty five Years, and been fourteen
> Years a Resident within the United States.

I really don't want to spend long on this because the basics of this entire work already address this issue. The truth is about the only thing I have not defined for you is the term *natural born*. The fact is, they like to use it interchangeably with *natural*, but it's clear when observing usage and taking into consideration the likelihood that the Founders who used the term *inhabitant* in every other position in the U.S. Constitution meant something specific by *natural born*.

So here it is simply stated. A *natural born Citizen* is a person born to a native mother and native father—two U.S. citizens born in the U.S. of American citizens, naturalized or otherwise. One parent being a U.S. citizen does not meet the need. I had a British man lose his mind at the idea of this when I said it on my old radio show. Several sources make it clear: John Bingham, "father of the 14th Amendment," in a comment that is actually quoting Emmerich Vattel's *Law of Nations* said:

> The natives, or natural-born citizens, are those
> born in the country, of parents who are citizens.

Keyword: "parents." Not father alone. Father alone has a lot to do with native citizens in the old works, but I believe the use of "or" relates the term parents more directly with the term *natural born citizen* and it makes the most sense of assuring the head of the military is directly of American stock.

A *naturalized* person clearly isn't a native or natural citizen. They've been given the rights of an American by statute, yet no expert would think a naturalized citizen would be like a natural-born citizen and free to be President after residing in the U.S. for 14 years. It would just be nonsensical and counterintuitive to any level of domestic security. Many think it applies to any person born in the U.S. to a U.S. citizen, or just born on U.S. soil. Again, I think this is counterintuitive to any level of domestic security. It seems reasonable that a naturalized and native-born American could hold any of the other offices for their positions are clearly limited in what they can do and what it takes for them to qualify for office, but since a naturalized cannot hold the presidency, I do not think it makes sense that the child of that one would be able to hold the office of the presidency either.

There are a lot of sources that pretty well act as though the definition used by those who think the 14th Amendment and current "experts" is wholly dependent on if/when the Supreme Court directly addresses this term specifically to the presidency. Since that has not been done, I'm going to be that arrogant scholar and say I'm right. Your parents need to be born American citizens for you to be President, and we'll move on from there.

Now, back to the Bill of Rights.

The Bill of Rights is agreed to in the end as being needed. For, even State Sovereignty is not to override personal independence, natural liberty, or the right of persons to freely protest. Freedom of protest in assembly is an absolute must in *every single* Liberty Republic. So, the Bill of Rights intended on providing the people with a guard of some kind against what was being designed. So government couldn't refuse them the power to meet up, or openly petition grievances and such.

THE AMENDMENTS

The amendments passed read as:

Amendment I

Congress shall make no law respecting an establishment of religion, or prohibiting the free exercise thereof; or abridging the freedom of speech, or of the press; or the right of the people peaceably to assemble, and to petition the Government for a redress of grievances.

Amendment II

A well-regulated Militia, being necessary to the security of a free State, the right of the people to keep and bear Arms, shall not be infringed.

Amendment III

No Soldier shall, in time of peace be quartered in any house, without the consent of the Owner, nor in time of war, but in a manner to be prescribed by law.

Amendment IV

The right of the people to be secure in their persons, houses, papers, and effects, against unreasonable searches and seizures, shall not be violated, and no Warrants shall issue, but upon probable cause, supported by Oath or affirmation, and particularly describing the place to be searched, and the persons or things to be seized.

Amendment V

No person shall be held to answer for a capital, or otherwise infamous crime, unless on a presentment or indictment of a Grand Jury, except in cases arising in the land or naval forces, or in the Militia, when in actual service in time of War or public danger; nor shall any person be subject for the same offence to be twice put in jeopardy of life or limb; nor shall be compelled in any criminal case to be a witness against himself, nor be deprived of life, liberty, or property, without due process of law; nor shall private property be taken for public use, without just compensation.

Amendment VI

In all criminal prosecutions, the accused shall enjoy the right to a speedy and public trial, by an impartial jury of the State and district wherein the crime shall have been committed, which district shall have been previously ascertained by law, and to be informed of the nature and cause of the accusation; to be confronted with the witnesses against him; to have compulsory process for obtaining witnesses in his favor, and to have the Assistance of Counsel for his defence.

Amendment VII

In Suits at common law, where the value in controversy shall exceed twenty dollars, the right of trial by jury shall be preserved, and no fact tried by a jury, shall be otherwise re-examined in any Court of the United States, than according to the rules of the common law.

Amendment VIII

Excessive bail shall not be required, nor excessive fines imposed, nor cruel and unusual punishments inflicted.

Amendment IX

The enumeration in the Constitution, of certain rights, shall not be construed to deny or disparage others retained by the people.

Amendment X

The powers not delegated to the United States by the Constitution, nor prohibited by it to the States, are reserved to the States respectively, or to the people.

With comparisons to reasons for their implementation:

AMENDMENT I

Congress shall make no law respecting an establishment of religion, or prohibiting the free exercise thereof; or abridging the freedom of speech, or of the press; or the right of the people peaceably to assemble, and to petition the Government for a redress of grievances.

Many bastardize this amendment more than any other aspect of the governing doctrines. The first part is not just so the government cannot create a church like the Church of England. It is literally so the government makes no law respecting any religious position and doesn't subvert any religious adherence whatsoever. As was noted the differing sects of Christians would undermine each other with the use of terms like "Our Lord Jesus Christ," while other sects do not see him as God embodied, or "Lord." Doing so in legal writing invokes that sect's religious authority in the Spirit of the Law. A no-no in a republic, like the criminal laws that exclude a religion or church from paying taxes everyone else paid. This is respecting a religious establishment. Thomas Jefferson had even banned churches from owning land, so they wouldn't buy up swaths and institute religious cities like in Europe. It then keeps the government from favoring one faith while banning another, making no religion's practice ban-able at the government level, nor allowing any religions behavioral laws to be implemented over the whole. That, however, does not protect an anti-liberty religion from facing the tumults of war when it oppresses the free people of the republic, or the government from taking a position of war against a religion that is trying to manipulate or infiltrate the political body.

Proof to this? Jefferson Query XVII:

> By our own act of assembly of 1705, c. 30, if a person brought up in the Christian religion denies the being of a God, or the Trinity, or asserts there are more Gods than one, or denies the Christian religion to be true, or the scriptures to be of divine authority, he is punishable on the first offence by incapacity to hold any office or employment ecclesiastical, civil, or military; on the second by disability to sue, to take any gift or legacy, to be guardian, executor, or administrator, and by three years imprisonment, without bail. A father's right to the custody of his own children being founded in law on his right of guardianship, this being taken away, they may of course be severed from him, and put, by the authority of a court, into more orthodox hands. This is a summary view of that religious slavery, under which a people have been willing to remain, who have lavished their lives and fortunes for the establishment of their civil freedom.

Remember these are pro-British Common Law judges/laws:

> At the common law, heresy was a capital offence, punishable by burning. Its definition was left to the ecclesiastical judges, before whom the conviction was...

In his push for religious freedom, which he succeeded in by the passing of the Virginia Bill of Establishing Religious Freedom in 1786, he said in Query XVII:[107]

> Our sister states of Pennsylvania and New York, however, have long subsisted without any establishment (of religion) at all. The experiment was new and doubtful when they made it. It has answered beyond conception. They flourish infinitely. Religion is well supported; of various kinds, indeed, but all good enough; all sufficient to preserve peace and order: or if a sect arises, whose tenets would subvert morals, good sense has fair play, and reasons and laughs it out of doors, without suffering the state to be troubled with it. They do not hang more malefactors than we do. They are not more disturbed with religious dissensions. On the contrary, their harmony is unparalleled, and can be ascribed to nothing but their unbounded tolerance, because there is no other circumstance in which they differ from every nation on earth. They have made the happy discovery, that the way to silence religious disputes, is to take no notice of them. Let us too give this experiment fair play, and get rid, while we may, of those tyrannical laws. It is true, we are as yet secured against them by the spirit of the times. I doubt whether the people of this country would suffer an execution for heresy, or a three years imprisonment for not comprehending the mysteries of the Trinity.

Further, the 1st Amendment recognizes you can speak as you wish, insult who you wish, disperse whatever media you wish. Only

---

[107] http://teachingamericanhistory.org/library/document/notes-on-the-state-of-virginia-query-xvii-religion/

other citizens *personally* can act against you, not the government, nor the courts (without a complaint by another free individual). You can protest any political body and any entity licensed by the government (including so-called private businesses), and your petitions against the government are to not be ignored or impeded.

AMENDMENT II

A well-regulated Militia, being necessary to the security of a free State, the right of the people to keep and bear Arms, shall not be infringed.

To assure the people can respond to any threat to their personal liberty and keep their political bodies independent, the right to have a weapon in any capacity is not to be infringed. When understanding these issues do you think the Founders erred on the side of *safety* or *freedom*? Then, for this to be the case you would also have to be able to execute the law. This isn't about militia being regulated by proclamations and codes. It is about the people being at-the-ready. As such the militia cannot be a permitted body by government decree, but an active, ever-vigilant fact of the individual of the society. Some try to state it is solely about regulating the militia and making sure guns are accessible to it. However, the important part reads:

... the right of the people to keep and bear Arms, shall not be infringed.

Not "the right of the *militia* to keep and bear arms." The People *are* the militia. An opinion series sent in to the *Virginia Independent Chronicle* by an author that when by the Impartial Examiner wrote:[108]

---

[108] http://www.constitution.org/afp/impar_exam.htm

It has ever been held that standing armies in times of peace are dangerous to a free country; and no observation seems to contain more reason in it. Besides being useless, as having no object of employment, they are inconvenient and expensive. The soldiery, who are generally composed of the dregs of the people, when disbanded, or unfit for military service, being equally unfit for any other employment, become extremely burthensome. As they are a body of men exempt from the common occupations of social life, having an interest different from the rest of the community, they wanton in the lap of ease and indolence, without feeling the duties, which arise from the political connection, though drawing their subsistence from the bosom of the state. The severity of discipline necessary to be observed reduces them to a degree of slavery; the unconditional submission to the commands of their superiors, to which they are bound, renders them the fit instruments of tyranny and oppression. — Hence they have in all ages afforded striking examples of contributing, more or less, to enslave mankind; — and whoever will take the trouble to examine, will find that by far the greater part of the different nations, who have fallen from the glorious state of liberty, owe their ruin to standing armies. It has been urged that they are necessary to provide against sudden attacks. Would not a well-regulated militia, duly trained to discipline, afford ample security? Such, I conceive, to be the best, the surest means of protection, which a free people can have when not actually engaged in war. This kind of defence is attended with two advantages superior to any others; first, when it is necessary to embody an army, they at once form a band of soldiers, whose interests are uniformly the same with those of the whole community, and in whose safety they see involved everything that is dear to themselves:

> secondly, if one army is cut off, another may be
> immediately raised already trained for military
> service. By a policy, somewhat similar to this, the
> Roman empire rose to the highest pitch of
> grandeur and magnificence.

He was greatly concerned about the lack of a Bill of Rights, and though I believe this quote carries the misnomer at the end of implying the Roman Empire in place of the Republic the entire concept is sound. As you no doubt see another example of a Foundational work vindicating much of what has been described as a factor in collapsing a republic. Instituted specialized military over dispersed public military skills. The military man even today is known to be limited in his ability to think for himself. Often after retiring they are hard-pressed to find jobs in which to apply their skills, though claiming to be highly skilled in engineering, and physical labor. They have a skewed view of the society in a couple of ways.

One, they pretend to be members of the general society, yet, their conditioning is of loyalty to their brotherhood of soldiers first, making most of their well-meaning action in public events and activities more about nationalist ideals and pro-government sentiments than a true liberty mentality of personal freedom. They do not exhibit true patriotism.

Another is in the fact they often ignore the reality they receive multiple pay checks. They are accustomed to violence as their job. When they do get a "civilian" job they see themselves as working hard for what they earn based on their civilian job. They tell themselves their comfortable lifestyle is a result of this hard work. Yet, they receive a second entire paycheck they think they earned in a service they no longer render for what in any proper republic would be a duty and service rendered and pay finished after the event was completed. Not to mention it makes them welfare recipients for a field they *chose* to serve in. Without this income most couldn't afford any type of the lifestyle they are used to, which most of us don't experience as our livelihood either.

The standing army and their soldiery tend to have no other focus but war, and it will convince itself and its former servicemen that the duty they accomplish is somehow never complete and security their ever-vigilant duty, robbing you—the citizen—of your natural authority to be the first responder to invaders and insurrection, and the skills necessary for making sound judgment upon such things. A perfect environment of useful idiots for the tyrant to employ their low-minded, under-skilled mentalities to the securing of despotism over the people of a republic. As such, and when this is the case, who is to defend you if such men side with the tyrant?

There was also an argument made during the debates which noted that at one point, France was considering an invasion, but upon learning the citizens were armed and military-knowledgeable their king changed his mind. These foreign and domestic examples of threat should provide enough evidence as to the need of the average person being armed and skilled.

AMENDMENT III

> No Soldier shall, in time of peace be quartered in
> any house, without the consent of the Owner, nor
> in time of war, but in a manner to be prescribed
> by law.

The Crown would require troops be allowed to stay in private homes at a whim. This bans this, but notice the fun loophole added "but in a manner to be prescribed by law." Again, the real law is the Common Law called the Constitution. This is why so many Anti-Federalists hated how the document allowed for what the Impartial Examiner called *arbitrary government,* the power for Congress to make rules as it saw fit when it needed them. This is why the Anti-Federalist was clear that the Constitution must be interpreted *as written per intent,* and the Federalist magically finds it interpretable to the issue at hand or terminology of the current times.

Oh, these next Amendments are so fun. Why? Because if you ask a judge or a lawyer, or a cop about them they'll pretty well lie to your face. Why? Because if Amendments like the 4th and 5th were adhered to and enforced by the people most government agents would be dead.

AMENDMENT IV

The right of the people to be secure in their persons, houses, papers, and effects, against unreasonable searches and seizures, shall not be violated, and no Warrants shall issue, but upon probable cause, supported by Oath or affirmation, and particularly describing the place to be searched, and the persons or things to be seized.

You do not have to reveal information about yourself or your things. Most everything they do to make you identify yourself is criminal. They claim the license is theirs and that's why they can request it from you. The Supreme Court has found many times in the past that licensing is not lawful. This criminality includes making you pull over and expose who you are during a traffic stop, for example. In nearly every instance they must get a warrant, unless they saw the crime committed. An ordinance violation is not a crime. Crimes require a victim. The line "no Warrants shall issue, but upon probable cause, supported by Oath or affirmation" means that in order to get a warrant *from a judge* they must have likely cause stated upon a document they swear is true. They cannot act before that. The courts and agents lie about this line and literally mutilate it to claim probable cause supported by an officer's verbal claim or claim after the fact is enough for an officer to search and seize your things at the point of accusation. Bullshit!

AMENDMENT V

No person shall be held to answer for a capital, or otherwise infamous crime, unless on a presentment or indictment of a Grand Jury, except in cases arising in the land or naval forces, or in the Militia, when in actual service in time of War or public danger; nor shall any person be subject for the same offence to be twice put in jeopardy of life or limb; nor shall be compelled in any criminal case to be a witness against himself, nor be deprived of life, liberty, or property, without due process of law; nor shall private property be taken for public use, without just compensation.

Any high crime like murder, treason, or insurrection requires a jury sees the evidence and agrees to a case occurring or there is no hearing. Unless you are in the activated military, or due to a server public danger. You cannot be forced to admission against yourself (self-incrimination), which is exactly what a cop is doing when he pulls you over. He begins a case investigation in which he is accusing you, and as a government officer cannot force you to implicate yourself, which he does by saying, "License and registration?" and "You know why I pulled you over?" When a cop guns a citizen down in the street over fleeing, the citizen is "deprived of life, liberty, and property, without due process of law."

Cops are not the law. They are agents. The reality of republics and freedom is that you have ample opportunities to get away with something and the agents have few openings to bust you. Thus, why self-government is so important, because you the citizen who is a freeman and not an agent have ample opportunities to nail one another, and equal opportunities to nullify each other's actions. When this power is parted out to collective will it always rigs the rule so that it can seem justified in breaking the law, and most half-wits will praise such actions. None of this is new. The Founders were well aware of these tactics which the Crown regularly employed.

AMENDMENT VI

In all criminal prosecutions, the accused shall
enjoy the right to a speedy and public trial, by an
impartial jury of the State and district wherein the
crime shall have been committed, which district
shall have been previously ascertained by law,
and to be informed of the nature and cause of the
accusation; to be confronted with the witnesses
against him; to have compulsory process for
obtaining witnesses in his favor, and to have the
Assistance of Counsel for his defence.

Every criminal crime, which means the *capital crimes* listed above and other crimes like theft, assault, or anything where there is a *physical victim* requires it be tried quickly so the accused is returned to their freedom if innocent (which you are until proven otherwise) under a jury trial in the place where the crime was committed which must already be asserted by law. No district established before the crime occurred, no legal authority for the government to prosecute. You must be informed of the accusation, what cause led to the accusation — including the evidence against you — and by whom, a process they regularly violate as well.

When they issue a traffic offense (this is the best example to use as many have had an interaction with it) they *arraign* you at court and get a plea before any evidence is presented. They claim the ticket defines the accusation and cause against you. To put things simply here, they are required to present a proper complaint which a ticket is not. The complaint must fully define the action you did, the law you violated (you never violate a *law* in traffic matters, they are *infractions* and *violations* with no victim) and the accuser who must be the effected party. How convenient the State defines itself a victim in action which has yet to result in harm of any kind.

AMENDMENT VII

> In Suits at common law, where the value in
> controversy shall exceed twenty dollars, the right
> of trial by jury shall be preserved, and no fact tried
> by a jury, shall be otherwise re-examined in any
> Court of the United States, than according to the
> rules of the common law.

We now have three tiers of law noted capital (high crimes), criminal (anything involving harm of a victim), and now common law, customary in nature and in republic above statue law. It is the unwritten law. Many of the issues defined within the power of the Supreme Court fall under this manner and where large sums for fines or recoupment are at play a jury is assured and no fact tried by the jury can be observed beyond the power of the common law. Which means a case be judged on the merits of the issue(s) and the restrictions on the artificial managing power. Modern definition tries to imply a relation to British Common Law which is only true to the extent that Common Law is that which is generally done customarily upon such an issue as what is brought before the court. However, we are a liberty society and England isn't and was not. Customarily we address issues *republicly,* not monarchically, and so judges and juries cannot use precedence as anything other than an example. A case in our society must be decided upon based on the event/issue at-hand. So, when a citizen sues another citizen the issue at hand is weighed, the statutory laws examined, but the reality of freedom held to the highest and supreme point first and by the will of a jury. Mind you, they don't do this.

As evidence Section. 11 of the Virginia Declaration of Rights, written by George Mason says:

> That in controversies respecting property, and in
> suits between man and man, the ancient trial by
> jury is preferable to any other, and ought to be
> held sacred.

Madison wrote to Peter S. Du Ponceau on the relation of Common Law in America:

> I must say at the same time that I have not been made a Convert to the doctrine that the "Common Law" as such, is a part of the law of the U. S. in their fœdero-national capacity. I can perceive no legitimate avenue for its admission, beyond the portions fairly embraced by the Common law terms used in the Constitution, and by Acts* of Congress authorized by the Constitution as necessary & proper for executing the powers, which it vests in the Government.

He considered the Common Law reaching over all members of the Union, and... (pay close attention to this for what I've already been telling you...):[109]

> If the Common Law has been called our birth right, it has been done with little regard to any precise meaning. It could have been no more our birth right than the Statute law of England, or than the English Constitution itself. If the one was brought by our ancestors with them, so must the others; and the whole consequently as it stood during the Dynasty of the Stuarts, the period of their emigration with no other exceptions, than such as necessarily resulted from inapplicability to the colonial state of things. As men, our birth right was from a much higher source, than the Common or any other human law and of much greater extent than is imparted or admitted by the Common Law. And as far as it might belong to us as British subjects it must, with its correlative

---

[109] https://founders.archives.gov/documents/Madison/04-03-02-0353

obligations, have expired when we ceased to be such. It would seem more correct therefore, & preferable in every respect to say) that the common law, even during the Colonial State, was in force not by virtue of its adhesion to the emigrants & their descendants in their individual capacity, but by virtue of its adoption in their social & political capacity.

How far this adoption may have taken place through the mere agency of the Courts can not perhaps be readily traced. But such a mode of introducing laws not otherwise in force ought rather to be classed among the irregularities incident to the times & the occasion, than referred to any rightful jurisdiction of those Tribunals.

Read this letter. He is very clear on the same thing I have noted for you prior and this position is echoed by most influential Founders. The Common Law (capitalized) of Britain has nothing to with us, but for its followers' own deceitful claims to garner authority where it didn't rest. In the Alien Sedition Acts he makes the point the common law includes the Ecclesiastic Laws, and that since we are not *one* community this cannot be held across all States and municipalities, another point to the reality we're not religiously bound to one type of religious law or nationalism.

In our case, the common law is that of *liberty*. What assures a man is not wrongly imprisoned or robbed? What assures personal freedom of the individual? What assures an autonomous community? These would be the key primary intentions behind anyone ascertaining the American "common law." The jury can nullify a law if it is inapplicable to the case or not within the powers of the court's assigned power by the common law, which is the power of the sovereign individuals jurying the case—as always in Natural Law which overrides everything.

AMENDMENT VIII

> Excessive bail shall not be required, nor excessive
> fines imposed, nor cruel and unusual
> punishments inflicted.

You can't be thrown in the iron maiden, tortured, held by an unpayable amount, or fined an unpayable amount risking you ending up out of freedom imprisoned for any "crime." This is to minimize indentured servitude and liberty violations. Obviously, history is riddled with examples of the king or the church (as noted in the Jefferson quote under the 1st Amendment breakdown) of destroying people for personal belief and political opinion which threatened the despotic construct. Further, consider the amounts charged for most traffic and code violations nowadays. Hundreds to thousands of dollars aren't "excessive fines imposed"?

In a lot of these Amendments you should notice a reinforcement of Solon Law. For example, the empowerment of the banking system at one point brought debtor prisons back to much of Europe. Such a prison is extremely criminal in a republic and robs a man of real freedom for perceived valuable non-living things, a value standard many republics understood was a form of madness.

AMENDMENT IX

> The enumeration in the Constitution, of certain
> rights, shall not be construed to deny or disparage
> others retained by the people.

The listing of the rights in the Constitution (or the Bill of Rights) does not allow for any right to be undermined from the people that isn't listed. It also has powers to act against someone who interferes with government permitted powers. Those powers cannot impede any not defined. Yet, the fact is this is a Bill of Restricted Rights on the government. As a republic, if the government can do it, the people can do it. If an official has a right, *you the citizen* have the right. More importantly, where government may have power to effect property or finances of membered States or agents, the property protections of the individual's holdings are absolute and not to be considered applicable. Thus, a nod to how the government's rules managing its agents' rights do not apply to non-agents… You. For if you can do it, government cannot intrinsically do it. If it's not listed government cannot necessarily punish one for infringing upon it.

AMENDMENT X

> The powers not delegated to the United States by the Constitution, nor prohibited by it to the States, are reserved to the States respectively, or to the people.

Anything the Union was not told it could do in the specific words in the Constitution or authorities the States gave up, the State, or the people personally can do. This is why soooo many Anti-Federalists desired the Constitution speak plainly and leave no vague loopholes for implying power where it had none. The people being at liberty can do anything the government can and can't do, but the States membered in the Union are absolutely limited in their power by the Union they joined and the powers they gave up to the General Government for protections the Union assures the people, first.

There is an additional power the People retain that the States do not. That is, no State or States may form a new State without the permission of Congress. Specifically, Article IV Section 3 of the U.S. Constitution says:

> Section. 3. New States may be admitted by the Congress into this Union; but no new State shall be formed or erected within the Jurisdiction of any other State; nor any State be formed by the

Junction of two or more States, or Parts of States,
without the Consent of the Legislatures of the
States concerned as well as of the Congress.

This section applies to the forming of a State by a State/States and
the Union. The People can freely establish a new state at any time for
they are over the jurisdiction of a State, not under it. This goes back
to Madison's and other Founders' resistance to consolidation and
charters. One way he discussed this was in Charters:

As compacts, charters of government are superior
in obligation to all others, because they give effect
to all others. As truths, none can be more sacred,
because they are bound, on the conscience by the
religious sanctions of an oath. As metes and
bounds of government, they transcend all other
land-marks, because every public usurpation is an
encroachment on the private right, not of one, but
of all.

Being republicans, they must be anxious to
establish the efficacy of popular charters, in
defending liberty against power, and power
against licentiousness; and in keeping every
portion of power within its proper limits; by this
means discomforting the partizans of anti-
republican contrivances for the purpose.

And...

How devoutly is it to be wished, then, that the
public opinion of the United States should be
enlightened; that it should attach itself to their
governments as delineated in great charters,

derived not from the usurped power of kings, but
from the legitimate authority of the people;[110]

The idea of a Bill of Rights is sound. It makes since to addendum
in clarity to the populace their un-waiverable power and immutable
protection from that which serves them. Yet, what do people think
enforces such a thing? Do they really believe outing those violating
such a doctrine is going to make those violators snap to sanity with,
"Oh my! So sorry! Whatever was I thinking?" Do most think it is self-
enforcing? That the page itself will jump to life, cut down
perpetrators, or shout in a court, "Hear ye, Hear ye! I am the Bill of
Rights protector of the people!"? It often appears so.

The Bill of Rights is literally violated every minute of every day
by the government. But the *only thing* that can enforce a Bill of Rights
are *those it applies to protecting,* and they must be ready to use force at
a moment's notice, for the auxiliary given a power will often use its
force much more quickly than the individual. There is no regress
before a corrupt body, especially one well-versed in law and well-
aware of such a doctrine's existence, as it would then be clear they are
already knowingly and likely happily violating the protection.

Only forceful reprisal will snap them into fear to behave.

I cringe at how many times someone who thinks the best methods
in rights redemption are to "use the rules of the courts against the
courts" and not for things to be stated in the court on the *record* that
the judge is aiding the court in violating a liberty. Judicites love to say,
"The judges do not like being made fools of, or being exposed in open
court to their treason against the Bill of Rights" which really means
you're just a slave playing by the master's current rules. In these
people's minds it is actually better to allow the abuse to continue and
accept some disempowerment to their real position and power of
immutability if it be quietly, and officially gets you off. Then it is to
make a loud stink on the record exposing the corrupt against the
actual law and being (criminally) held in contempt or directly
punished under our natural personal authority. Oh, and don't you

---

[110] http://oll.libertyfund.org/titles/madison-the-writings-vol-6-1790-
1802

dare be aware of your right to kill the criminal judges for their insurrection, because in the mind of the judicite that's what they want... Because you see how violence never works in controlling criminals in government and public... Except in every republic... Ever.

THE FINAL OUTCOME

The final outcome of the Constitution wasn't America's real success. Though the public flourished in many cities throughout the Union, rights violations in those cities were pretty regular. On the upside, in most places people were able to innovate and advance. They knew their rights from encroachment by authority for a long time and could get the court to submit. The great prize was knowledge of liberty in the peoples' minds. Especially, those who wanted to branch out into the frontier. They're our next greatest success. The Wild West is where many of the processes noted in this work so far were the regular operation for anyone there needing to bring justice to a situation. For example, the process of personally bringing in an accused, and filing complaints personally.

The division caused by Federalists caused in the old Revolutionary States eventually lead to massive Civil War, a war engineered to expand the system and enslave whichever side lost to some level of central government. In other words, it didn't matter which side won, the goal by most leaders was stronger central control. I would love to expand on this event, but it lacks the realities of republic and the trust that the event unfolded honestly is too ingrained in the general public. Suffice it to say, it was very much the Communist Revolution Karl Marx called for in 1848. Leadership on both sides were likely influenced by foreign socialist elements to some extent. Look into the 48'ers and know these were the opposite of everything you just learned about in the Anti-Federalists, and were people accepting of Federal power who were flooding here at the time they were uprising in Europe. They were very used to accepting centralized power in Romanic Germany and the Old World. In the end, the Federal Government swallowed up State powers and the people were made subjects under the unlawful 14th Amendment, which as already noted, Polk vetoed, and the Congress criminally deemed as passed.

After this act of insurrection to the Law of the Land, the public being stressed, abused into military service, and dependent on government, became ignorant in their powers over the government, and criminal laws using subjugation were regularly upheld by Federal sympathetic judges. All in less than 80 years.

Banks and businesses then were able to more influence the government. The barons of the Era of Progressivism are evidence of this. Capitalism ran amuck in to corporateering, its natural evolutionary conclusion, and merchants using the bank system swept up the people into the maelstrom of tyranny though industrially-produced conveniences and provided needs they had to work for others to gain. We get focused on the advancements they made, but abuses by the likes of Big Oil, and Ma Bell's monopolization (which many Founders always desired an amendment to protect against) allowed for large power grabs, and public theatre made the appearance of these bodies being broken up seem like a citizens' wins. When in many cases the former owners just ended up on the boards of most the branch entities and were paying off the elected official that drafted the rules against their monopolies.

The greatest example of how corporate America of the late 1800's into 1900's was nothing but a merchant theft of invention, innovation, and personal freedom, is the theft, concealing, and destruction of inventions and innovations by people like Nikola Tesla, by patenteers like Thomas Edison, and later the U.S. intelligence agencies, and the subversion of inventions like the Stanley steamer (the water powered engine), advancements to make us comfortable were put out, because the fact is American fascists realized early on *a happy slave is peaceful slave*. Anything that would allow one to succeed independently, like say personal power generators so we're not on a joint grid, were buried.

Yet, the need to maintain a work force in a communist style of authority over the individual, where the people doing the jobs felt they needed to work and bring in income to live, versus a life prior where people grew their own food, and provided their own raiment, became our norm due to ignorant and dependent city dwellers. Freemen, who once could do the basic of most skills needed to keep their homes up and feed their families, have since been specialized into unions and compartmentalized private and public fields of employment instead of making modern skills — general skills taught in public education, creating a public incapable of operating in multiple fields with multiple attributes to be able to competently govern their own lives. Actions committed by tyrants you'll notice you've already read about in the history of other republics as to maintain their power.

Since the Civil War, every national emergency, coupled with international entanglement (which our Founders were very clear we were to stay out of) have expanded Federal power. A power that in no way, shape, or form lawfully exists in this republic. The military is a strong standing army consisting of men who—socialized and brainwashed—believe they stand against communism, socialism, and enemies of the people, all while having everything from their paycheck to their gear supplied from the public treasury (the commonly held wealth of the public) but materiel denied to the people at large for this preferred class of persons. Making the military, effectively, a communist organization that will secure the State before it secures you. If you said to yourself, but "They have to pay for their gear!" Some of it. Which they do with a paycheck... from the public treasury. Them paying something out is a psychological tactic to make them feel they have put additional monetary skin into the game.

Now, sure I have noted all long a republic pays for the armories via public funds to be readied, and it can fund the troops. However, *they are not a standing military force*. They are freemen who are not to still be paid by the public after their mission is accomplished. If they cannot end the enemy, it does not mean they can be ever-standing in case of the threat. For as armed freemen they are always that.

The *official* State militias that would have stood against such usurpations were happily handed over by the States to Federal "Government" as part of the criminally Standing Army under the guise of a "National Guard."

The politicians work tirelessly to expand their power, complaining there is always more to be done when they have very little to lawfully do. The State governments are in cahoots via political parties that have unified the local, state, and national political bodies under regulations of election and governing operations they co-operatively agreed to while pitting the voters against each other in their Orwellian nightmare. The whole way using the judiciary to nullify the Purpose of the Constitution under legal jargon disguised as rightful power delegated under no authority but for their own opinion and the will of whatever party the judicial hack is attached to. All of this is protected by a jealous public of party members all wanting to use the government to their own ends of what they think the best behavior of individuals is. Cowards screaming for their preferred tyranny. A People who wave flags every 4th of July feigning independence while praising their government, all ignorant of the fact that their forefathers restricted the government power, and never wanted the People to trust it to do what was best.

> "God forbid we should ever be twenty years
> without such a rebellion."
>
> —Thomas Jefferson

Standards of Education in Republic

Education

Speaking of the people's ignorance, we must take quick recap of the Lycurgan standards. The people both need to be the military force, capable of fighting, and the provider of goods, which Americans *were*, and though once forced to be in a battalion, the true tenets of a free society would be to make the tool of war available to anyone interested in practicing military tactics at any time, as well as publicly announcing whenever a (public) training drill is being held. Such drills amount to a necessary skill—knowing how to fight or understanding battle tactics.

More important than understanding battle tactics is being competent in language, history, mathematics, and sciences. The American education system is based on Jefferson's call for *diffused knowledge:*

> Whereas it appeareth that however certain forms of government are better calculated than others to protect individuals in the free exercise of their natural rights, and are at the same time themselves better guarded against degeneracy, yet experience hath shewn, that even under the best forms, those entrusted with power have, in time, and by slow operations, perverted it into tyranny; and it is believed that the most effectual means of preventing this would be, to illuminate, as far as practicable, the minds of the people at large, and more especially to give them knowledge of those facts, which history exhibiteth, that, possessed thereby of the experience of other ages and countries, they may be enabled to know ambition

under all its shapes, and prompt to exert their
natural powers to defeat its purposes; And
whereas it is generally true that that people will be
happiest whose laws are best, and are best
administered, and that laws will be wisely
formed, and honestly administered, in proportion
as those who form and administer them are wise
and honest; whence it becomes expedient for
promoting the publick happiness that those
person, whom nature hath endowed with genius
and virtue, should be rendered by liberal
education worthy to receive, and able to guard the
sacred deposit of the rights and liberties of their
fellow citizens, and that they should be called to
that charge without regard to wealth, birth or
other accidental condition or circumstance; but the
indigence of the greater number disabling them
from so educating, at their own expence, those of
their children whom nature hath fitly formed and
disposed to become useful instruments for the
public, it is better that such should be sought for
and educated at the common expence of all, than
that the happiness of all should be confided to the
weak or wicked:[111]

As we read with Sparta, diffused knowledge was an invaluable
public trust. However, it can and currently is being used for evil. A
State-forced education easily begins to indoctrinate the student in the
way of the government by the existing rulers' standards, and not
necessarily by the intention of the foundations of the society.

Jefferson's concept was that the first few years of education
through a public structure was just the basic of the above-mentioned
curriculum. After that it was up to parents to get their children better
educated. This could be done by private tutors and private schools
whose funding is done privately or provided through grants from a

---

[111] Thomas Jefferson, "A Bill for the More General Diffusion of
Knowledge"

multitude of sources. The local municipalities can offer extended public schooling, but as per any republic, anything funded by public treasury is to be accessible to the public, from elementary to university facilities. However, you can't force people to fund it. Which is not what we do. Today if you don't fund the local school, which is often done through forced property taxation, your land and assets are criminally seized by the government. How is that in line with the Founding intentions? We can bet Jefferson would not support such schemes.

His intention was to assure the ability for one to examine information personally and determine the truth in it themselves, that an education in liberty would grow the freedom the revolution fought for, and to help one better understand the limitations on the political body created, industries, sciences, and the religions all at play too. In fact, as I write this book, the political battle of parents angry about leftists teaching their children about sexual orientations is hot. The reality is, not only should teachers not discuss their sexual leaning and personal "gender" choices, but the only reason the government at any level has the ability of legislation for or against such things started with religious conservatives violating the purpose of public education to impress their viewpoint and beliefs that induce thinking the U.S. is a nation of Christian laws. The Founders nipped this in the bud and deceivers since the Civil War have been violating that wall by preying on ignorance and zealotry. What is seen as Jefferson's concept goes back to a few places, but his idea is built upon the Virginia public school concept and observation of the bill on it exposes my point:[112]

> Another object of the revisal is, to diffuse
> knowledge more generally through the mass of
> the people. This bill proposes to lay off every
> county into small districts of five or six miles
> square, called hundreds, and in each of them to

---

[112] Thomas Jefferson, Notes on the State of Virginia, Query XIV: Justice | Teaching American History

establish a school for teaching reading, writing, and arithmetic.

And...

> Instead therefore of putting the Bible and Testament into the hands of the children, at an age when their judgments are not sufficiently matured for religious enquiries, their memories may here be stored with the most useful facts from Grecian, Roman, European and American history. The first elements of morality too may be instilled into their minds; such as, when further developed as their judgments advance in strength, may teach them how to work out their own greatest happiness, by shewing them that it does not depend on the condition of life in which chance has placed them, but is always the result of a good conscience, good health, occupation, and freedom in all just pursuits.

As well-meaning as they may be, the people who violated this ideal in the first place were just as bad as the thing they were attacking, and the direct cause of it, even having a claim to such action being allowed in public schools. There is further evidence to this in Jefferson's works. In "From the Minutes of the Board of Visitors, University of Virginia, 1822-1825," found in Jefferson's *Letter's and Writings* he discusses the university's focus on adherence to the Separation of Church and State to assure religious freedom and the university's goal of intentionally not allowing a *professor of divinity*:[113]

---

[113] Minutes of the Board of Visitors of the University of Virginia (archives.gov)

In the same Report of the Commissioners of 1818. it was stated by them that "in conformity with the principles of our constitution, which place all sects of religion on an equal footing, with the jealousies of the different sects in guarding that equality from encroachment or surprise, and with the sentiments of the legislature in favor of freedom of religion, manifested on former occasions, they had not proposed that any professorship of Divinity should be established in the University; that provision however was made for giving instruction in the Hebrew, Greek, and Latin languages, the depositories of the Originals, and of the earliest and most respected authorities of the faith of every sect, and for courses of Ethical lectures, developing those moral obligations in which all sects agree. That, proceeding thus far, without offence to the Constitution, they had left, at this point, to every sect to take into their own hands the office of further instruction in the peculiar tenets of each.

It was not however to be understood that instruction in religious opinions and duties was meant to be precluded by the public authorities, as indifferent to the interests of society.

When the education system is hijacked by persons who are subservient to the State (and or a religion) and hold it in regards above the individual, they will teach that process to their students. Currently in U.S. law the virus of State supremacy through lesser codes, regulations, and ordinances with the power of courts to legislate from the bench and ignore personal liberties clearly stated in State and the U.S. Bill of Rights is rampant throughout the U.S. education system. I have had a lawyer refer to Lockean principles as rudimentary philosophy not applicable in our system despite the overwhelming evidence to the contrary. This is a poison which began even in Jefferson's day. He was flabbergasted by the amount incompetence to liberty-based law there was in lawyers and had concern they would fail to uphold the University of Virginia's standards in adhering to the Revolution, and fact that the U.S. was its own legal system and structure, by one of them becoming a law professor in his own college, teaching Blackstonian tactics and interpretive law.

Here are the Standards:[114]

> Resolved that it is the opinion of this board that as to the general principles of liberty and the rights of man in nature and in society, the doctrines of Locke, in his 'Essay concerning the true original extent and end of civil government,' and of Sidney in his 'Discourses on government,' may be considered as those generally approved by our fellow-citizens of this, and of the US., and that on the distinctive principles of the government of our own state, and of that of the US. the best guides are to be found in 1. the Declaration of Independence, as the fundamental act of union of these states. 2. the book known by the title of 'the Federalist,' being an authority to which appeal is habitually made by all, and rarely declined or denied by any as evidence of the general opinion of those who framed, and of those who accepted the Constitution of the US. on questions as to it's genuine meaning. 3. the Resolutions of the General assembly of Virginia in 1799. on the subject of the Alien and Sedition laws, which appeared to accord with the predominant sense of the people of the US. 4. the Valedictory address of President Washington, as conveying political lessons of peculiar value. and that in the branch of the school of Law, which is to treat on the subject

---

[114] Meeting Minutes of University of Virginia Board of Visitors, 4 ... (archives.gov)

of Civil polity, these shall be used as the text and documents of the school."

And here is Jefferson's concern for the law student coming to his school:[115]

In selecting our Law-Professor, we must be rigorously attentive to his political principles. you will recollect that, before the revolution, Coke Littleton was the universal elementary book of Law Students; and a sounder whig never wrote, nor of profounder learning in the orthodox doctrines of the British constitution, or in what were called English liberties. You remember also that our lawyers were then all whigs. but when his black-letter text, and uncouth, but cunning learning got out of fashion, and the honied Mansfieldism of Blackstone became the Student's Hornbook from that moment that profession (the nursery of our Congress) began to slide into toryism, and nearly all the young brood of lawyers now are of that hue. They suppose themselves indeed to be whigs, because they no longer know what whiggism or republicanism means.

This only was made worse over time by Federalists, and by 1902 the infiltration of Fabian Socialists into Columbia University was well underway, where most teachers in the Union were being educated out of. When education is to teach basics of knowledge and inform the student of where public influences are coming from, but not to blindly follow those influences, it can be a powerful cultural security. *It is also the greatest weapon an enemy can use against the people*

---

[115] From Thomas Jefferson to James Madison, 17 February 1826 (archives.gov)

because it lumps all the children into one giant indoctrination center, especially when parents expect others to raise their children for them.

Making homeschooling quite a powerful tool in being self-sufficient. The enemies know this and have hijacked education to get persons focused on their narrative and limit their ability to critically think through information. I laugh when recent graduates use terms like "logical fallacy" and think the related concepts equate to they themselves being capable of deep critical thinking, when all they can do is parrot such phrases against concepts they "dislike."

Just as with Sparta, by you knowing all the basics, *you* can govern your daily activities. Thus, a further truth to the fact that we are self-governed, not because we vote and elect officers, but because were managing our own personal, and interpersonal affairs as wise, informed free men.

THE INFORMED REPUBLIC

CONCLUSION

Before we wrap things up, I must reiterate that I hate going over the aspects of the Constitution and general political agreements and protections like the Bill of Rights, because in the scope of personal liberty it is meaningless and only applies to that body and participants, but We the People do not understand this. Having gotten through all that, I hope you take more from the points on the culture of the general people, and not the outcome of their appointed representatives. The history is clear there was a long conspiracy of minds working towards getting to the New World to reestablish a society of freemen away from the Old World powers, and that any usurpation of community agreement to create a central power is simply criminal piracy which needs to be acknowledged and extricated from us.

That stated, even if one finds my interpretation of *republic* in Greek and Roman era incorrect, even if they believe the term centralizes around the concept of government by the people's representatives in a central house, the facts of the American Republic, the Enlightenment that laid its road map, and the numerous quotes like this one by Thomas Jefferson:

> The policy of the American government is to leave their citizens free, neither restraining nor aiding them in their pursuits.

... make it quite clear the *Republic* the Founders created meets the definition I have stated all along in this work. Though admittedly, many men of even that time period and some of the strongest voices of liberty fell into the trap that *republic* equated specifically to *government* of some kind, even though they had a regular tendency of noting it always fell under liberty for the individual. The citizen in the natural republic is always at liberty and never to be restrained until they have caused a negative event, and even then they can only be taken for punishment by the willing hand of other free men, not civil servants (servants of government), and not because there is a *risk* of a fellow freeman causing an event that never unfolded.

The modern actions of politics can disclose to us the reality of Jefferson's words. The United Nations currently has termed *Peoples* and *People* to mean two different things. *Peoples* are, according to the U.N. Declaration of Indigenous Peoples:

> Indigenous communities, peoples and nations are those which, having a historical continuity with pre-invasion and pre-colonial societies that developed on their territories, consider themselves distinct from other sectors of the societies now prevailing on those territories, or parts of them.

> — U.N. Department of Economic and Social Affairs document[116]

116

https://view.officeapps.live.com/op/view.aspx?src=https%3A%2F%2Fwww.un.org%2Fesa%2Fsocdev%2Funpfii%2Fdocuments%2Fworkshop_data_background.doc%23%3A~%3Atext%3D%25E2%2580%259CIndigenous%2520communities%252C%2520peoples%2520and%2520nations%2520are%2520those%2520which%252C%2520having%2Cterritories%252C%2520or%2520parts%2520of%2520them.&wdOrigin=BROWSELINK

CONCLUSION

If you understood this correctly, what you read is that "We the People of the United States of America," are told by an institute the Federal Government helped create (the United Nations), America does not house indigenous peoples. This is important because it means we are viewed by them as beholden to the Global and National government and its agreements with the U.N. Whereas, indigenous peoples receive a bevy of protections from required adherence to a multitude of governments. In other words, they used an external global agency to redefine the legal terminology of *our* sovereign documentation to place anyone who fled the Old World back under their dominion.

Yet, our forward thinking Founders named us a new race of people. They made a preexisting legal declaration that made us "legally" indigenous, and it is why we must understand the liberty men who settled here were undermined by the colonial immigrants of England. We the freemen did not come here to invade or colonize. This kills the U.N.'s position over us. We can think and even know this U.N. claim is meaningless in reality, but politicos believe in and give power to this fiction.

Besides, the global implication that "We the People" are not indigenous to the U.S. by International Code. Jefferson and Franklin referred to us as a *new race of man*, placing us under the United Nations' definitional clause:

> ... consider themselves distinct from other sectors
> of the societies now prevailing on those territories,
> or parts of them.

Other attacks to our Republic come from within the U.S. legal structure. In the current language of U.S. legal definitions, the term "declaration" is no longer viable in a way that if you wrote the Declaration of Independence today, it would be illegal. If codes and legalese superseded the Spirit and the Purpose... but they don't.

TheFreeDictionary.com's legal section defines a declaration as such:[117]

> The first Pleading in a lawsuit governed by the rule of Common-Law Pleading. In the law of evidence, a statement or narration made not under oath but simply in the middle of things, as a part of what is happening. Also, a proclamation.
>
> A declaration is the plaintiff's statement of a claim against the defendant, formally and specifically setting out the facts and circumstances that make up the case. It generally is broken into several sections, which describe the different counts of the Cause of Action. The declaration should give the title of the action, the court and place of trial, the basis for the claim, and the relief demanded. The defendant then answers with a plea. Common-law pleading has been abolished in the United States, and modern systems of Code Pleading and rules based on federal Civil Procedure now provide for a complaint to accomplish the same purpose as did the declaration in former times."

A *complaint* is not as powerful as a *declaration*. The definition even admits that without understanding so. In the case of the Declaration of Independence the case was taken before the Court of Nature's God in General Congress. We the plaintiff defined our claim and took our own action to remedy our plight as the Earthly human power that would have otherwise been appealed to was corrupt and would have assured we stayed in chains it fashioned, so we appealed to the Supreme Judge. What competent man asks his slave driver to free him? The Declaration is not done under "oath" because it should always be presumed in republic that the Citizen is honest (honorable) and the Government lying even with the declaration is done *on record*. That's why governing officials must take Oaths of Office. The

---

[117] https://legal-dictionary.thefreedictionary.com/declaration

human (artificial) authority thus, cannot allow this course to be acceptable. Did you notice the most imperative keywords there too? "Federal Civil Procedure," the implication of a national centralized command over the civic law, even at local levels.

In the republic Common Law (Constitution or common contract) is God (supreme power). The people Sovereign. If the government has judicially abolished the Common Law position on Declarations, they have killed the power of Public Record and forced any "declaration" to be accepted by their Code based Courts by "complaint." Like we're some kind of business with workers and not a community of competent freemen. It was stated by Judge Frank Easterbrook before Harvard Law on a video titled "The Inaugural Scalia Lecture | Judge Frank Easterbrook: Interpreting the Unwritten Constitution" that the Code Law must fall to the Common Law. There are many contracts that exist under legal structures not in place, but their validity is absolute. Judges must know this. How will it fall to the Common Law if the modern system has convinced the civil servants *it* is the only authority in which a matter or procedure *can* be addressed? That is literally the slaveholder telling a man he can only come to him to have it decided if his chains can be removed... which draws us right back to the Solonian Reforms.

Here I can return you to the falsehood of the first definition I shared with you on *republic:*

> a democratic style system where the leader is
> elected through popular vote, to an oligarchical
> form of democracy where the elite rule through
> representatives in Checks and Balances.

If this were true why is it the American Founders, whose educations and culture are directly part of the Enlightenment, are clear that *democracies do not work,* and is not what they established?

One of the best examples of this view being the case is by Fisher Ames:

> Democracy is a volcano, which conceals the fiery
> material of its own destruction. These will
> produce an eruption, and carry desolation in their
> way.

Though Ames was a Federalist his, statement is echoed by his Revolutionary Era peers, as well as Jefferson, Madison, and a horde of Anti-Federalists. Again I remind you, Federalist leader and famed dictionary creator Noah Webster even stated:

> Do you not know that in this country almost every
> farmer is the Lord of his own soil? That instead of
> suffering under the oppression of a Monarch and
> Nobles, a class of haughty masters, totally
> independent of the people, almost every man in
> America is a Lord himself...

So, if I'm a Lord myself, who should think so highly of themselves that they are my trustee with power over me? Who is then my leader? Who thinks that they can say and make the will of every other man's concern of their own supersede my will? Should I succeed in my endeavors of personal achievement that trustee may come and command me? If we consider a democratic leader under an oligarchy that means "few rules" instead of an oligarchy of men, do we not end up back at a republic where there is only so much they can do?

The one area both Federalists and Anti-Federalists agreed upon was that *democracy destroys a nation's sovereignty*, and thus, its own and all peoples' freedom.

A populace driven by a officiate under perception they rule it when it rules them is one of the greatest threats and best tools for a tyranny.

The only solution to such egregious assaults on liberty is a new system altogether. I recommend a Stateless Republic of many Forums limited in capacity of members through which only rare dangerous events need bring together very temporary alliances which should be immediately disbanded after the danger is dealt with, and which said associations should be seen as *an enemy* when claiming the danger is ever-present, and the association in need of permanence. To each of us the knowledge of birthright sheriffdom to enforce the natural and common law in line with the Lycurgus, Laws of Solon, and Brutus' republican concepts. The total and utter reduction of "civil" and "statutory" law to at-will functions, but for over *public servants*. Our power to self-govern and self-prosecute, to be self-sufficient in all dealings, is the most imperative skill and ability we can possess to live happy fulfilled lives.

Be free.

The Battle of Long Island, a National Guard Heritage Painting by 21st century artist Domenick D'Andrea that was created for the National Guard Bureau. The painting depicts the Delaware Regiment at the Battle of Long Island on August 27, 1776.[118]

---

[118] https://en.wikipedia.org/wiki/Battle_of_Long_Island#/media/File:BattleofLongisland.jpg

ABOUT THE AUTHOR

C.D. Ginsburg is a native Coloradan with a background in analytics, quality assurance, customer service, and radio. He worked for the world's top video game companies in the early 2000's, and had his own political talk radio show in Colorado Springs, which was broadcast across the globe. He was instrumental in providing 2010 gubernatorial candidate Tom Tancredo with on-air coverage, aiding him in garnering over 36 percent of the state's vote as a third-party candidate.

Largely a stay-at-home dad in recent years, he returned to radio during the 2020 lockdown scheme to serve as an advocate for individual freedoms against the criminal activities of our destructive, over-reaching government.

Despite his willingness to engage in political circles, Ginsburg is not part of groups for groupthink's sake. Independence and liberty are his primary ideals, and he prefers to stand alone rather than clumping with the masses shouting collective slogans. Regardless, he's not above a good public rally in support of the true ideals that America was founded on—life, liberty, and the pursuit of personal happiness.

THE DECLARATION OF INDEPENDENCE

In Congress, July 4, 1776.

The unanimous Declaration of the thirteen united States of America, When in the Course of human events, it becomes necessary for one people to dissolve the political bands which have connected them with another, and to assume among the powers of the earth, the separate and equal station to which the Laws of Nature and of Nature's God entitle them, a decent respect to the opinions of mankind requires that they should declare the causes which impel them to the separation.

We hold these truths to be self-evident, that all men are created equal, that they are endowed by their Creator with certain unalienable Rights, that among these are Life, Liberty and the pursuit of Happiness.--That to secure these rights, Governments are instituted among Men, deriving their just powers from the consent of the governed, --That whenever any Form of Government becomes destructive of these ends, it is the Right of the People to alter or to abolish it, and to institute new Government, laying its foundation on such principles and organizing its powers in such form, as to them shall seem most likely to effect their Safety and Happiness. Prudence, indeed, will dictate that Governments long established should not be changed for light and transient causes; and accordingly all experience hath shewn, that mankind are more disposed to suffer, while evils are sufferable, than to right themselves by abolishing the forms to which they are accustomed. But when a long train of abuses and usurpations, pursuing invariably the same Object evinces a design to reduce them under absolute Despotism, it is their right, it is their duty, to throw off such Government, and to provide new Guards for their future security.--Such has been the patient sufferance of these Colonies; and such is now the necessity which constrains them to alter their former Systems of Government. The history of the present King of Great Britain is a history of repeated injuries and usurpations, all having in direct object the establishment of an absolute Tyranny over these States. To prove this, let Facts be submitted to a candid world.

He has refused his Assent to Laws, the most wholesome and necessary for the public good.

He has forbidden his Governors to pass Laws of immediate and pressing importance, unless suspended in their operation till his Assent should be obtained; and when so suspended, he has utterly neglected to attend to them.

He has refused to pass other Laws for the accommodation of large districts of people, unless those people would relinquish the right of Representation in the Legislature, a right inestimable to them and formidable to tyrants only.

He has called together legislative bodies at places unusual, uncomfortable, and distant from the depository of their public Records, for the sole purpose of fatiguing them into compliance with his measures.

He has dissolved Representative Houses repeatedly, for opposing with manly firmness his invasions on the rights of the people.

He has refused for a long time, after such dissolutions, to cause others to be elected; whereby the Legislative powers, incapable of Annihilation, have returned to the People at large for their exercise; the State remaining in the mean time exposed to all the dangers of invasion from without, and convulsions within.

He has endeavoured to prevent the population of these States; for that purpose obstructing the Laws for Naturalization of Foreigners; refusing to pass others to encourage their migrations hither, and raising the conditions of new Appropriations of Lands.

He has obstructed the Administration of Justice, by refusing his Assent to Laws for establishing Judiciary powers.

He has made Judges dependent on his Will alone, for the tenure of their offices, and the amount and payment of their salaries.

He has erected a multitude of New Offices, and sent hither swarms of Officers to harrass our people, and eat out their substance.

He has kept among us, in times of peace, Standing Armies without the Consent of our legislatures.

He has affected to render the Military independent of and superior to the Civil power.

He has combined with others to subject us to a jurisdiction foreign to our constitution, and unacknowledged by our laws; giving his Assent to their Acts of pretended Legislation:

For Quartering large bodies of armed troops among us:

For protecting them, by a mock Trial, from punishment for any Murders which they should commit on the Inhabitants of these States:

For cutting off our Trade with all parts of the world:

For imposing Taxes on us without our Consent:

For depriving us in many cases, of the benefits of Trial by Jury:

For transporting us beyond Seas to be tried for pretended offences

For abolishing the free System of English Laws in a neighbouring Province, establishing therein an Arbitrary government, and enlarging its Boundaries so as to render it at once an example and fit instrument for introducing the same absolute rule into these Colonies:

For taking away our Charters, abolishing our most valuable Laws, and altering fundamentally the Forms of our Governments:

For suspending our own Legislatures, and declaring themselves invested with power to legislate for us in all cases whatsoever.

He has abdicated Government here, by declaring us out of his Protection and waging War against us.

He has plundered our seas, ravaged our Coasts, burnt our towns, and destroyed the lives of our people.

He is at this time transporting large Armies of foreign Mercenaries to compleat the works of death, desolation and tyranny, already begun with circumstances of Cruelty & perfidy scarcely paralleled in the most barbarous ages, and totally unworthy the Head of a civilized nation.

He has constrained our fellow Citizens taken Captive on the high Seas to bear Arms against their Country, to become the executioners of their friends and Brethren, or to fall themselves by their Hands.

He has excited domestic insurrections amongst us, and has endeavoured to bring on the inhabitants of our frontiers, the merciless Indian Savages, whose known rule of warfare, is an undistinguished destruction of all ages, sexes and conditions.

In every stage of these Oppressions We have Petitioned for Redress in the most humble terms: Our repeated Petitions have been answered only by repeated injury. A Prince whose character is thus marked by every act which may define a Tyrant, is unfit to be the ruler of a free people.

Nor have We been wanting in attentions to our Brittish brethren. We have warned them from time to time of attempts by their legislature to extend an unwarrantable jurisdiction over us. We have reminded them of the circumstances of our emigration and settlement here. We have appealed to their native justice and magnanimity, and we have conjured them by the ties of our common kindred to disavow these usurpations, which, would inevitably interrupt our connections and correspondence. They too have been deaf to the voice of justice and of consanguinity. We must, therefore, acquiesce in the necessity, which denounces our Separation, and hold them, as we hold the rest of mankind, Enemies in War, in Peace Friends.

We, therefore, the Representatives of the United States of America, in General Congress, Assembled, appealing to the Supreme Judge of the world for the rectitude of our intentions, do, in the Name, and by Authority of the good People of these Colonies, solemnly publish and declare, That these United Colonies are, and of Right ought to be Free and Independent States; that they are Absolved from all Allegiance to the British Crown, and that all political connection between them and the State of Great Britain, is and ought to be totally dissolved; and that as Free and Independent States, they have full Power to levy War, conclude Peace, contract Alliances, establish Commerce, and to do all other Acts and Things which Independent States may of right do. And for the support of this Declaration, with a firm reliance on the protection of divine Providence, we mutually pledge to each other our Lives, our Fortunes and our sacred Honor.

ADDITIONAL SOURCES

- https://en.wikipedia.org/wiki/Jamestown,_Virginia
- https://en.wikipedia.org/wiki/Plymouth_Company
- https://en.wikipedia.org/wiki/London_Company
- http://www.history.org/foundation/journal/autumn01/james i.cfm
- https://en.wikipedia.org/wiki/Roanoke_Colony
- https://en.wikipedia.org/wiki/Walter_Raleigh
- https://historicjamestowne.org/history/virginia-company/
- https://www.landofthebrave.info/royal-colonies.htm
- Cestui Que Vie Act 1666: http://www.legislation.gov.uk/aep/Cha2/18-19/11#commentary-c919468